EVENT MANAGEMENT IN SPORT, RECREATION AND TOURISM

Now in a fully revised and updated second edition, *Event Management in Sport, Recreation and Tourism* provides a comprehensive theoretical and practical framework for planning and managing events. Focusing on the role of the event manager and their diverse responsibilities through each phase of the event planning process, this is still the only textbook to define the concept of knowledge in the context of event management, placing it at the centre of professional practice.

The book is designed to encourage critical thinking on the part of the student to help them develop the skills that they will need to become effective, and reflective, practitioners in the events industry, and every chapter contains a rich array of real-world case studies, data and practical examples from sport, recreation and tourism contexts. This second edition has been significantly strengthened with the inclusion of two completely new chapters – on environmental sustainability, and on the politics of event management – and is essential reading for any student or practitioner working in event management, sport management, leisure management, outdoor recreation or tourism.

Cheryl Mallen: Associate Professor in the Department of Sport Management at Brock University, Canada. Her research involves knowledge and environmental sustainability. She is well published, with articles in the *Journal of Sport Management*, *Sport Management Review* and the *European Sport Management Quarterly*.

Lorne J. Adams: Associate Professor in the Department of Kinesiology at Brock University, Canada. He is the recipient of four teaching awards, including the 3M Teaching Fellowship. He has been a coach and served as Athletic Director for 10 years.

EVENT MANAGEMENT IN SPORT, RECREATION AND TOURISM

THEORETICAL AND PRACTICAL DIMENSIONS

SECOND EDITION

EDITED BY CHERYL MALLEN AND LORNE J. ADAMS

Routledge
Taylor & Francis Group

LONDON AND NEW YORK

First published 2008
by Butterworth Heinemann

This edition published 2013
by Routledge
2 Park Square, Milton Park, Abingdon, Oxon OX14 4RN

Simultaneously published in the USA and Canada
by Routledge
711 Third Avenue, New York, NY 10017

*Routledge is an imprint of the Taylor & Francis Group, an
informa business*

© 2013 Cheryl Mallen and Lorne J. Adams

British Library Cataloguing in Publication Data
A catalogue record for this book is available from the
British Library

Library of Congress Cataloging in Publication Data
Event management in sport, recreation and tourism : theoretical
and practical dimensions / edited by Cheryl Mallen and Lorne Adams.
p. cm.
1. Special events–Management. 2. Sports–Management. 3.
Recreation–Management. 4. Tourism–Management. I. Mallen, Cheryl. II.
Adams, Lorne James.
GT3405.E9 2013
394.2068--dc23
2012023535

ISBN: 978-0-415-64100-5 (hbk)
ISBN: 978-0-415-64102-9 (pbk)
ISBN: 978-0-203-08228-7 (ebk)

Typeset in Melior and Univers
by Keystroke, Station Road, Codsall, Wolverhampton

Printed and bound by CPI Group (UK) Ltd, Croydon, CR0 4YY

CONTENTS

1 TRADITIONAL AND NICHE EVENTS IN SPORT, RECREATION AND TOURISM   1

CHERYL MALLEN AND LORNE J. ADAMS

2 THE CONCEPT OF KNOWLEDGE IN EVENT MANAGEMENT 10

CHERYL MALLEN

vi

6 THE EVENT PLANNING MODEL: THE EVENT IMPLEMENTATION, MONITORING AND MANAGEMENT PHASE   127

LORNE J. ADAMS

7 THE EVENT PLANNING MODEL: THE EVENT EVALUATION AND RENEWAL PHASE   145

SCOTT FORRESTER AND LORNE J. ADAMS

8 SAFEGUARDING THE NATURAL ENVIRONMENT IN EVENT MANAGEMENT   166

CHRIS CHARD AND MATT DOLF

9 FACILITATING QUALITY IN EVENT MANAGEMENT 181

CRAIG HYATT AND CHRIS CHARD

10   EVENT BIDDING   198

CHERYL MALLEN

11   POLITICS IN EVENT BIDDING AND HOSTING   212

TRISH CHANT-SEHL

12   CONCLUSIONS   227

LORNE J. ADAMS

xi

CONTRIBUTORS

Lorne J. Adams: Associate Professor, Department of Kinesiology, Brock University, St. Catharines, Ontario, Canada.

Cheri Bradish: Associate Professor, Department of Sport Management, Brock University, St. Catharines, Ontario, Canada.

Trish Chant-Sehl: Director, University Advancement, McMaster University, Hamilton, Ontario, Canada.

Chris Chard: Assistant Professor, Department of Sport Management, Brock University, St. Catharines, Ontario, Canada.

Maureen Connolly: Professor, Department of Kinesiology, Brock University, St. Catharines, Ontario, Canada.

Amy Cunningham: a musician and recording artist at Independent, Victoria, British Columbia, Canada.

Matt Dolf: Manager of the Centre for Sport and Sustainability, Vancouver, British Columbia, Canada.

Scott Forrester: Associate Professor, Department of Recreation and Leisure Studies, Brock University, St. Catharines, Ontario, Canada.

Craig Hyatt: Associate Professor, Department of Sport Management, Brock University, St. Catharines, Ontario, Canada.

Joanne MacLean: Dean, Faculty of Health Sciences, University of Fraser Valley, Abbotsford, British Columbia, Canada.

Cheryl Mallen: Associate Professor, Department of Sport Management, Brock University, St. Catharines, Ontario, Canada.

PREFACE TO THE SECOND EDITION

This second edition responds to the feedback from student usage and the evolving field of event management. Student input in particular has produced a modification of the overview of type of events in Chapter 1 and a reworking of the chapter on knowledge, Chapter 2. Students told us that they were studying research processes in other required courses, and so the chapter on that subject has been replaced with new material on environmental sustainability, Chapter 8. Further, it was clear in class discussion about event bidding that the problems of the politics involved in the process needed to be made more explicit. This has resulted in another new Chapter 11, which follows the revamped chapter on event bidding, Chapter 10.

While all of the chapters have been updated, and some new ones developed, the chapter on environmental sustainability represents a new and increasingly important responsibility of the event manager. From small local events to world-class spectacles, environmental concerns are becoming a focal point of event hosting.

Sport, recreation and tourism event management is a vibrant, complex and growing industry. Growth around the world in this diverse field has stimulated the need for skilled event managers. This edited text is intended to guide learners to assimilate knowledge for use in the event industry. There are four objectives for this text upon which the chapters are based.

OBJECTIVES

The first objective of this text is to provide a foundation of sound theoretical and practical principles in sport, recreation and tourism event management. The second objective is to encourage learners to develop an understanding of the concept of knowledge. This understanding involves the construction of critical interpretations of defining knowledge and determining knowledge requirements for the field. The third objective focuses on presenting an event management planning model, including progressive phases of the model, and the key elements within each phase. The fourth and final objective involves an emphasis on the role of the event manager as a facilitator. The facilitation role involves "thinking through" the requirements for each phase of the event planning model and utilizing a variety of strategies to guide those assigned the task of planning to stage an event.

AN OVERVIEW OF THE FOCUS OF THIS TEXT

This text focuses on sport, recreation and tourism event management and emphasizes the complex role of an event manager as a facilitator. In addition, emphasis is placed on defining traditional and niche events, the concept of knowledge, the planning phases to be gone through when one is organizing components for staging an event, the critical factors for event bids, the concept of quality, and experiential learning.

EVENT ELEMENTS OUTSIDE THE FRAMEWORK OF THIS TEXT

The event manager has a complex role in the staging of an event that necessitates managing a multitude of activities within a changing event environment. In performing this role, both depth and breadth of knowledge are necessary. Thus, an event manager's training needs to be diverse and to extend to areas that are beyond the focus of this text. Examples of additional areas within the realm of event management are ethics, financial management, marketing, sponsorship, facility management and law. Each of these areas of expertise can be applied to the organizing and production of an event. Each aforementioned area is sufficiently important to the staging of an event that they would require far more emphasis than a single chapter in this text could provide. However, a study of the above-listed topics will provide a fuller understanding of the broad scope of requirements in event management. For example, understanding the application of law from the perspective of legal liability, risk management, dispute resolution and contract development for athletes, facilities, entertainers, staff and volunteers is a vital aspect of event management. In addition, marketing and sponsorship have a direct application to the viability of events. There are multiple texts on the market that discuss facility management, marketing, sport law and other such subjects that relate to event management. There are only limited resources, however, on the event manager's role as a facilitator for the key phases that involve planning for an event. Therefore, this text is intended to concentrate on that gap in the literature.

Cheryl Mallen and Lorne J. Adams

ACKNOWLEDGEMENTS

Cheryl Mallen would like to acknowledge a lifetime of support from her parents Bob and Betty Brown; the friendship and love from husband Paddy that underpin her life; and her children, Bob and Sarah, who are always the priority in her world.

Lorne J. Adams would like to acknowledge his co-editor for this edition, whose enthusiasm for this project was contagious. For "Lili," 9, 12, 25. To his family, thanks for the care and support, which have been unwavering.

CHAPTER 1

TRADITIONAL AND NICHE EVENTS IN SPORT, RECREATION AND TOURISM

CHERYL MALLEN AND LORNE J. ADAMS

Traditional events and hybrid or *niche* events are both prevalent in the sport, recreation and tourism industries. This chapter examines the unique characteristics that differentiate traditional events from niche events and provides an explanation for the contemporary rise of niche events. The discussion leads to a conclusion concerning the demand for skilled traditional and niche managers in the burgeoning field of event management.

CHARACTERISTICS OF TRADITIONAL EVENTS

For ease of this discussion, each traditional event is considered to be a sport event staged for recreational or competition purposes and/or acts as a driver for tourism. Traditional events exhibit two key characteristics. The first characteristic is a governing body. The second characteristic is that the activity is a recognizable and time-honoured sport.

A traditional event has a governing body

Traditional events have a governing body that sanctions events and establishes and enforces standardized rules and regulations to be followed during the production of the event. This governing body can be structured as an organization, association or federation that governs the event. Its rules and regulations specify elements such as the competition area, the number of participants, their dress and acceptable actions for participation.

The governing body can operate in a range of markets and in small- to large-scale events. Examples include governing bodies for traditional events held in particular countries, such as netball in Australia, box lacrosse in Canada, high kick and leg wrestling competitions in the Arctic, hurling and Gaelic football in Ireland, rodeo and jai alai in the United States and sumo wrestling in Japan. Additional examples include governing bodies for traditional events that engage multiple countries and tourism markets, such as the Olympic Games, the Youth Olympic Games and Paralympic Games, the Arctic Games, the Asian Games, the Commonwealth Games, the International Children's Games, the Highland Games and the Mediterranean Games.

A traditional event is a recognizable and time-honoured sporting activity

The second characteristic of a traditional event involves the utilization of an activity that is a recognizable and a time-honoured sport. Adaptations can be made to the rules and regulations in a traditional event based upon a range of pressures, such as the requirements of a particular culture or country, the need to adapt for the age of the participant population or the availability of new technologies. A traditional event may undergo adaptations or transformations over time; however, the transformations do not give rise to an entirely new event. Change is limited. There is universality in the implementation of the rules and regulations. From generation to generation the event is conducted repeatedly in the same manner. The event is practised to follow the rules and regulations, including the traditions, customs and routines, of a consistent, mature, respected and recognizable event. The general rules for a traditional event are followed even as the focus changes from a recreational activity to a high level of competition and/or tourism event.

An example of a traditional event is what is called football in a large part of the world and soccer in North America. This sport event can be played on a range of levels from a large elite competition to a local recreational activity that uses a homemade ball and makeshift fields whereby the players emulate the characteristics of the traditional event. The consistent use of rules and regulations at any level makes the event a time-honoured and recognizable game of football/soccer. If played as a single game, league or circuit format, the rules and regulations for the football/soccer events are

2

standardized by the bodies that govern such elements as the playing field, number of players, their dress and the conduct of each player. Multiple bodies govern football/soccer throughout the regional, provincial or state, national and international levels of focus throughout the world. Some bodies adapt the rules for their particular purposes, such as creating age levels for competition. However, the event itself resembles the football/ soccer that is played worldwide.

Overall, a traditional sporting event is regulated by a governing body and involves a recognizable and time-honoured sporting activity. Each traditional event, whether it is small or large, needs an event manager. The demand for event managers, however, does not end there, as the world of event management extends beyond the traditional events to include niche events.

CHARACTERISTICS OF NICHE EVENTS

In contrast to a traditional event, anyone can design and host niche events by setting new directions and offering event opportunities. Each niche event is forged through innovations that alter or renew an event or create a completely new kind of event. Many niche events are progressive hybrid events that generally stem from the roots of a traditional event. This means that niche events can be founded by altering or renewing a traditional event to produce the "next generation" of the event. This type of niche event may use a traditional sport event surface such as a rugby pitch or volleyball court, or traditional equipment such as a lacrosse helmet or rugby ball, or rules and regulations that are derived from a traditional event such as basketball. A niche event has no requirement for the number of traditional components that could be utilized or the form in which they can be combined. Yet a niche event can exhibit elements that are recognizable as those of a traditional sporting event.

There are three key characteristics of niche events. The first is that the event is created and adapted for a particular sport, recreation or tourism audience. The second characteristic is that there does not have to be a traditional governing body that has established time-honoured rules and regulations, although an organizing body may exist that can provide rules and regulations. The third characteristic is that the event may exhibit recognizable traditional event components or may be unconventional in its form.

A niche event is created or adapted for a particular audience

A niche event can be continuously adapted for a particular audience. The event can be adapted at any time to meet innovative designs or the changing needs of the participants and tourists or spectators. Adaptations can be made to any individual element of the event, or the entire event can be adapted at any given time. Niche events involve the freedom to design an event with the use of conventional or unconventional components or activities. This type of event, thus, can be adapted to another generation of the event at any time for a particular audience. Whatever the focus – an individual event, a circuit of events or a league at the local, regional, national or international level – the possibility remains for full-scale changes to the niche event at any time, depending on the needs of the audience.

A niche event has no traditional governing body

One of the reasons a niche event can adapt to a particular audience quickly is that it does not have a traditional governing body establishing rules and regulations that have been devised over time. The rules and regulations established are not expected to be traditional or passed down from generation to generation or from event to event – they can be brand new! There is always the potential for adapting the rules and regulations because of the influences of culture, the movement to incorporate new equipment technology, the need to accommodate the requirements of a particular age group or type of abilities, or the creative genius of the event management.

A niche event can take an unconventional form

Niche events are springing up throughout the world and each in an unconventional form. For example, in the United States, basketball is being played on a series of trampolines instead of a traditional basketball court. In Canada, a niche event has extended snowmobile racing to the summer months by competing on grass instead of snow, as would be done in winter. Canada also hosts a World Outdoor Hockey Championship with adapted rules to award a goal for each penalty called, to avoid having a participant sit out in the cold when serving a penalty. Around the world, niche skiing and snowboarding events are being conducted on hills of sand instead of

4

the traditional mountains of snow. Football/soccer events are being staged in a three-on-three format played on sand instead of grass. Cricket events have been held with adapted rules in the West Indies, England, New Zealand and South Africa. Skill-testing events have sprung up, such as the golf long ball drive, putting and hole-in-one contests, baseball home run derbies, ice hockey shooting and skating skills competitions, and American football throwing and kicking skills competitions. Further, niche adventure races involve trekking, horseback riding or scaling mountains.

Niche events can also exist in multiple forms, such as innovative festival, conference, media event, banquet, skills competitions and/or charity events. The use of innovative designs can form new niche sport, recreational or tourism events.

Niche events can evolve into traditional events

Niche events can evolve into the traditional event realm. The triathlon is an example of a niche sport that has become a traditional event. This triactivity sport event combines swimming, cycling and running. The combination of traditional sports established a niche event that grew from a local to an international phenomenon. The Ironman Triathlon, held in Hawaii in the United States, is also an example of a triathlon that is a successful tourism event. Over the course of time, the triathlon developed rules and regulations that were practised in a consistent manner. The event was eventually accepted into the group of sports to be staged at the Olympic Summer Games. This acceptance meant that participants were selected from a series of events conducted with standardized rules and regulations. In addition, there was recognition of the event as a triathlon at every level from local to internationally staged events. At this point, the triathlon entered the realm of a traditional event.

Even as some triathlons evolve into traditional events, the triathlon continues to develop as a niche event. The niche triathlon event has been spurred on by organizers' continuing to adapt the multi-activity event elements. This includes adapting to use two sport activities, such as walking and cycling, or adjusting to allow a team of three members to compete, each completing one of the sport activities. This continual use of adaptations to the triathlon keeps the event in the niche event realm; however, it is possible for an event to be produced in both the traditional and the niche event realms simultaneously.

Other examples of events that were born as niche events and evolved to traditional event status can be found in the sport of skiing or snowboarding. Niche events began as moguls competitions, the half-pipe, ski cross and ski dancing – and then these events became transformed into traditional events. Volleyball is a further example of a traditional event that generated a niche element in beach volleyball that has now become a traditional event. Today, all of these events with niche roots have been included in major traditional events such as the Olympic Games and have standardized traditional rules and regulations.

DESIGN A NICHE EVENT

Niche events continue to emerge and they may or may not move to the realm of traditional events in the future. Regardless, they are expanding the array of sport, recreation and tourism events being produced annually. Event managers are needed to stage each of these small and large niche events around the world.

Examine the niche events that are springing up in your area. Next, consider adaptations or innovations that could be made within a local traditional event to give rise to a niche event. This niche event does not have to be a wholesale innovation to generate a new event. It can involve basic, simple adaptations. Remember, someone designed each niche event and had the courage to host such an event. Many event managers have developed their own careers through this avenue. Can you design a niche event that could potentially be implemented in the future? If so, what would you do to generate an innovation for a traditional sport in your hometown? Read the next section to develop understandings of why niche events will continue to expand the event industry into the future.

WHY ARE CONTEMPORARY NICHE EVENTS ARISING?

This text proposes that niche events stem from an outgrowth of our need to learn about, and to practise for, change. According to Gallagher (2012), we mentally seek change, as it is just the way humans are "wired." We need change or novelty to develop the skills necessary to improve our chances of survival during evolutionary change. Jensen (1999) stated that survival is contingent on the individual or group that "is most adaptable

6

to change" (p. 16). We thus adapt elements in our lives as part of a cycle to acquire opportunities to practise for change (Gallagher, 2012).

Our current period of contemporary change has been described as a postindustrial era (Bell, 1973; Zuboff, 1988). The impact of postindustrial change on contemporary society has produced an environment of complexity and unpredictability (Choo & Bontis, 2002). According to Homer-Dixon (2001), contemporary change impacts all aspects of contemporary society. This impact demands a process of active and continuous learning in order to accommodate change (Hirschhorn, 1984; Sproull & Kiesler, 1991). Adapting to this challenge of change necessitates a mindset for adapting and innovating.

In the process of learning to accommodate change, a new concept has surfaced that Limerick, Cunnington and Crowther (1998) call "collaborative individualism" (p. 103). This concept involves a group or a collective of responsible individuals being "held together by common cultures, shared world meanings and values" (p. 128). This new form of collective encourages a mindset that one must "embrace individualism, collaboration, and innovation" (p. 22). Each of these elements must be embraced simultaneously, and all members within the collective have a voice. As these individuals retain and develop their personal voice, they are encouraged to collaborate in order to develop innovations for managing in our contemporary environment.

Applying the concept of collaborative individualism to niche events requires a change-based mindset, an individual voice and a push for individuals to collaborate and to be innovative. At the grassroots level, collaborative individualism is occurring as groups are using innovative design to create niche events. Bound together by common threads from an event's culture, meaning and value, groups are capable of creating, sharing and nurturing adapted meanings and values to create niche events. These niche events can be described as design experiments.

Cobb, Confrey, diSessa, Lehrer and Schauble (2003) describe design experiments as "test-beds for innovations" (p. 10). Cobb and his group of researchers indicate that design experiments offer the opportunity to complete a series of cycles of development and allow for regular revisions to an event. The notion of a test-bed implies that not all innovations will succeed. However, the test-bed concept for events suggests that opportunities to design niche events abound. Niche event experiments can explore and reflect designs and activities that offer new understandings and innovations which create niche events. In sport, recreation and tourism event management, design experimenters are producing a growing body of dynamic and creative niche events.

THE NEED FOR SKILLED TRADITIONAL AND NICHE EVENT MANAGERS

The sport, recreation and tourism industries have undergone phenomenal growth since the 1960s. The combination of increased traditional and niche events is changing the sport, recreation and tourism event landscape, in that each event needs one or more event managers.

Consider the potential number of event managers that could be needed in the world on an annual basis. Event managers are necessary for local recreational and competitive events that extend to regional, provincial/state, national and international events, including leagues, circuits or tours for a variety of age groups and abilities. In addition, these traditional events can include a wide variety of sports ranging from archery to yachting. The number of niche events is growing annually in the form of tourism-focused festivals, banquets and shows. Add to this the number of sport and recreational events that are being altered or renewed to produce the next generation of events, and the number of event managers required increases concomitantly.

The exact number of events held annually is an unknown. Calculations are difficult, owing to the complex conditions of the sport, recreation and tourism industry. However, a general estimation is that millions of traditional and niche events are staged annually around the world. Well-informed, prepared and knowledgeable managers are in high demand – hence the need for this text.

CONCLUSION

A growing body of traditional and niche sport, recreation and tourism events drive the demand for experts who are knowledgeable and experienced in the field of event management. Today's event managers need skills to advance beyond using pre-established lists that dictate the replication of actions used to stage previous events. *Contemporary event managers must be able to think through and self-determine the requirements of*

8

staging traditional or niche events. This requirement demands knowledge of, coupled with experience in, event management.

We now head to Chapter 2, where the concept of knowledge and a knowledge transfer race is discussed. Also, a uniquely formed definition of knowledge for sport, recreation and tourism event managers will be presented. Chapter 2 aims to guide event managers in their pursuit of knowledge for use in the event industry.

CHAPTER QUESTIONS

1 What are the two key characteristics of traditional events?
2 List three traditional events and explain why they qualify as traditional events.
3 What are the characteristics of a niche event?
4 Describe three niche events that are being hosted in your area and explain the characteristics that make them niche events and not traditional events.
5 Can an event move from being traditional to becoming a niche event? If not, why not? If it can, what changes are necessary for it to make the transition?
6 Why are niche events growing in number at present?
7 What does the dual growth of traditional and niche events mean for the field of event management?

CHAPTER 2

THE CONCEPT OF KNOWLEDGE IN EVENT MANAGEMENT

CHERYL MALLEN

This chapter discusses the concept of knowledge and, in particular, the elements that make up *common and advancement knowledge* within the event management industry. In addition, a unique definition of knowledge designed for event management is provided and suggestions are offered concerning how to acquire event knowledge. Further, this chapter indicates that we are all in a "knowledge transfer race" (English & Baker, 2006), and the relevance of this race is discussed as it affects the event industry. The underlying issue within this chapter is that if you cannot articulate your definition of knowledge, then how can you obtain the necessary knowledge to be a valuable member of the event management field? Or how can you know in what types of knowledge you will need to be accomplished, in the fields of sport, recreation and tourism in event management?

It is important to note at the beginning of this chapter that the terms *knowledge*, *information* and *data* have been used interchangeably in some contexts. However, in this text the opinion of Boisot (2002) is followed, whereby you "think of data as being located in the world and of knowledge as being located in agents [within your mind], with information taking on a mediating role between them" (p. 67). In this view, knowledge, information and data are considered to be three separate entities.

THE CONCEPT OF KNOWLEDGE

As far back as 1973, Bell noted that knowledge is situated as a "central" feature within our advancing society. Over the past several decades, the

10

value of knowledge has continued to increase rapidly. One reason for the meteoric rise in the value of knowledge is the recognition that knowledge is a resource that aids productivity (Grant, 1996). Thus, productivity and, ultimately, success in event management are, in part, contingent upon the knowledge that you acquire, create, share and apply.

DEFINING KNOWLEDGE

How do you currently define knowledge? Think about your currently held definition of knowledge and record your answer. Review your definition of knowledge and be sure that you have listed the key dimensions, features or characteristics of knowledge, and then consider how these dimensions apply to event management in sport, recreation and tourism (Figure 2.1).

This is a difficult exercise. Researchers have been trying to define knowledge for decades. No single definition of knowledge that you can adopt exists in the literature; the concept has been elusive. The difficulty in arriving at a consensus on a definition of knowledge stems from the intangible nature of knowledge and the fact that one definition for all purposes is simply not available (Edvinsson & Malone, 1997). Although researchers cannot agree on a definition of knowledge, there is no reason for not articulating contextual understandings of knowledge. This is because researchers offer tangible components that mark one's knowledge and can be applied to event management in sport, recreation and tourism. I will now review a number of these definitions as they relate to two categories of knowledge that I shall call *common knowledge* and *advancement knowledge*.

---

1 Record how you currently define knowledge.
2 List at least three key dimensions, features or characteristics of knowledge in your definition.
3 Apply your definition of knowledge to one of the fields of sport, recreation or tourism event management.
4 Review your definition and consider the question: If you have knowledge in the field of event management, this means you have knowledge in what?

Figure 2.1 Defining knowledge in event management

COMMON KNOWLEDGE IN EVENT MANAGEMENT

Common knowledge involves *general understandings* that are gained as it "grows – emerges – out of . . . interactions" (Spender, 2002, p. 160). This means that the development of your common knowledge is dependent upon the interactions that you obtain concerning event management. *This type of knowledge is gained through interactions – including interactions such as taking event management classes, reading research, participating in short experiences in the field and having conversations with individuals in event management.* Instructors in the classroom and those individuals in the industry can describe, teach and guide the development of your common knowledge. Each interaction helps you to contextualize, interpret and conceive options concerning event management knowledge.

Common knowledge is explicit and provides a foundation that is necessary for your participation, including the judgments that you make. This is because common knowledge is "the platform for everything else. It lies deep and brings together, in contextualized thought and action, all the other types of knowledge that are judged relevant – for it is the sources of such judgments" (Spender, 2002, pp. 157–158). The more varied your common knowledge, the greater the foundational base of event management knowledge you develop. This base of knowledge is used to judge the value of new knowledge and facilitates the integration of one's currently held knowledge with new knowledge.

Common knowledge is defined in a number of ways. We will now examine definitions of common knowledge in order to delineate the multiple dimensions within common knowledge that are applicable to event management.

Common knowledge means *acquiring systemic knowledge*

One definition of common knowledge involves systemic knowledge. This type of knowledge involves having a general understanding of the overall organization and its methodological systems, technological systems and general processes. This type of knowledge extends to include understandings of the general procedures, schemes and techniques, and the contents of the organization's manuals and information packages (Nonaka, Toyama & Konno, 2000). Each dimension described within systemic knowledge is

12

applicable to the knowledge one would require in the production of sport, recreation and tourism events. Understanding one organization does not mean that one has a full understanding of all event organizations. The systemic knowledge could be different for a variety of event organizations, and, thus, systemic knowledge can involve acquiring knowledge of multiple organizations within the broad base of the event industry.

Common knowledge means understanding of *what one does*

Another definition, by Blackler (1995), defines common knowledge as what one does. This implies that a dimension of common knowledge includes an overall understanding of the human resource structures and the multiple roles that are played by people in event management. These roles include the event manager and the managers of the multiple event components, such as the accommodation manager, accreditation manager, the ceremonies manager (the ceremonies include opening, closing and awards ceremonies), the drug testing or doping manager, the food and beverage manager, along with the managers of protocols, public relations, transportation, venue and warehousing. Further, many of these management roles are supported with staff and/or volunteers, and this knowledge extends to understandings concerning what one does within each of these supporting roles. This knowledge also encompasses understandings in terms of the facilitation role to ensure that what one is supposed to do within each of these roles gets completed. For example, one may facilitate event operational planning or volunteer program development. Knowledge of what one does, therefore, encompasses a multitude of roles in event management.

Common knowledge means *"know-how"*

Common knowledge is described by English and Baker (2006) as the basic "know-how" or theoretical knowledge and *the understanding of how to apply the theory to event practices, processes and procedures*. This type of knowledge implies that one needs to understand key characteristics of contemporary theories. Examples of these theories include agency theory, complexity theory, contingency theory and systems theory. Beyond knowing the characteristics that make up each theory, knowledge includes being able to have a general ability to apply the characteristics within professional event practice.

Common knowledge involves *understanding the basics of culture, politics and personalities*

Gupta and MacDaniel (2002) describe having common knowledge as possessing basic understandings of culture, politics and personalities. This type of knowledge requires one to be able to participate in the event management environment, including being able to conduct oneself in the social culture(s) that have been established. Additionally, there is a need to be able to recognize, understand and apply one's knowledge to political situations and to be able to assess the impact of such political manoeuvres. Consequently, this type of knowledge requires a talent for understanding and deciding on how to manage differing personalities in event management, including any cultural associations.

Common knowledge includes *basic conceptual understandings*

Nonaka, Toyama and Konno (2000) indicate that common knowledge can be conceptual (ideas are conceived and understood mentally) and that this type of knowledge is obtained on the basis of abstract capabilities. Conceptual knowledge includes ideas that are expressed or visualized. An example includes generating the initial designs concerning entertainment elements in event opening and closing ceremonies.

Common knowledge means having *common sense* for the event management industry

Common knowledge has been described as common sense for a particular context or field (Spender, 1996). This type of knowledge means gaining general knowledge of the language, including common terms used within the event field. It also means having a basic awareness and understanding of the feelings and meaning within the language that is shared (Grant, 1996). Further, there is a sense of knowing how to apply the common knowledge at the appropriate time.

ADVANCEMENT KNOWLEDGE IN EVENT MANAGEMENT

In contrast to common knowledge, advancement knowledge is *in-depth experiential knowledge* that can be acquired through long-term experiences that include high levels of responsibility in the industry. These

14

experiences generate perspectives and understandings that provide a competitive advantage and offer value with a high level of knowledge sophistication.

Advancement knowledge provides highly framed quick insights, understandings and intuition, and is used for decision-making (Leonard & Sensiper, 2002). This type of knowledge, however, is difficult to obtain as it is tacit in nature (Nonaka & Takeuchi, 1995).

Tacit knowledge is what an individual holds in their mind about perspectives, beliefs and models (Nonaka & Takeuchi, 1995). This mental capacity can take decades to develop through personal experience (Winter, 1987). Time is necessary, as this type of knowledge is difficult to articulate and discuss. Because of this difficulty, advancement knowledge has been described as a type of "iceberg" (Schorr, 1997, p. 29). This means that much of advancement knowledge is buried in one's memory, but cannot be easily explained. Therefore, because of its hidden nature, acquiring advancement knowledge from someone else can be challenging, as the knowledge holder has generally never expressed the knowledge, either verbally or in writing (Spender, 1996). No solution capable of fully alleviating this issue has been found. A person can have advancement knowledge that is deep, intimate and personal, but they may not realize that they possess the knowledge. Therefore, the process of transferring the knowledge to someone else continues to be difficult.

Overall, advancement knowledge has multiple definitions. We will now examine a number of definitions of advancement knowledge in order to delineate the multiple dimensions within event management.

Advancement knowledge *involves an in-depth understanding of event management routines gained through practice*

According to Nonaka et al. (2000), advancement knowledge is an in-depth awareness concerning routines in the event processes and procedures, including the best sequential order of events. This "know-how" concerns insights into daily activities that are acquired through years of hands-on participation in practices or long-term experiential opportunities. Advancement knowledge of routines means knowing the subtle details of how to be efficient, effective and successful, and this is learned with practice. This definition is supported by Nelson and Winter's (1982) seminal work, which indicates that the gaining of intimate understandings of daily routines and practices comes from analyzing situations and making decisions. This type of knowledge can lead to the pioneering of ideas for efficiencies and effectiveness in routines for progress, and ultimately success in event management.

Advancement knowledge includes *"enbrained" knowledge in event management gained through practice*

Enbrained knowledge comprises high-level conceptual understandings and encompasses cognitive abilities that are produced with practice (Collins, 1993). According to von Krogh and Grand (2002), this "knowing means holding certain beliefs about the world, this knowledge being justified in experience and current observations as well as conceptual reasoning and thinking" (p. 172). Enbrained knowledge thus requires the development of a keen awareness, the ability to think through requirements that underscore actions and the sensing of needs. This definition of advancement knowledge implies that beliefs of what constitutes knowledge are affected by experiences, observations and abilities to conceptually reason and to think.

Advancement knowledge involves *"encultured" knowledge in event management gained through practice*

Encultured knowledge also encompasses cognitive abilities, but in this case these abilities consist of intimate understandings of the subtleties required for full participation in a particular culture (Collins, 1993). Encultured knowledge is derived from being immersed within a specific culture – even if it is just for a period of time. For example, one can immerse oneself by living in North American culture, an Asian culture or any of the European cultures. This type of knowledge requires deep understandings of the thought processes, practices and social norms of the particular culture.

Advancement knowledge is foundational for *the generation of your new knowledge*

For years, we have understood that creating new knowledge does not occur disconnected from our current abilities and understandings (Kogut &

16

Zander, 1992). Rather, new knowledge in the form of innovations arises from "a firm's *combinative capabilities* to generate new application from existing knowledge" (p. 390). This implies that, generally, to create new knowledge, it is the combination of what you already know, along with the application of this knowledge to a new situation, that aids in the generation of new knowledge. Overall, the process of creating new knowledge requires individuals to synthesize their current knowledge for different applications or situations.

THE VALUE OF BEING ABLE TO DEFINE KNOWLEDGE

The value of being able to define knowledge is that it can guide you in seeking and acquiring the knowledge you need for successful event management. Overall, obtaining common knowledge in event management is important in order to manage the multiple aspects of an event; however, it is advancement knowledge that can provide the difference when one is managing arising issues or when event situations do not have well-defined parameters. Thus, advancement knowledge is the foundation for high-level judgments or decisions.

Earlier in this chapter you were asked to record a definition of knowledge. Now go back and review your initial definition of knowledge and the dimensions or features of knowledge that you were able to describe, and compare them to the definitions and features of common and advancement knowledge described so far in this chapter. Rework your definition.

A UNIQUE DEFINITION OF KNOWLEDGE TO GUIDE YOU IN THE CONTEXT OF EVENT MANAGEMENT

To further aid your understandings, a definition specifically for knowledge in event management is provided. This definition was constructed by applying the multiple definitions and descriptions of common and advancement knowledge offered above. The ensuing definition of knowledge is outlined in Figure 2.2.

Based on the definition of knowledge outlined in Figure 2.2, a synergy, or the confluence of common and advancement knowledge, involves more than just adding up your knowledge to create a total level of knowledge. The synergy gives rise to a personalized combination of types of knowledge that can be achieved through interactions for use in practice. The aim is, therefore, to acquire personalized knowledge.

The author of this chapter provides the following definition of knowledge for the context of sport, recreation and tourism event management:

> Event management knowledge = The synergy of common knowledge and advancement knowledge in the sport, recreation and tourism event industry that leads to perspicacity (quick insights and understandings) for competence (in actions and ability).

Figure 2.2 An umbrella definition of sport, recreation and tourism event management knowledge

THE ADVANTAGE OF YOUR *"FLEXIBILITY EFFECT"* OR PERSONALIZED KNOWLEDGE

A knowledge advantage can be derived from what Conner and Prahalad (2002) call the *flexibility effect*. This effect includes knowledge that is personalized by intertwining one's personal perspectives, opinions, approaches, experiences, ideas and options. In addition, personalization includes the impact of one's skill, personality, motivations, abilities, perceptions and interpretations on those elements. This impact creates differentiation, or one's flexibility effect. According to Zack (1999), a flexibility effect includes differentiated ideas, interpretations and responses that provide a competitive advantage (Figure 2.3). This advantage is produced through the personalization process that leads to insights, understandings and the development of new knowledge.

Your flexibility effect includes the use of personal perspectives, opinions, approaches, experiences, ideas and options to create knowledge differentiation, or one's "flexibility effect[s]." Differentiated ideas, interpretations and responses provide a potential competitive advantage in the contemporary change-based environment (Zack, 1999).

In other words . . . it is important to be yourself!

Figure 2.3 Flexibility effect

18

The personalization of knowledge facilitates the production of ideas and new knowledge. This is because differentiation ensures that ideas are varied, and not limited to one particular person's viewpoint (Carney, 2001). Accepting and nurturing the personalization of your knowledge encourages the development of options, varied interpretations and solutions. When you are sharing or exchanging knowledge, it is important that you develop your flexibility effect for potential advantage.

YOU ARE IN A KNOWLEDGE TRANSFER RACE

An emphasis on knowledge in society has stimulated what English and Baker (2006) call "the knowledge transfer race." In this race, each individual has a primary role in creating knowledge. Individuals and collaborative groups race competitively to continuously develop more knowledge. The key activity in the continuous development of knowledge is the sharing of this knowledge. There is a race to transfer or share knowledge in order to facilitate the creation of more knowledge.

The value of knowledge transfer, or a sharing process, was highlighted by George Bernard Shaw in 1930 when he expressed the following in his play *The Apple Cart*:

> If you have an apple and I have an apple and we exchange these apples then you and I will still each have one apple. But if you have an idea and I have an idea and we exchange these ideas, then each of us will have two ideas.

An application of Shaw's exchange concept to knowledge implies that transference aids the development of all parties in the knowledge-sharing process. This sharing concept was expressed by Shaw decades ago, but it has become a requirement for participants in today's knowledge-based environment.

Knowledge has been described by Boisot (2002) as being personal in nature, yet there is a critical dependence between the knowledge holder and the development of more knowledge with the use of a sharing process (Hall, 2001). Individual effort simply does not provide enough knowledge to fully compete in the knowledge transfer race. A connection to others is needed to further one's knowledge development.

For years, transferring knowledge has been seen as a top priority because "the fast and effective transfer of knowledge is the only truly sustainable competitive advantage" (Drucker, 1994, p. 10). However, English and Baker (2006) posit that only those who acquire the appropriate knowledge to share can participate and gain additional knowledge through the transferring process. This is because you need to have knowledge to share with others so they will, in return, share their knowledge with you.

An application of this transference process indicates that those in sport, recreation and tourism event management must share knowledge in order to advance their own personally held knowledge. The development of knowledge within a process of sharing can develop even more knowledge for the staging of events, including the development of innovations for the event industry and the solving of contemporary event problems.

To be competitive in event management, it seems logical that a strategy is needed for knowledge transfer. In this chapter, the strategy proposed is a self-directed plan to develop the ability to become efficient and effective in the process of acquiring and transferring a variety of types of knowledge for event management.

At the core of this strategy is the definition of knowledge as it applies specifically to sport, recreation and tourism event management. Once knowledge is defined, a strategy for participating in the knowledge transfer race can be developed. However, the defining of knowledge is not a clearly articulated process. Difficulties arise as one attempts to establish a definition of knowledge and the key characteristics that it entails.

YOU NEED A KNOWLEDGE TRANSFER RACE STRATEGY

A knowledge transfer race strategy is a plan to guide you in gaining the common and advancement knowledge for a successful career in event management (Figure 2.4). It is a self-directed plan to assist you to become efficient and effective in the process of acquiring and transferring knowledge in event management. This strategy articulates a deliberate means to guide you to develop your capacity for knowledge for competitive use. In event management, a knowledge transfer race strategy aims to increase your common knowledge, to acquire advancement knowledge, to advance your perspicacity (quick advancement insights and understandings) and to advance your competence (actions and ability) for use in the event management field.

20

> Knowledge transfer race strategy is a deliberate means to act to develop your capacity for knowledge for use in the fields of sport, recreation and tourism event management.

Figure 2.4 Defining a knowledge transfer race strategy

To effectively participate in a knowledge-sharing process, you need to establish an overview of the types of knowledge you are looking to acquire. Complete Figure 2.5 to set out a path as to how you can acquire common and advancement knowledge for the event industry. This ongoing assignment should be revisited over time to update the knowledge you specifically require for your particular involvement in event management and to establish the path for obtaining this knowledge. Implement your knowledge transfer race strategy and pursue the knowledge that will make you a valuable and successful participant in event management.

Features of "common knowledge"	Guidance to assist you to determine the common knowledge you require for the event management industry
1 Systemic knowledge: understandings about the overall organization	List a minimum of two local/regional event organizations and two national or international event organizations that you would like to investigate. Next, determine what can be read to gain basic knowledge about these organizations.
	Who could you talk to and what questions could you ask to advance your common knowledge about these event management organizations (generate a minimum of five questions)?
2 Systemic knowledge: understandings of organizational systems	What methodological systems are used to aid the event management organizations you listed above? For instance, what procedures, schemes, techniques, manuals and/or information packages are utilized, or describe these systems?
	How can you gain common knowledge about these systems?
	Consider listing upcoming events by the organizations you provided above and find out how you could gain volunteer or work experience on some of these events.

▼

Features of "common knowledge"	Guidance to assist you to determine the common knowledge you require for the event management industry
3 Understanding what one does in event management	Fully describe what one does if one is an event manager.
	Consider the managers of event accommodations, accreditation, ceremonies (including opening, closing and awards ceremonies), drug testing, food and beverage provision, media management, protocols, public relations, results, transportation, venue and warehousing.
	Where can you obtain written job descriptions and/or who can you talk to about the role played by each of these event managers to advance your common knowledge?
	Each manager needs to facilitate event activities. What is involved in this role and how can you obtain experience in facilitation?
4 Understandings of theories	Record the dimensions or characteristics of a minimum of three theories that relate to event management (such as agency, complexity, contingency, legitimacy and systems theory). Next, record how each of these theories can guide an event manager or what the theories indicate that can be applied by an event manager.
5 Understandings of the basics of culture, politics and personalities	Determine the cultures potentially involved in the event organizations that you listed above. Next, state at least three ways in which you can advance your understandings about the beliefs and practices within each of these cultures.
	Determine whom you could talk to about political issues that can arise in event management and how they can be handled . . . and what this individual has learned in hindsight.
	Also, determine whom you could talk about difficult personalities in event management that they have encountered and their strategies for handling these situations to ensure excellent coordination and cooperation between workers.
6 Conceptual understandings	Create a list of the types of conceptual understandings found in event management. Consider your conceived understandings concerning planning events and working with a number of people.
7 Common sense	Record three commonsense decisions that you may encounter in event management.

Features of "advancement knowledge"	Guidance to assist you to determine the advancement knowledge you require for the event management industry
8 In-depth understandings of routines	Outline a potential career path for you to pursue over the next 15 years in event management. This path should contain at least four career changes, and you should consider traditional and niche events. Next, record the types of routines that are pertinent to each career option and indicate a long-term strategy for learning these routines.
9 "Enbrained" knowledge or an awareness & ability to think through the requirements to complete tasks	Develop a strategy for participating in the hosting of events and start practising thinking through the task requirements and implementing plans.
10 "Encultured" knowledge or deep understandings of a particular culture	Develop a strategy for gaining intimate knowledge of cultures. Consider travel to work on events and home stay options.
11 New knowledge	Continuously seek to advance new knowledge with the application of what is already known to new situations.

Figure 2.5 Ongoing assignment: develop a strategy for advancing your knowledge in event management

SOCIAL NETWORKS SUPPORT THE KNOWLEDGE TRANSFER STRATEGY

A description from Castells (2000) indicates the following:

> Networks are dynamic, self-evolving structures, which, powered by information technology and communicating with the same digital language, can grow, and include all social expressions, compatible with each network's goals. Networks increase their value exponentially as they add nodes.
>
> (p. 697)

The combination of individual member relationships creates the structure of a network. The social nature of networks employs communication as their key characteristic. Communication is a constant requirement for the formation and maintenance of the network. The key role of every member in the network is to communicate.

Each member within the network needs to develop the competence to be a valuable communicator. Harris, Coles and Dickson (2000) indicate that network competence includes the ability of each member to

> share their understanding of issues and devise ways to relate to each other in carrying out the work necessary to bring about a shared vision of the future. This vision provides the context that orients all network activity. Retaining this orientation is critical to developing and maintaining networks.
>
> (p. 6)

The sharing within the network provides opportunities for ideas to be generated and knowledge to be created (von Krogh & Grand, 2002).

To form an event management knowledge transfer network, members are necessary to encourage the relationships for a knowledge-sharing process. This requires an investment of the necessary time, attention and competence to develop and maintain the network relationships. A key component in a knowledge transfer race strategy is *network activism* (Figure 2.6). This involves a conscious effort to expand your personal network, to encourage contacts between the members in the network and to advance the quality of the network relationships for exchanging knowledge.

You should seriously consider creating your own network for knowledge sharing. To develop a network, consider the following questions:

- Whom would you contact to begin a personal network in order to pursue event management knowledge?
- What do you expect from each network member in terms of the transfer of knowledge, and what are you providing in return?

Network activism is a conscious effort to (a) expand the number of nodes (people or groups) within your personal network, (b) encourage contacts between the nodes and (c) advance the quality of the network relationships.

Figure 2.6 Network activism

24

- How will you encourage a greater number of contacts between you and others in your network?
- How will you advance the quality of the network relationships to gain more knowledge?

CONCLUSION

Those in event management cannot expect to be exempt from the knowledge requirements emphasized in contemporary society. To begin to gain the necessary knowledge, you need to develop your personal definition of knowledge and create a knowledge transfer race strategy to guide you in the acquisition of the multiple dimensions of knowledge needed for the event management industry. The implementation of your knowledge transfer race strategy includes the search for knowledge with the expansion of your relations in event management, advancing the contact and the quality of the network relationships. Your participation in a network that encourages collaboration and sharing of knowledge aids in the effort to obtain more knowledge.

To support the concept of a knowledge transfer race strategy, this text *does not* provide a list of elements that you can follow to produce a sport, recreation or tourism event. A list of elements is not conducive to the traditional and niche events being hosted. This is because all events are not alike, and the contemporary environment of change means that you will be working on events in the future that have not yet been conceived. It is important, therefore, to be able to "think through" the particular requirements for the context and event. It is perspicacity that you are seeking – the constant advance of quick insights and understandings that position you well for a future in event management.

CHAPTER QUESTIONS

1 Describe the characteristics of common knowledge in event management.
2 Describe the characteristics of advancement knowledge in event management.
3 Why is advancement knowledge more difficult to obtain compared to common knowledge?
4 What is a knowledge transfer race and how and why do you need to participate in this race?

CHAPTER 3

THE EVENT PLANNING MODEL: THE EVENT DEVELOPMENT PHASE, PART I

AMY CUNNINGHAM AND JOANNE MACLEAN

This chapter examines the first phase of a four-phase event planning model (Figure 3.1), the *event development phase*. In the discussion of this phase, the event manager is positioned as a facilitator. A definition of facilitation is provided, along with the theory of facilitation. The facilitation role is outlined as guiding the development of the event structures for governance. Theories, including systems theory, contingency theory and complexity theory, are applied to the facilitator's role.

THE EVENT MANAGER AS A FACILITATOR (by Amy Cunningham)

One of the most exciting aspects of event management is the requirement to produce a team effort. The event needs a facilitator to guide the process of *sharing of knowledge* between members. In addition, the event manager is responsible for *facilitating* event processes. These are the processes that are found within the collaborative effort of planning and implementing an event, where all members of the group need to feel equally a part of the team effort.

The role of the event manager as a facilitator is established in the development phase of the planning model. This facilitation role will be discussed in more depth in what follows, but first let us take a step back and investigate the meaning of facilitation itself. The concept of facilitation is crucial to the role an event manager must play, and will provide the theoretical framework upon which we will draw our understanding within this section and the overall text.

26

Event development phase

The event manager facilitates the development of event structures for governance, event networks, policies, volunteer practices and participation in a corporate social responsibility program

Event evaluation and renewal phase

The event manager facilitates the selection of event components to be evaluated, the completion of the evaluation tasks and the implementation of the evaluation recommendations

Event operational planning phase

The event manager creates and facilitates the development of written operational plans that are logical, sequential, detailed and integrated, along with contingency plans and the activation of a plan refining process

Event implementation, monitoring and management phase

The event manager facilitates the implementation of the written operational plans, monitors activities, looking for deviations, and manages all deviations from the plans

Figure 3.1 An event planning model

What is facilitation?

Bens (2000) defines facilitation as "a way of providing leadership without taking the reins" (p. 7). Facilitation theory assumes that learning will occur with the aid of one who facilitates the process of learning as opposed to one who simply provides knowledge to a group (Laird, 1985; Lambert & Glacken, 2005). Within this theory of facilitation, it is believed that since change is constant, the greatest teachers are those who have learned how to learn, and can lead others in self-directed learning and critical thinking (Lambert & Glacken, 2005; Peel, 2000). This style of leadership encourages the development of empowered learners and contributors to group processes, where the creation and dissemination of knowledge are dependent on all members of the group.

To be an effective facilitator and supporter of this theory, one must subscribe to certain assumptions. According to Bens (2000, p. 8), believers in facilitation theory and practice assume that:

- People are intelligent, capable and want to do the right thing.
- Groups can make better decisions than any one person can make alone.
- Everyone's opinion is of equal value, regardless of their rank or position.
- People are committed to the ideas and plans that they have helped to create.
- Participants can and will act responsibly in assuming true accountability for their decisions.
- Groups can manage their own conflicts, behaviours and relationships if they are given the right tools and training.
- The *process*, if well designed and honestly applied, can be trusted to achieve results.

Now that we have a general understanding of what is meant by the theory of facilitation, the role of an event manager acting as a facilitator can be explored.

The role of an event facilitator

If we look back to Figure 3.1, "An event planning model," the event manager has an important role to play as a facilitator throughout all of the planning phases. As a facilitator, your job is to *get others to assume responsibility and to take the lead.* Rogers and Freiberg (1994, p. 21, after Lao Tzu) expressed this facilitation leadership role in the following way:

A leader is best
When people barely know that he exists,
Not so good when people obey and acclaim him,
Worst when they despise him.
Fail to honour people; they fail to honour you
But of a good leader, who talks little,
When his work is done, his aim fulfilled,
They will all say, "We did this ourselves."

A facilitator becomes the director of the performance, where each participant plays a central role (Vidal, 2004). By the end of this performance, with the creation of group synergy, which should be one of the main goals of true facilitation, participants will have had "the pleasure of working creatively and collectively to achieve some goals" (p. 394). Overall, facilitators aim to make specific processes easier during all phases of the event.

28

There are many specific skills, experiences and knowledges that the event manager must possess to facilitate an event (Peel, 2000; Thomas, 2004). This array includes advancement knowledge, which involves intuition about the processes that they are guiding to help them "act on their feet" and make quick decisions with regard to the needs of a group or process (Peel, 2000). By making these processes easier, specific tasks will be completed, goals will be met and the team will feel a pleasurable synergy after a job well done (Vidal, 2004).

A good facilitator empowers the group and the individuals within it to rise to their own potential and have the confidence to be an equal player on the team so that no one becomes dependent on a "teacher." Everyone is shown to be their own developer of knowledge, and the strengths of each individual within the collective can be drawn out and their benefits maximized within the overall process (Peel, 2000). Review Figure 3.2 for an overview of the difference between teaching and facilitating.

Figure 3.3 offers a comprehensive outline of some of the specific roles that a facilitator would play during the event-managing process.

Facilitating the communication requirements

Greenberg (2002) explains, "Communication is the process through which people send information to others and receive information from them" (p. 217). This process can be a difficult one to facilitate, as it is made up of numerous interactions between various members of a team, all of whom bring their individual personalities, knowledge, skills and communication styles to the table. It is a key role of the event manager, then, to act as a facilitator and to make sure that communication lines are open, that members of the team feel that they are being supported and that specific processes and requirements are articulated and managed throughout the overall process (Bens, 2000).

Describe the difference between *teaching* and *facilitating*.

Determine the *advantages* and *disadvantages* of teaching compared to facilitating.

Figure 3.2 Questioning the difference between teaching and facilitating

A facilitator

- Helps the group define specific goals and objectives
- Provides processes that assist members to use their time efficiently to make good decisions; helps group members understand these processes
- Guides group discussion to keep things on track
- Keeps accurate notes that reflect the ideas of the group members
- Supports members in assessing their current skills and the building of new ones
- Uses consensus to help the group make decisions that take all members' opinions into account
- Supports members in managing their own interpersonal dynamics
- Helps the group communicate effectively
- Helps the group access resources
- Creates a positive environment in which members can grow and work together toward attaining group goals
- Fosters leadership in others by sharing leadership responsibilities
- Supports and empowers others to facilitate

Source: Bens (2000); Peel (2000); Vidal (2004).

Figure 3.3 The event manager as a facilitator

In organizational settings, the communication process can be extremely complex, depending on the design of the organization. In many cases, information may need to flow up or down through the "ranks" or be transmitted to certain individuals via other individuals (Greenberg, 2002). The complexity of these links can lead to communication breakdowns and confusion if not managed properly. The wonderful thing about facilitating a group of individuals with whom you are considered a part of the team is that most of the communication in this process will move horizontally. As Greenberg states, "Messages of this type are characterized by efforts at coordinating, or attempts to work together" (2002, p. 201). By focusing and guiding group members' communication and decision-making processes in a structured form, a facilitator can reduce the chances of engaging in faulty processes and harness the strengths of the group. If the proper communication requirements have been articulated and set in place by the facilitator at the onset of the event planning process, the facilitator should fade into the collective, merely to be called upon to manage problems and situations as they may arise.

As a facilitator, the event manager is constantly listening, thinking and reflecting throughout the process as problem solving and decision making are occurring between group members. In any group situation, decisions will need to be made, and any conflicts will need to be resolved. While the overall process of task completion is equally the responsibility of each member of the group, it is the role of an effective facilitator to guide the group to a synergy that is born of effective communication (Vidal, 2004). In this regard, historically a facilitator would act as a neutral party who reminds the group of the aims, guides the group communication requirements, sets specific strategies at the onset of the process and interjects as necessary to guide the group back into synchronicity (Laird, 1985; Rogers & Freiberg, 1994).

Now that the importance of facilitating the communication requirements is understood, Figure 3.4 shows some helpful tips to consider.

The case of group rhythm and facilitation
According to a seminal work by Drucker (1946), "an institution is like a 'tune'; it is not constituted by individual sounds but by the relations

---

- Be a supportive communicator
- Focus on the problem instead of the person
- Match words with body language and encourage group members to do the same
- Encourage the group to acknowledge each other's ideas
- Keep the conversation going
- Encourage open feedback
- Encourage the use of simple language
- Paraphrase to clarify; repeat what people say to assure them they are being heard and to make sure each member of the group has understood and is clear
- Walk the talk; don't say one thing and do another, and watch for this behaviour in group members
- Be a good listener and encourage the group to be good listeners too; consider the use of a "talking stick" to ensure that everyone has a chance to speak and be heard
- Stay neutral, and avoid sharing your personal opinion unless it is requested; focus on your *process* role of communication
- Ask questions; this will invite participation, help to gather information, test assumptions and get to the root causes of problems
- Synthesize ideas; encourage group members to comment and build upon each other's ideas
- Stay on track; set time guidelines for each discussion
- Summarize clearly

Source: Bens (2000); Greenberg (2002).

Figure 3.4 Facilitation tips

between them" (p. 26). An event can exhibit institutional characteristics and requires the facilitation of the relations between the many individuals involved to create a coordinated tune.

Lulu Leathley, from Vancouver, British Columbia, Canada, is an individual who specializes in facilitating group rhythms (group drumming circles) and promotes the importance of facilitated communication in group processes. The teachings of Leathley position the facilitator's role as beginning with the act of being a conductor. In music, the goal is to reach a moment in the facilitation of group music-making where everyone (whatever their musical background and experience) feels empowered and collectively reaches a place of group synergy. It is her goal to slowly fade into the background and become a part of the group so that the music created is dependent upon each person and no one becomes dependent on her as a leader. To accomplish this goal, she sets certain communication requirements (both verbal and nonverbal) at the beginning of the group drumming circle. She very clearly articulates the importance of listening to each other, making eye contact and getting in touch with inner intuitions and rhythms. In other words, she encourages and empowers group members to look inside of themselves for the knowledge that she believes they already possess in order to create something that is a sum of all parts of the collective. Throughout the facilitation process, she encourages the group to bring their own inner rhythms and strengths forward in order to contribute to the collective song. She makes sure to keep the rhythm going, despite the ups and downs, and provides ample room and encouragement for feedback. At the completion of a successful event, there is the energy of connection.

In musical collaboration, there is an overall feeling by the musicians when everything culminates in a satisfying "click" (Sawyer, 2006). This synergistic click is a challenge to attain, as it takes the cooperation and ability of all group members working together to reach this goal. The facilitator's job is to communicate with the group both verbally and nonverbally in the beginning and then to re-enter and guide the group and *sense* what is needed throughout the process.

Experience in facilitation helps you become quicker with your intuitive decision-making abilities, and your flexibility effect includes personalizing your knowledge, perceptions and ideas for an advantage. A facilitator's role, therefore, is to use their knowledge to facilitate the event process. This facilitation includes recognizing when certain group members are overpowering others, when people are not listening to each other or when

32

the group is approaching a collective musical disaster. In this situation, Leathley responds and reacts to the needs of the group on the basis of her own experience, knowledge, skills and intuition – the *flexibility effect* she has acquired as a music teacher and facilitator.

If the group has succeeded in coming together and clicking, there is an overwhelming sense of empowerment, pride and accomplishment as a collective at the conclusion of the event. As has already been mentioned, this is a sign that the event facilitator has been effective and successful in their role. Facilitating communication within the group process, then, can be seen as one of the most important roles of the event manager.

A sport, recreation or tourism event manager facilitates the communication processes. Their experience, knowledge, skills and intuition contribute to the ability to create a collective synergy in event production.

We have now reviewed the meaning of facilitation and the role of the facilitator, specifically regarding communication process requirements. Now let us consider another important role in facilitation, the transfer of knowledge.

Facilitating knowledge transfer

We have discussed the role of the event manager as a facilitator and what that entails during group processes in the organizing of an event. It is your job, as facilitator of a collaborative group effort, to make sure knowledge is transferred between group members and built upon. This transfer helps ensure that the best and most informed decisions are made in the pursuit of task completion, drawing on the collective knowledge of the group. But how does the facilitator go about ensuring that their own knowledge is transferred to inform the field as a whole?

The sharing of knowledge with others invites other facilitators to share their knowledge in return and assumes they will do so, and as a result the knowledge apex will broaden and expand. This broadening has very positive outcomes if we are to assume that the goal of sharing and receiving new knowledge is to continuously work toward honing our effectiveness and expertise as facilitators.

Within a practical setting, let us revisit Lulu Leathley's facilitation of rhythm-based events. As a facilitator within a network of other facilitators, Leathley engages in many specific knowledge transfer strategies that enable her to inform her field, contribute to the expansion of the knowledge pool and broaden her own knowledge base. Some of these strategies include:

- building relationships and sharing dialogue about experiences with other facilitators;
- attending rhythm facilitation conferences;
- continuously attending training sessions with other facilitators with varying levels of experience;
- joining discussion groups and posting information on various websites;
- becoming an active member in the rhythm facilitators' guild;
- aiding others to develop facilitation skills by lending her talents and experiences to mentorship programs.

In these activities, there is a climate of cooperation and support that aids in the important transfer of knowledge. As a result of this enthusiasm and support, the community of facilitators continues to grow, and individuals are able to develop their *perspicacity* (quick, advanced insights and understandings) through the knowledge that is shared. There are many ways in which an event manager may facilitate this knowledge transfer, and we have examined various examples within one particular case. I have also outlined the specifics of facilitation, the role of the event manager as a facilitator, the importance of facilitating communication requirements and ways in which this may be done. Let us now begin a discussion on another area of interest in the development phase of the planning model, the facilitation of structures for governance when staging an event.

FACILITATING EVENT STRUCTURES FOR GOVERNANCE
(by Joanne MacLean)

Let us consider an event of huge magnitude, for example the Olympic and Paralympic Games. In July and August 2012, London hosted the Games. The previous Games were held in February and March 2010, when the communities of Vancouver and Whistler welcomed the world to Canada for a massive winter sporting festival. Competition is generally conducted over a 17-day period, with another 10 days of Paralympic competition following. The event organizers have, as their mission, inspiring the world through this event. The Vancouver Organizing Committee indicated that

34

the mission is to touch the soul of the nation and inspire the world by creating and delivering an extraordinary Olympic and Paralympic experience with lasting legacies. The vision is to build a stronger Canada whose spirit is raised by its passion for sport, culture and sustainability.

(Vancouver 2010, 2007)

The 2012 Olympic Games held in London also had a motto of "Green and Secure" (Scribd.com). This motto indicated an emphasis on safeguarding both the natural environment and the participants and spectators throughout the Games.

The missions, visions and mottoes were to be met through organizing a variety of sporting competitions and cultural festivities. Thousands of employees and volunteers staged the Games, and the images of athletes from hundreds of countries around the world were televised and followed intently by fellow citizens. Organizing the Olympic Games required an enormous planning process.

Now turn your attention to a smaller event run in your community, such as a community tourism event or a team sport championship being hosted at your university or college. Even though it is of smaller magnitude and duration than the Olympics, it still involves many of the same components. Event components in sport, recreation and tourism can include elements such as:

- accommodation;
- accreditation;
- ceremonies;
- communications;
- drug testing or doping control;
- food and beverages;
- hospitality services;
- media management;
- official management;
- participant management;
- results and awards;
- spectator services;
- transportation.

In each case, a considerable amount of work is devoted to planning and staging a successful event.

Events within sport, recreation and tourism have levels of magnitude, appeal and complexity that require well-designed event structures that contribute to successful delivery. Oftentimes, the structure and governance of event management are "silent," somewhat behind the scenes as compared to the main program of activities that are consumed or watched. However, in reality the elements of effective structure and governance are foundations to success. Successful events simply cannot be achieved without a structure for planning and delivering the event that enables effective communication, decision making and appropriate amounts of flexibility among event managers. In order to understand this in further detail, the purposes of the following sections include:

1   defining the concepts related to event structures and good governance of event management;
2   outlining the theoretical dimensions of event structures that will enable the delivery of successful events, without identifying the specifics of that structure;
3   identifying principles that result in the creation of effective event structures;
4   applying the theoretical dimensions and principles of event structures identified above to different types of events currently popular in the business of sport, recreation and tourism.

By following the topics identified above, students will gain an appreciation of two important fundamental principles about facilitating event structures for event management: first, different kinds of events require different event management structures that provide the management best suited for the particular event; and second, we believe that event managers are better served learning the *guiding principles* that will enable them to make decisions about the most appropriate and effective structure for the event being planned, as opposed to duplicating the structure from another event. You may label these two fundamental principles *flexibility* and *specificity* regarding event management structures. The following sections will help you understand these and other principles and their application in creating effective event structures.

A. Cunningham and J. MacLean

Event structures

So what exactly do we mean by the term *event structure*? This term refers to breaking down the tasks associated with delivering the event such that employees or volunteers have specific roles and an understanding of how these roles interrelate. The structure involves individual positions or groups of individuals in committees that control tasks and understand the authority they have to make which decisions, and the reporting relationships between individuals and committees. Typically, event leaders publicize a management structure in the form of a chart with boxes and connecting lines outlining the task areas, with proximity between areas that need to cooperate and/or collaborate, and reporting directions.

Theoretically, the structure of an organization is usually examined from three points of view (Slack & Parent, 2006). The first viewpoint is *formalization* (the degree to which rules and regulations, policies and individual and committee roles are defined to guide the activities of event managers). The second viewpoint is *complexity* (the scope and number of different individual committees and sub-units required to deliver the event and the density of the hierarchy of authority involved). The third viewpoint is *centralization* (the degree to which decision making is controlled by those in charge of the event or delegated to individuals working at the level of committees or individual jobs). The event structure can be designed to be high or low in each of formalization, complexity and centralization, depending on the type of event.

Event structures are developed to aid the governance of an event. Governance refers to exercising the authority to define policy regarding how the event will be run, who does what, and when and how they do it. If an event is to be successful, then the structure created to deliver it must provide for effective transfer of knowledge and decision making. Facilitating event structures means that you have the knowledge necessary to create the most appropriate organizing structure for your event.

In addition to the theory discussed above regarding event structure, there are a number of other important theories that have been developed which aid in understanding effective event structures. The theoretical dimensions of event structures that we have chosen to include in this discussion involve systems theory, contingency theory and complexity theory. The following subsections will briefly introduce each theory in the context of understanding effective event structures for good governance and successful event management.

Theoretical dimensions of event structures

Event structures vary considerably. For concrete local examples, examine how your educational recreational events are structured. Compare the recreational event structure to a local tourism event and a locally held elite sport championship. Each event can be unique in its structure. The structure dictates the hierarchy, which in turn influences the freedom to act in the process of making, relaying and implementing decisions and actions when an event is being staged.

When creating an event, you will need to consider a structure that will lead to the most effective and efficient delivery for staging the event. In order for you to achieve this goal, there are several theoretical perspectives that relate information about effective organizations and event structures. The theoretical dimensions outlined next are largely complementary, in that parts of each theory may apply in specific ways to the event structure you develop.

Systems theory

Systems theory stresses that event management structures rely on the environment within which they operate for many of the materials that will be required for hosting the event. Materials include a wide variety of items such as people, equipment, technologies and facilities, to name a few. Systems theory suggests that the event will have three different systems working together: *input systems*, *throughput systems* and *output systems*. In order to run an event, you must take in resources (inputs), create the event activities (throughputs) and generate end results for participants or others (outputs). The three systems are interrelated and depend on each other for success. A change in one inevitably affects the other parts of the system. Any event you are organizing involves inputs or the acquisition of raw materials (competition facilities) and human resources (volunteers) to organize the event; throughputs might include the application of technology (a website designed for managing communication and registration) and information (the number of participants who can be accommodated); and outputs include the enjoyment of participants and the money raised for the charity of choice. The overall event system interacts within its component parts and with its environment. Understanding the application of systems theory identifies the importance of component parts of the organization structure depending on and influencing one another.

38

Contingency theory

A rational extension to systems theory in understanding the organizing structure and management of an event is *contingency theory*. This theory suggests that the effective structure of an organization is contingent on contextual factors of the environment within which it operates, such as size, competition, strategy, resources and so on. As such, the design of the event structure and its units must "fit" with the environment and work well in coordination in order for the event to succeed. Therefore, there is no "best way" to organize an event structure, as it depends on factors within the environment of operation. For example, in a charity recreational event the structure of the event organizing system will need to account for how many competitors register. However, the size of registration may be wholly contingent on what facilities exist, how much time can be acquired within facilities and how many referees are available. These factors may be impacted by other tournaments running proximal to yours in timing or location. Such factors are often termed constraints, and understanding event constraints and contingencies will lead to optimal organizing structure, decision making and leadership.

Complexity theory

In keeping with systems and contingency theories, complexity theory works to identify how organizations optimally adapt to their environments. Using this theory, managers focus on the required complexity of structure that can achieve the mission of the event while retaining the ability to adapt and make strategic decisions quickly. Complexity theory identifies the importance of complex adaptive systems, structures that commonly consist of a small number of relatively simple, partially connected structures. In our recreational charity event example, a simpler structure involving committees for scheduling, facility organization, registration and volunteers that connect to each other via a tournament leaders' committee will be better able to communicate, make effective decisions and adapt to its environment.

Theories expand our understandings

In academic study, the word "theory" is used to describe the logical explanation for a phenomenon that has been studied systematically, an explanation thought to expand our understanding. The theories briefly described above provide a foundation for understanding why and how event structures may be optimally designed. How can we facilitate effective structures? What makes one event structure effective and another ineffective? How do event structures come to influence good governance, such that the decision making, policy development and efficiency of the event are optimized? Understanding the above theories sheds some light on answering these questions. And from these theories, along with trial and error concerning what works in practice and the transfer of this knowledge, a variety of principles in event structures have been identified. Let's look at these in further detail.

Principles in event structures

Principles can be likened to rules or understandings that have resulted from theory and practice regarding how and why things work. In developing effective organizing structures for event management, a number of principles are identified that will help event organizers create the optimal structure for the particular event and environment within which the event is being delivered. The following are some of the major principles applying to event structure development:

- *Form follows function.* This principle suggests that the type of structure created to manage the delivery of an event should be predicated on the purpose of the event and the definition of governance roles (for example, developing policy, managing, operating) within the event management design. Copying the event structure from a previously successful event does not necessarily result in a workable structure for another event. For example, using the structure developed to deliver the Olympic Games would be ridiculous when you are delivering a high school basketball tournament, because the former event is so much larger and more complex than the latter.
- *Operating specialization.* Optimal event structures identify the activities required to deliver the event and cluster similar or like activities together into sub-units to encourage communication and decision making. By so doing, efficiency is created by maximizing interconnections among managers with responsibilities that impact one another, leading to more autonomous but interconnected work groups.
- *Increasing complexity increases both the amount of planning and the amount of time required for planning.* The more complex an organizing structure, the more planning is required to ensure that the structure functions optimally. It stands to reason that this will take more time than with a simple structure. An example of this

40

principle is the organizing of the Olympic Games. Games operating committee structures are designed a minimum of six to eight years in advance of the competition, and the extent of planning is exceptionally broad.

■ *Communications efficiency*. Planning does not take place in the brain of one person in isolation from others. Therefore, the structure for event management must create linkages and liaisons for individuals to communicate their activities and decisions, and this communication must be formally arranged in order to be efficiently enacted. The speed and number of communications can be enhanced depending on the type of event structure created.

■ *Synergistic outcomes*. Synergy refers to the phenomenon of the greater efficiency and better outcomes that occur when two or more agents work together as compared to what could be achieved had each completed the same tasks in isolation. Event structures that create opportunities for synergistic outcomes are said to be efficiently lean and more effective for task accomplishment (Kilmann, Pondy & Slevin, 1976). The accruing synergistic outcome results from the idea that the overall accomplishment is more than a simple summation of output, meaning that the whole is greater than the sum of its parts.

Understanding the theories and principles relative to facilitating effective event structures is very important, but knowing how to apply the ideas presented to create actual event structures is perhaps even more critical for the success of the event and its managers. Next we move to a discussion of the application of key characteristics of the above theory.

Application of theory and principles in event structures

The theory and principles outlined earlier in this chapter regarding the development of effective event structures apply to both traditional and niche events. In practice, traditional events may involve more formality of structure compared to niche events as a result of the dictates of the governing body and its established policy regarding how the event is to be organized. Systems theory suggests that the environment within which the event is hosted be considered for both traditional and niche events. The required resources needed to create the event, the anticipated outcomes of the event, and the event activities will also need to be considered. Contingency theory holds that the importance of fitting the event structure to both its purpose and its environment – creating a structure that fits appropriately with the size, resources and intent of traditional and niche sporting events – is paramount. Complexity theory also establishes the importance of matching the structure for organizing the event to its environment and purpose in order to create a structure that matches the strategy and adaptability that might be required in the environment. Being able to adapt to unforeseen problems, pressures and changes is a fundamental requirement for traditional and niche event structure frameworks. This adaptability can be optimized when the structure created for the event is directly linked to its purpose (for example, form follows function). While it might seem straightforward, an obvious decision, to use the structure of another, successful event when planning a new event, it is actually a risky proposition. Linking form and function – creating an event structure that identifies the intent and governance roles that most specifically meet the needs of the actual event – is highly important. Doing so is critically important for traditional sport event structures, but the need to link form and function must necessarily be stressed even further with niche events, where the event structure is without the guidance of a governing body, established policy or other comparable events. Similarly, creating a clear understanding of the operating specialization for the event and linking the activities of sub-units with common or dependent roles will encourage effective communication and create efficiency. This is the case with both traditional and niche sport events. The complexity of the event structure will surely impact the amount of planning that is required to enable effective communication and decision making, along with the time it will take to make this a reality. Planning with the specific intent of ensuring coordination among the parts of the event organizing structure is an important role for event managers; it can have a multiplied, synergistic outcome of much greater magnitude than the impact of the work of an individual or committee. Event leaders need to take a role in creating synergy among the parts of the event organizing structure, where the impact will be a positive result in both traditional and niche sport event structures.

Creating event structures so that good governance will result is the ultimate goal of understanding and applying the theory and principles discussed in this chapter to the management strategies within your event. A structure that is flexible provides for effective levels of communication, decision making and exchange of information among the individuals delivering the event. The structure created, while being specifically designed for the

42

purpose of the event, will best serve the needs of event managers and contribute to overall success. Effective event structures for governance go hand in glove with facilitating effective event networks that bring additional groups or constituent organizations relationships and resources to aid in the development of an event, our next topic of interest.

CONCLUSION

In this chapter, the key role of an event manager as a facilitator was introduced. A definition of facilitation was provided, along with the theory of facilitation. The role of the event manager was outlined as that of a facilitator who guides the development of the event structure for governance established in the first phase of the planning model, the development phase. Further, systems theory, contingency theory and complexity theory were applied to the key role of event facilitation.

CHAPTER QUESTIONS

1   What does someone do when they "facilitate" event activities and what types of knowledge does one need to facilitate successfully?
2   How is facilitation different from teaching personnel involved in an event?
3   An event structure can be examined from three points of view: formalization, complexity and centralization. Describe each of these.
4   Describe systems theory, contingency theory and complexity theory and relate these theories to the development of event structures.
5   What does the principle *form follows function* imply?

CHAPTER 4

THE EVENT PLANNING MODEL:
THE EVENT DEVELOPMENT PHASE, PART II

MAUREEN CONNOLLY, LORNE J. ADAMS AND CHERI BRADISH

This chapter continues the discussion on the first phase in the planning model, the event development phase. In this chapter, the event manager is positioned as a facilitator for the development of policies, volunteer practices and participation in corporate social responsibility. We begin with a section on facilitating the development of event policies.

FACILITATING EVENT POLICY DEVELOPMENT

(by Maureen Connolly and Lorne J. Adams)

As an event manager, you will come face to face with both established policy and the need to develop new policy. Sometimes you will feel constrained or limited by policy and at other times you will wish that you had a policy in place to help you deal with one of the contingencies that has arisen from an event you are managing. Such is the life of an event manager. You have to negotiate a world that is at once well defined and perhaps restrictive in some matters, but ill defined and fluid in others. As these issues arise, you will need to ask yourself whether existing policy helps with the present situation or needs to be modified. You might also have to ask whether new policy needs to be developed or whether the issue can be dealt with without a formal policy.

Graff (1997) has done much work with volunteers and has identified that there are four general purposes or types of policies. She has put them in the context of volunteer programs, but they are germane to your role as an event manager. She describes the four functions of policy as follows:

44

1   policy as a statement of belief, position or value;
2   policy as a method of risk management;
3   policy as a rule;
4   policy as an aid to program effectiveness.

The Brock University website at www.brocku.ca provides a document entitled "The Administration of Board Policies." This document extends the above concepts a little further and indicates that:

■ Policies follow a prescribed format for consistency and ease of reference.
■ Policies state the position on a particular subject that has institutional implications.
■ Policies mandate or restrict actions to ensure compliance with governing principles, laws and regulations.
■ Policies provide guidelines, alternatives and limits to decision makers.
■ Policies promote operational efficiency and/or minimize risk consistent with the objectives.

Similarly, the University of Alberta indicates on its website (https://policies online.ualberta.ca/PoliciesProcedures/Policies/Policy-Development-Framework.pdf) that "policies need to be clear and concise statements of expected behaviors, practices and standards. As policy reflects the values of the institution it is important that new and existing policy be developed or revised using an effective and consistent approach."

It should now be clear that policy forms the foundation on which your event should unfold. While that may seem self-evident, as Graff (1997) has indicated, policy decisions are made on a regular basis; however, they might not be called policies, nor are they necessarily committed to paper. In her terms, then, writing policy is the formalizing of decisions that may have already been made concerning an event. Doing so will provide clarity and indicate the importance of the matter. Further, the fact that a policy appears in written form may encourage people to be more compliant with the written rule than with an unspoken expectation. Having a written policy also ensures that decisions are not made on an ad hoc basis (Graff, 1997).

It is true that many policies are written in response to crises or problems (Graff, 1997). When there is deviation from the plan or something goes wrong, you will see the gaps in existing policy. The need to develop new policy to deal with what is going on now and/or to prevent adverse circumstances from reoccurring in the future will be evident.

The process of policy development, then, is yet another responsibility that must be facilitated by an event manager. While it might seem to be a daunting task initially, you have already been exposed to the processes required to create effective policy. To this point in the text, you have been advised to understand the nature and intent of your particular event, as well as the audience, the participants and the stakeholders involved. Doing so will provide the context for writing policy. However, as we now point out, many times effective policy can only be formulated if it is in response to clearly written and realistic goals and objectives. When it is conceived in that context, it is possible to achieve the goals that Graff (1997) has set out for policies, namely that responsibility is clarified and lines of communication and accountability can be established. In her terms, policy, then, can ensure continuity over time from manager to manager and event to event.

A source that summarized some of the policy literature is the Ontario Health Promotion Resource System. The online document is no longer available, but those concerned concluded that policy development is not a linear process but consists of four stages: *initiation*, *action*, *implementation*, along with *evaluation and reformulation*. Thus, policy development is an ongoing cycle of activity without a final end point. The authors also provided a series of key questions that are very helpful as you begin to develop policies:

■ Have you identified and analyzed the issues your policy needs to address?
■ Are your policy goals reasonable and your policy objectives measurable?
■ Does your policy specify who is responsible for what?
■ Have you identified the barriers to implementation you are likely to encounter?
■ Do you have a plan for dealing with barriers?

Consistent with the theme of this text, what follows is a theoretical orientation by Dr. Maureen Connolly on the development of policy. This author has focused her theoretical lens on the development of policy using a variety of perspectives. As you will see, these theoretical perspectives allow you to position in a much larger context the practical elements we

46

have discussed above, which will guide your behaviour as an event manager. While Dr. Connolly makes her theoretical framework clear, it is by no means the only way to approach policy development. You should, as she encourages, explore and think through how you would establish your theoretical framework for a practical and tacit approach to policy development in event management. The theoretical orientation and practical scenario by Dr. Connolly is now presented.

First, I want you to realize that there is no such thing as unguided or unpremised action. That is, there is always a policy at work. It is up to you (and me) to be aware of the forces, values and beliefs guiding our actions; or we can behave in the absence of that awareness, and be unconscious of what is guiding our actions. Either way, it's a decision.

Second, I cannot have you walking away from this section of the chapter without your having something different to think about; so, when I present you with the theory or model that I propose as a dignified approach to policy development, I will be adding a slight twist to it. Given the thematic of much of the work written in this text, contingency theory will be guiding my discussion of policy development. This involves adding consideration of bodily contingency to the human relations considerations typically associated with contingency models.

Third, my pitch, then, is this: there really is nothing more practical than a good theory. If you want to do the right thing at the right moment, know what guides your action and be able to step back in the midst of the confusion and connect with that guiding principle. I will provide an example and will offer you an opportunity to think, learn and reflect.

Human relations models of organizational behaviour seem to be the appropriate models to apply when examining events that are dependent on interpersonal relations. Human relations models recognize professionals and clients as complex persons who make choices about how to act and what to believe based on their perceptions of a number of interrelated personal goals and organizational or event characteristics. Given the endless array of variables that are free to vary, or "contingent" on people's choices and subsequent actions, human relations models are frequently referred to as contingency models (or theories).

Contingency models indicate that individual satisfaction and performance, and overall organizational effectiveness, depend more on an appropriate "fit" among an array of situational, technological, environmental, social, relational, cultural and personal variables than on the use of any single approach. Contingency models are also concerned with the processes by which people manage ambiguities, uncertainties and complexities.

An important task in the development phase of a planning model involves facilitating the creation of policies for the particular structure, network, staff and volunteers in an event. Event policy development involves the generation of statements or premises that direct personnel involved in an event. Policies direct (or guide) expected approaches, actions, accountability and the consequences of actions. The combination of event policies provides the foundational framework for all actions and desired outcomes. The goal of policy development is to guide event personnel by providing direction in those key areas: approach, procedures and actions/protocols.

According to *Webster's New Collegiate Dictionary* (1985), policy is prudence or wisdom in the management of affairs; sagacity. Sagacity means discernment or the ability to do the right thing at the time. As was mentioned earlier, curriculum and policy are analogous allies. When I plan curriculum, I ask:

- What are the intentions?
- What are the assumptions?
- Who or what are the resources, how will they be distributed and under what authority?
- What are the relationships necessary for things to work and what is the authority structure for advancing the relationships?
- What has or has not worked, and how do I know?
- What or how shall I learn from this and what is the process for adapting for the learning?

These questions can also be used to initiate the development of policies. Answering questions such as those posed above can aid in revealing topics that can be used to develop policies for an event. For example, if the event curriculum or program includes multiple committees, then the intention of the relationship between committee members might be that these committees are to work in tandem as an efficient group. Policies are needed to provide the foundational framework for how committee members are to interact to be efficient. Procedural policies are needed to guide actions during the interactions. Protocol policies are necessary to provide rules of behaviour during the interactions. The intertwining of policy between and among these factors increases accountability.

48

Complementary concepts in policy development

Wendell's (1996) "paradigm citizen" (p. 41) is an idealized, young, cease-lessly productive individual who can keep a technological and machine pace and whose body does not make visible the inability of event planners and policy developers to come to terms with contingency and diversity. Wendell also articulates what she refers to as "the myth of control":

> Refusal to come to terms with the full reality of bodily life, includ-ing those aspects of it that are rejected culturally, leads people to embrace the myth of control, whose essence is the belief that it is possible, by means of human actions, to have the bodies we want and to avoid illness, disability, and death.
>
> (p. 9)

A key concept at work here is the reality of the body. Events and policies which do not take seriously the bodies of the organizers, resource people, support staff and volunteers as well as the eventual participants or attendees are doomed to the vagaries of unacknowledged but usually foreseeable contingencies.

Bain's (1990) work on the invisible curriculum in physical education is highly applicable to event contexts, and resonates remarkably well with contingency models, and bodily contingencies in particular. In speaking of the "hidden curriculum," Bain is referring to what is taught to students by the institutional regularities, by the routines and rituals of teachers' and students' lives. The dynamics of power or expectations are not explic-itly or didactically promoted, but rather are lived as normal, familiar and unquestioned. Three themes that emerge from Bain's work on the hidden curriculum are meritocracy, technocentric ideology and construction of social relations. Meritocracy is the use of a standard to regulate goal-directed behaviour through the myth that hard work will get what it deserves – or, put another way, that compliant behaviour will be rewarded accordingly. The emphasis is actually more on order and control than on achievements, and usually creates a two-tiered system of hard workers. One set believe they will be rewarded but seldom receive the resources or training they require in order to achieve at a higher level. The other group consists of talented and/or clever individuals who do receive resources and continue to achieve regardless of how hard they work. Technocentric ideology constructs ends or goals as taken for granted and unexamined.

Emphasis is then placed on the development of increasingly effective and efficient means of achieving these goals. In such an ideology, existing social arrangements tend to be reproduced rather than challenged, and the body tends to become a commodity to be exchanged for admiration, security or economic gain (Bain, 1990, p. 29). Construction of social relations is also a reproduction of power dynamics through unquestioned patterns of interaction, exemplifying a cavalier lack of awareness of diversity and contingency.

If, as an event manager, you want to enact an authentic meritocracy, build into the event and its policies accountability and consequences structures that can make it so. If the ends justify the means, then expect short cuts and various other forms of "hacking" in the name of efficiency rather than holistic and innovative problem solving. If reproducing inequitable power differentials goes unchecked, then expect apathy and lack of commitment in the realms of respect, courtesy and public relations.

Lanigan's (1988, 1992) cultural attunement is a strategy for meta-analysis, or understanding the big picture. He gives us three things to think about: normative logics of a culture (the implicit and explicit rules), the signs or indicators that those rules are important (how people behave to uphold or break or stretch the rules) and the larger overarching codes that keep all of this working. Taking this structure to an event and the policy development that guides it, we would see protocol policies as the normative logics, procedural policies as the signs or indicators, and foundational framework policies as the larger systemic or code level.

Merleau-Ponty's (1962) concept of the lived body finishes off our complementary concepts section. The "lived body" is an actual body in the everyday world of time, space and relationships of people, places, objects and happenings. Here is an example which I hope allows you to distinguish between the lived body and the abstract or disconnected body. If we are in a space together and I am too hot, you may be too cold. It does not matter what the measured temperature reading is; my lived experience is "too hot." Likewise, we might have different lived experiences for things such as chair comfort, lighting, sound, odours, chemical sensitivities. *It is the lived bodies that fill out the event evaluations and decide to hire you for their next event*, so taking lived bodily contingencies into account in your planning and policy development is more than a courtesy, it is an economic and reputational necessity.

50

Application: policy becomes praxis

As you read the following example, make a note of which policies need to be made more explicit, and where gaps may appear in written policy. The example makes clear the link to contingency theory. Once you have completed reading the example, from your knowledge and by thinking through the issues and how it affected the participants, you should be able to indicate the type and the context of policies that you would need as an event manager.

This example is an annual meeting and conference for Active Living Alliance for Canadians with a Disability (ALA). Approximately 120 participants included 65 youth with disabilities, an organizing team of 10–12, a conference services team of four, various support staff and 65 student volunteers. There was also significant liaison with the surrounding city and region.

As far as sport, recreation or tourism events go, a five-day, 350-person event is hardly extravagant; however, the contingencies were intriguing, to say the least. Chief among these were the heavy construction projects scattered across the area hosting the event, making entrances, exits, way-finding and overall access a challenge for non-disabled participants and a nightmare for participants with disabilities.

There were obvious explicit rules. The safety and dignity of all participants was a priority. People with disabilities were consulted on how needs were to be met. No effort was spared to make campus spaces accessible. Planning began 15 months in advance of the event. Unspoken rules were more subtle, of course. Assume that everyone has good intentions; all stakeholders get equal credit; no one argues or fights – we have mature disagreements; reputational impact is significant; promised activities will unfold as they have been described; all volunteers and support personnel will show up and know what they have to do. Deeper subtexts were anxiety over injuries, ignorance of the disabilities, fear of saying the wrong thing or being inadvertently offensive, food allergies, getting lost on the way to activities, missing buses and planes, and no-shows.

The larger system at work for this event to be successful was an authentic meritocracy – that is, a code of conduct by which people do indeed work hard for the good of the event, feel a sense of pride in that work ethic and are publicly appreciated for that work ethic.

Within our experiences in life, including the features of the people we meet, the places we go, the objects we encounter and the happenings with which we must contend, we need to consider how each of these elements impacts our personal space, our time and our relationships. Within the conference, there were several prominent happenings, including an opening ceremony, various receptions, excursions to the surrounding region's tourist sites, a closing banquet, an annual general meeting, the conference sessions, keynote and plenary speakers, and an activity and social program for youth delegates.

One youth delegate activity was sailing. The sailing activity had been organized months ahead of time, with the number of kids who needed special seats or partners being discussed, the number of boats available, along with the number of support personnel needed to be present on-site. There was one-to-one volunteer support for the delegates, but none of the volunteers had expertise in sailing. The City provided free bus transportation for the delegates and their volunteers, and medical support and coordinators for the three buses. Directions to the site were in hand. The weather was perfect. We had mistakenly assumed that the weather was our only uncontrollable contingency, and at the outset it was cooperating. As one contingency after another presented itself, we realized in hindsight that we had not taken seriously enough the lived experience of body, space, time and relation. The saga unfolds.

The greater than typical numbers of persons using wheelchairs and ambulatory assists meant that boarding the buses took an hour longer than we had planned. Although we had phones, there was no phone contact at the site, so we could not inform the people there of the late arrival. This is an example of non-disabled people underestimating the time it takes for a person with disabilities to access a transportation vehicle. Further, the delegates on the buses were experiencing the hour of waiting in a hot space in close quarters with other bodies, so the lived experience of that hour probably felt much longer and the bodily experience of sweating on vinyl seats with 30 of your close friends was also a less than exhilarating start to the activity.

Finally the buses departed, and air-conditioning and motion dismissed the previous frustrations. Directions to the site were excellent; getting from the site entrance to the boats was more complicated, as there was no signage, no familiar humans; no obvious signs of a sailing activity for youth with disabilities. Thanks to innovative and observant volunteers, we were able

52

to make our way to the dock, where three boats and three sailing support personnel awaited 65 children and youth as the weather developed into the hottest day on record.

Results included dehydration leading to seizures and adverse medication reactions in several delegates (unanticipated lived-body responses). Numerous non-event people in the general area volunteered their boats, drinking water and a variety of play objects (balls, Frisbees, kites). This was an unanticipated but welcome experience of lived relations. Once again, lived time reared its ugly head as waiting for turns felt endless; however, volunteers maximized the waterfront site, thereby utilizing lived space in an innovative and safety-conscious fashion. The coordinators learned from the earlier lived time bus-loading adventure and began a phased return to the campus once groups of delegates had completed their recreational sailing and tourism experience. As a planning team, we had woefully underestimated lived time and lived bodies and had overestimated the lived relation preparedness of our sailing program team. Our volunteer and citizen lived space and relation contributions were pleasant surprises.

This one happening within a larger event is a dramatic example of how considering the lived body allowed us to plan, adapt and evaluate our behaviour. However, it did not allow us to turn back the clock and pretend that all was well and that our planning and policies had been adequate to the challenges of our highly (bodily) contingent population.

It must also be said here that even if our group had not been a group of children and youth with disabilities, several significant errors occurred long before the sailing day happened. I challenge you now to revisit these earlier-posed questions in light of the event just described:

- What were the intentions?
- What were the assumptions?
- Who or what were the resources?
- What materials were needed?
- What were the relationships that were necessary for it to work?
- What did not work and how did I know?
- What, or how, shall I learn from this?
- What can be done better next time?

Now, add to your reconsideration of these questions one final reflective activity: assume that your overall approach is a contingency-based model with a serious consideration of bodily contingency. Suggest one procedure and one protocol, along with required policies, that might have made a difference for the sailing day. Embracing contingency will allow you to anticipate and respond in ways that make your policies coherent and your events memorable for all the best reasons, including actions that promote dignity and respect.

One challenge in event management is the facilitation of the generation of policy statements that direct personnel in their expected approaches, actions and accountability, and the consequences of actions. Overall, the practice of generating policies is used to guide activities within the structure of an event, including the multiple staff and volunteers.

Another important area for consideration in the development phase of the planning model is volunteer management. Participation in facilitating event volunteer management can enhance an event, and we shall now discuss this valuable area in event management.

FACILITATING EVENT VOLUNTEER MANAGEMENT

(by Lorne J. Adams)

Who is a volunteer? That is a most basic question that you as an event manager need to address. The answer is as simple as the question itself: anyone can be a volunteer. While the research generally collects data on people aged at least 15, there are many ways to involve those much younger than that. Volunteers are as diverse as the society in which we live – rich and poor, employed and unemployed, professionals and labourers, moms and dads, young and old, friends. A volunteer provides their services and talents with no expectation of remuneration in return for their involvement, other than a sense of contributing to the greater good.

> Volunteering is the most fundamental act of citizenship and philanthropy in our society. It is offering time, energy and skills of one's own free will. It is an extension of being a good neighbour, transforming a collection of houses into a community, as people become involved in the improvement of their surroundings and choose to help others. By caring and contributing to change, volunteers decrease suffering and disparity, while they gain skills, self-

esteem and change their lives. People work to improve the lives of their neighbours and, in return, enhance their own.

(Volunteer Canada, 2006a)

If you are an undergraduate student, and hence part of the demographic target of this book, the chances are you have already been a volunteer. The Canadian Survey of Giving, Volunteering and Participating (2010) reported that 47% of the population aged 15 and over had volunteered their time through a group or organization. In fact, "Canadians volunteered nearly 2.1 billion hours in 2010, the equivalent of nearly 1.1 million full-time jobs (assuming 40 hours per week for 48 weeks)." These figures remained relatively unchanged from the last completed survey in 2007.

Perhaps you volunteered to help a friend with a project; perhaps you have volunteered with a community group; or you may even have been part of a large event such as the Pan American Games or the Olympics. Regardless of the venue, it is worthwhile to look back at your experience as a volunteer. Was it satisfying and fulfilling, or frustrating and perhaps stressful? Maybe you have experienced the range of emotions that come with being a volunteer.

Volunteering has changed over the years and has been likened to a living organism. "It grows, declines and changes in response to the stimuli surrounding it. Changes in society, changes in the way we view work . . . in the availability of free time . . . in motivations and attitudes about reciprocity have direct effects on volunteering" (Merrill & Associates, 2006).

The integration of the internet and the World Wide Web into daily life has enabled volunteers to participate remotely from their home or work computer. This virtual volunteering can be completed according to one's schedule, and the problems of travel in order to meet face to face can be avoided. However, a manager embracing this type of volunteer format needs to have the technical skills to deal with the unique problems of electronic communication (Merrill & Associates, 2006).

However, the form of volunteering that you are probably most familiar with has been described by Nancy Macduff as episodic volunteering. She has described it as a service of "short duration." In her terms, it indicates that volunteers prefer to engage on a one-time-only basis, or to work on specific projects, some of which may occur annually. She further indicates that, at least in the United States, episodic volunteering has become the pattern of choice across all age groups (Macduff, as cited in Merrill &

Associates, 2006). This has significant implications for you as an event manager. While volunteers may choose to work on selected projects and then move on, how they relate their experience to their peers or social group can create either viral goodwill or negative impressions.

In a similar vein, Hustinx and Lammertyn postulate that societal change has produced a concomitant change in the willingness to volunteer. "Volunteering seems to be more dependent on personal interests and needs" (cited in Merrill & Associates, 2006). A reflexive volunteer of this kind is motivated by a search for self-realization and wants to have assignments with tangible outcomes.

Episodic volunteering, then, is concerned with individual availability, interests, skills, motivation and commitment (Merrill & Associates, 2006).

A volunteer management program

Unless you are involved in an already established program, you may need to be the driving force behind establishing a volunteer program that will benefit both your event and the volunteer. Starting from scratch may seem a little daunting, but, as with the rest of the concepts in this text, some careful planning will go a long way to ensuring that everyone's needs are met. Just as you have established values, goals and objectives for your project, the same thought processes will go into the creation of a successful volunteer program.

Why a volunteer management program should be developed

Quirk (2009) asked questions concerning the need for and value of the development of a volunteer management program. In response, I would say that there should be some direct service value to your organization. In addition, this service value extends to the individual volunteer, and the opportunity should be available to serve the larger community and to develop personal skills. It is through volunteering that you may make connections or linkages that would not otherwise be possible, or perhaps you simply have an increased profile locally and/or beyond.

The management of the volunteers should not be left to chance, but should be a well-planned and well-organized program. To begin this program, a code for volunteer management is needed.

56

A code for volunteer involvement

An organization called Volunteer Canada promotes the idea that the development of a code can "specify organizational values, guiding principles and the specific rules or standards, which align with these values. It can help ... make decisions based on the organization's values and principles" (Volunteer Canada, 2006b, p. 5). As such, the Canadian Code for Volunteer Involvement (CCFVI) consists of several important elements, including:

- values for volunteer involvement;
- core statements of the importance and value of volunteer involvement;
- guiding principles for volunteer involvement;
- principles detailing the exchange between voluntary organizations and volunteers;
- organizational standards for volunteer involvement;
- standards in developing or reviewing how volunteers are currently involved (p. 5).

Volunteer Canada (2006c) has also outlined some national standards for volunteer involvement in an audit tool that provides a sound basis for mounting a volunteer program.

Support for the volunteer management program

A volunteer management program needs to be established with the full support of the organization, including the Board of Directors and the Executive Committee (Quirk, 2009). Obviously, a program cannot be successful if only a small segment is committed to the enterprise. As Penner (2002) has pointed out, both individuals and organizations harbour a certain amount of neophobia – fear of something new. The amount of stress that change induces is related to the size and impact of the change, the amount of preparation for the change and the level of input from those affected by the change. This means that the introduction of a volunteer program requires that your communication skills are well developed and that you are equipped to be an agent of change. The benefits of your new program will need to be well articulated and should answer questions such as:

- What are your short-term goals?
- What are your long-term goals?
- What benefits will the organization accrue from this volunteer management program?

- How much money will be required to support the program?
- What human resources will the program require?
- Where are volunteers needed?
- What specific skills will volunteers need?

As Hager and Brudney (2004b) indicate, "Benefits and challenges are two sides of the same coin" (p. 2). Being fully aware of both will aid in gaining support from all sectors in the organization.

While they bring much to the table, "volunteers are not free" (Quirk, 2009, p. 2). This means that there is a need for financial and human resource support for the volunteer management program. It will be your job to determine what resources are needed for the program, and you will also need to develop those resources. Even if your organization is small, someone is going to have to provide training and supervision to those volunteers. As more volunteers are needed, the level of supervision, reporting and accountability also increases. This may mean that someone will have to be assigned to those responsibilities and, further, you may need to hire someone to assume that responsibility. Either way, event managers must address the fact that there are direct and indirect costs relating to the volunteers. There may be some training involved for the person who will supervise volunteers. You may wish to send that person to training workshops or conferences. In addition, a volunteer recognition program is not without cost. As the event manager, you will need to account for these costs. You will need to assess whether those costs provide you with the benefits you hope for. If the funds are not available, fundraising may be necessary.

The volunteer management program structure and processes
Next, you will need to think through how you would like the volunteer management program to function and how each volunteer role fits into the functional processes (Quirk, 2009). The functional processes can be established by asking the following questions:

- To whom will the volunteers report?
- How will volunteers report?

Consideration of the benefits of a volunteer management coordinator could be valuable. Hager and Brudney (2004a) looked at the net benefits accrued by an organization in terms of the investment in a paid staff person who

58

assumed volunteer management duties. Their research showed that the lowest level of net benefits was associated with not having a volunteer coordinator. Conversely, they found that net benefits to the organization increased as paid staff members (one-third time, one-third to two-thirds time, two-thirds time and above) devoted more time to volunteer management. They were surprised, however, to find that unpaid managers in the volunteer management role had net benefits just as high as those paid volunteer coordinators who spent a substantial amount of time on volunteer management. While they admitted that this phenomenon needed further study, it appears that in some organizations an unpaid volunteer can be just as effective as a paid staff member. Hager and Bruner hypothesized that unpaid volunteers have what Susan Ellis has called "the luxury of focus" (2004a, p. 9). That is, those volunteers were not constrained in their duties by other organizational duties and commitments. They further explain that unpaid coordinators may have a special rapport with their volunteers, which may improve the experience and performance of the volunteers. Having the right person in the right place appears to provide substantial benefit to an organization.

Volunteer roles

At this point, an assessment can be made as to the specific tasks that volunteers will complete. Again, answering a number of questions can aid in the development of this activity, including the following:

- Are there tasks that could easily be passed to a volunteer, thereby freeing up staff to carry out other activities?
- How will the volunteers assist us in achieving our mission goals and objectives?
- How many volunteers will be needed?
- How many different types of volunteers are needed and what specialized skills are required? What type of involvement will we be asking of the volunteers?

Hager and Brudney (2004b) have indicated that volunteers have different interests and ways that they can contribute. Their research indicated that organizations derive more benefits if they arrange for volunteers to perform a variety of functions within the organization. They concluded that using volunteers in a variety of assignments was positively linked with net benefits, even though the use of volunteers in various assignments "incur[s] greater demands on management and greater challenges" (p. 8).

Volunteer recruitment and assignment

The volunteer assignments should fit the specific needs of the organization and the volunteer. In order to get started, one of the things you can do would be to make a list of all of the different types of volunteers your organization will need and then develop a profile of the individual best suited for that type of job. Think about where you might come in contact with that type of individual and what would be the best way to get in touch with them. Quirk (2009) recommends identifying "recruiters" who can ask their friends and contacts to volunteer. "The number one way volunteers get involved is from being personally asked" (Quirk, 2009). This is a very powerful statement and reaffirms the need to constantly develop and expand our network. The more people we have in the network, the greater the resource pool on which to draw.

Before we can match profiles, though, it is imperative that for each volunteer assignment a clear and detailed position description must be created. Volunteers need to know specifically what their duties and responsibilities will be and what skills they need for a particular task. Volunteers should also be provided with a realistic estimate of the amount of time a particular assignment will entail. It is just as unfair to over-estimate the level of time commitment as it is to underestimate the level of time commitment. Given, as we have mentioned before, that volunteers tend to be episodic, and interested in satisfying their own needs, a realistic statement about what personal benefits might be gained from volunteering should be included. In summary, recruitment messages need to be clear and realistic, and to outline the expectations for each assignment.

Another consideration in volunteer recruitment is the level of risk associated with each position. The risk can be to either the organization or to the individual volunteer. Obviously, we want to minimize the risk for all concerned, but we probably cannot eliminate it entirely. This may mean that new policy will have to be developed, or that differential levels of screening and supervision will be required depending on the assessment of the level of risk. To that end, Volunteer Canada (2006b) recommends that "[s]creening procedures are delivered consistently with no exceptions made for certain individuals or positions" (p. 20).

As part of the recruitment process and in order to attract the best people, a list should be created of where best to post the call for volunteer positions. Some will require the use of broad-based media, while others, depending on the task, may need to be targeted at a very specialized audience.

60

As part of the recruitment process, an application form will obviously be needed, but in addition, taking the time to develop meaningful interview questions will help the process immensely. Well-thought-out questions will allow you as manager to assess what the volunteer has to offer the organization and whether they match the profile you have developed for the particular position. As well, good interview questions and a well-conducted professional interview allow the potential candidate to assess their own level of fit with the organization and whether or not their individual needs will be met by this particular assignment. They should also know at this stage that screening is an essential process and that the level of screening is concomitant with the level of risk inherent in the position.

Volunteer training

People volunteer because they have an interest in your particular event or cause. It is fair to assume that by doing so they want you to succeed, for your event to be a success or your cause to be recognized. It is also fair to assume that they too want to succeed at whatever assignment they have taken on. As the event manager, you need to provide them with the tools (resources) and the training required for them and you to succeed. Once the interview and hiring process is complete, the volunteer needs to know about the mission, goals and objectives of the organization. That is, they need to understand where the organization is going and how it is going to get there. Understanding the *core values* and being given an opportunity to discuss them formally or informally increases commitment and motivation. Informed people are cooperative people, and they may in fact become "advocates" for the organization, increasing your recruitment pool, your recognition in the community or your reputation.

A *policy and procedure manual* should be provided to each volunteer, or a copy made available via the website. Further, volunteers should be given an opportunity to review the manual, and there needs to be a mechanism for questions and feedback. In particular, the policies and procedure specific to their assignment should be highlighted.

Additionally, if the event is involved in corporate social responsibility, this needs to be incorporated within the volunteer training activities. It is imperative that all of the volunteers involved in the event are part of instituting the corporate social responsibility activities in order to aid in success in the program. This topic will be addressed in full in the next main section of the chapter.

Given the type of assignment and level of risk, volunteers should be given adequate training for performing their duties. For some jobs, that can be as simple as an orientation meeting with a small fact sheet referencing specific tasks. These procedural guidelines are relatively simple and should be easy to follow. Other jobs, with elevated risk, may require specialized or even intensive training. This may mean that those concerned are assigned a paid staff member as mentor or that they need to attend special training sessions. The goal is to be able to complete their assignment without putting themselves or others at risk.

Volunteers should also be made aware of where their job begins and where their responsibilities end. This is not to curtail the enthusiasm of the individual; rather, the fact that the volunteer understands the specific boundaries of a task prevents "job creep," communication problems and potential conflict. Going outside the intended boundaries may also increase the risk to the individual, others and the organization. Ongoing supervision and regular performance evaluation should, however, ameliorate the problem. They should also give the volunteer an opportunity to provide feedback and input for the organization. The popularity of reality TV shows like *Undercover Boss* has consistently pointed to the need for an opportunity to connect to the people "on the ground" doing the work and acting as the face and indeed spokesperson for the company. Training, supervision and feedback are big elements of satisfaction.

While it is unpleasant and not a desired outcome, there will be situations that require either a reprimand or in some cases outright dismissal. It is imperative that there is a well-delineated policy and procedure in place that clearly outlines what the grounds for dismissal are and how it will be enacted. These rules and regulations cannot be made up as they are needed, but must be predetermined. Each volunteer should be made aware of this at the time they are informed of the mission and goals, etc. Should the situation arise, it is imperative that the protocol is invoked and that the dignity of the individual is respected.

Volunteer retention and autonomy

As profession golfer Jack Nicklaus once said, "It is hard to excel at things you don't enjoy!" This quote is particularly germane to the notion of volunteer retention. How long do you persist at activities you don't enjoy? Given the wide array of activities available to provide us with enjoyment, we simply quit the activity in favour of something else. Volunteer retention

62

programs need to nurture environments that are conducive to keeping volunteers.

Organizations need to develop a culture that is both welcoming and respectful. As was indicated earlier, many organizations could not get by without volunteers. To treat them as valuable contributing members of the team is to create a symbiotic relationship that allows everyone to flourish. This relationship can be created by simply "managing," by walking around. Your presence, even if it is occasional, gives status to the work being performed and provides a sense that you are invested and that you care. Opportunities to provide feedback both formally and informally provide a sense of being heard and valued. Input from volunteers can be incorporated in planning and evaluation. If volunteers are considered to be equal and contributing members of the team, the likelihood of retaining them is enhanced. Similarly, staff who work frequently and effectively with volunteers should also be recognized for their commitment to creating a positive culture for the organization.

There are many things that might attract a volunteer's attention once they have selected your organization. We want to be able to keep them, particularly if there is a large investment of time, money and training. As Hager and Brudney (2004a) have indicated, to enhance retention, organizations should focus on "enriching the volunteer experience" by "recognizing volunteers, providing training and professional development, and screening [them] and matching them to organizational tasks" (p. 1). Hager and Brudney go on to say that volunteers have been widely used to meet organizational needs for services and administration. "Most charities could not get by without their volunteers. . . . Turnover of volunteers can disrupt the operation of the charity, threaten the ability to serve clients, and signal that the volunteer experience is not as rewarding as it might be" (p. 12).

Volunteer recognition
As we have indicated earlier, volunteers provide their skills, expertise and time with no expectation of monetary return. This does not, however, mean that we can abdicate our responsibility to acknowledge and recognize the significant contribution they make. As an event manager, you have an obligation to acknowledge publicly and formally the contribution of volunteers. This can be completed in a number of ways, such as printed materials, in personal letters, in mass media, when speaking publicly about the event and when talking to volunteers in person.

Formal methods of recognition such as dinners, receptions, certificates, reference letters or letters of commendation need to be provided both consistently and in a timely fashion.

Informal methods of recognition also need to be delivered in a timely and appropriate manner. Something as simple as an article of clothing that links the volunteer to the organization and the event goes a long way to creating a culture that increases the likelihood of their volunteering again.

A trained, motivated volunteer base that you can count on is an invaluable resource for an event manager. Like most other concepts in this text, that type of resource does not just happen. It takes pre-planning and attention to detail. It also calls upon your skills as a manager of people to ensure that volunteers feel that they have made a worthwhile contribution and that their involvement is valued and acknowledged.

On a broader scale, event managers are now being tasked with facilitating corporate social responsibility and providing leadership in harmonizing event goals and missions with the larger community's needs and well-being. Corporate social responsibility is the subject of the following pages.

FACILITATING CORPORATE SOCIAL RESPONSIBILITY

(by Cheri Bradish)

> Being a responsible corporate citizen in today's sports marketplace means being a vigilant steward of the emotional and financial investment made by individuals, companies and community groups into your sports organization. It is recognizing, valuing and nurturing the partnership that is fundamental to that investment.
> (VP, Maple Leaf Sport and Entertainment, 2005)

Corporate social responsibility (CSR), or social responsibility (SR), is a re-emergent and important strategic concept for modern managers and professionals. As such, it is important for event managers to understand the importance of "giving back" through their respective organizations and events. Whether through charitable links, employee wellness programs or even international outreach, event managers need to appreciate the importance of community well-being and to firmly commit themselves and their organization to taking an active lead in positive community actions.

64

Broadly defined and interpreted, CSR is regarded as an all-encompassing commitment of an organization to sustained community well-being both in theory and in practice. More generally, CSR can also be interpreted as an organization's commitment to behave ethically. A sound commitment to CSR may be accomplished through a number of means, including discretionary business practices, empowering accountability, and corporate resources, as well as community development and input (Kotler & Lee, 2005). CSR in principle can also be referred to as *corporate citizenship*: the obligation that an organization has to be ethical and accountable through positive action.

As broadly interpreted, CSR has come to be known for and associated with a number of "giving back" concepts and practices, which provide sport, recreation, tourism and event managers with a number of different possibilities for demonstrating a commitment to community well-being. As its core, a *true dedication to CSR MUST exist to make the commitment relevant and authentic.* Managers can adopt a number of related strategies under the greater CSR umbrella. Doing so will facilitate sound and ethical business practice, which includes the principles of corporate reputation, cause-related marketing, strategic philanthropy, community relations and even sport for development.

Corporate reputation is a complex mix of characteristics that identifies an organization's public "personality." Corporate reputation is a measure of the public and corporate perception of the organization, which is hinged to its practice of responsible business action and commitment to community well-being. It is important for sport, recreation, tourism and event managers to understand and interpret corporate reputation. A company that has a highly regarded reputation will find considerable favour with stakeholders, employees and consumers.

Cause-related marketing is, as the name suggests, primarily a marketing strategy which, when executed properly, can be positioned as a true commitment to community well-being. Cause-related marketing could be considered another important link to a company's CSR practice. By way of example, cause-related marketing is the support of a social cause by a firm through a developed affinity program for its consumers. A simple way to create a link, then, would be for Recreation Organization A to donate one dollar to the national cancer society for every registrant at a local event. There are many such programs in existence today. These programs are most effective when practised authentically and when demonstrating a true commitment to the cause by having company leaders and employees actually participate in the event in large enough numbers to be recognizable.

Strategic philanthropy is understood simply as strategic giving, most commonly in the form of financial support. An organization adopts a cause (or causes) that is in line with its mission and objectives, and supports that cause financially throughout the year. Again, as with cause-related marketing, it is important that there is a true commitment (for example, of money and time) to these causes and that the partnership genuinely seeks to improve the position of the cause.

Community relations as part of the greater marketing umbrella is also an effective outlet for CSR practice. Here, through community outreach programs, a sport, recreation or tourism organization can develop stronger relationships with the community. The opportunity then exists to highlight the positive actions of both the company doing the supporting and the community services receiving the benefit. Community relations, media relations and public relations can all work together to develop and execute sound CSR programs.

Sport for development is a concept whereby organizations understand and interpret sport and recreation as a vehicle for development, be it economic and/or community, and even, as is indicated in the International Olympic code of conduct, peace for all nations. Partnerships with Sport for Development organizations, such as Right To Play (Figure 4.1), add a global element and more international focus to an organization's overall CSR commitment.

For you as an event manager, understanding CSR gives you an advantage in terms of enhancing whatever event you may be organizing. Being aware of companies that have a well-developed CSR plan is another tool you can add to your tool box. Matching the right company to the event is your challenge, but once a match has been found, everyone, including you, stands to benefit.

On one level, if the company has been matched with the event, you may have access to resources, including human, technical and financial materials, that you might not otherwise have. On another level, the prestige or visibility of your event may be enhanced by your being able to link with a company that is highly respected. On yet another level, there may be a "trickle-down" effect where some will say, "If X is involved, then we should be involved as well."

66

The organization Right To Play uses specially designed sport and play programs to improve health, build life skills and foster peace for children and communities affected by war, poverty and disease. Working in both the humanitarian and the development contexts, Right To Play has projects in more than 20 countries in Africa, Asia and the Middle East.

Right To Play is a global-scale implementer of Sport for Development and Peace programs and takes an active role in driving research and policy development in this area and in supporting children's rights.

Right To Play focuses on four strategic program areas, including Basic Education and Child Development, Health Promotion and Disease Prevention, Conflict Resolution and Peace Education, and Community Development and Participation.

Working with partners, funders and the local communities, Right To Play tailors every program to meet identified needs. Each program has specific goals, impacts and outputs. To build each program, it draws upon specially designed sport and play-based resources, as well as the expertise of program development, research, monitoring and evaluation, policy and country office teams.

The principles of the Convention on the Rights of the Child underpin Right To Play, and they ensure that its programs benefit the most marginalized children, including girls, street children, former child combatants, refugees and children affected by HIV and AIDS.

Right To Play's Team of Athlete Ambassadors is supported by an international team of top athletes from over 40 countries. These athletes inspire children, are role models for healthy lifestyle choices and help raise awareness and funding for Right To Play projects. Led by four-time Olympic gold medalist and Right To Play president and CEO Johann Olav Koss, Athlete Ambassadors include Wayne Gretzky, Martina Hingis, Dikembe Mutombo, Haile Gebrselassie, Michael Essien, Frank Lampard, Anja Pärson, Chelsea Football Club and many more.

The global reach of Right To Play is extensive, as it works in Azerbaijan, Benin, Chad, China, Ethiopia, Ghana, Indonesia, Jordan, Lebanon, Liberia, Mali, Mozambique, Pakistan, the Palestinian Territories, Rwanda, Sierra Leone, Sri Lanka, Sudan, Tanzania, Thailand, Uganda, the United Arab Emirates and Zambia.

For further information on Right To Play, see http://www.righttoplay.com/site/PageServer?pagename=overview

Figure 4.1 Right To Play

The notion of giving back to the community creates a symbiotic relationship. The event gains support and recognition from the community, and the community stands to gain both tangibly (such as via economic infusion) and intangibly (such as gaining an enhanced reputation as a tourist destination). Events that have a well-defined CSR plan, and a commitment to the plan, can increase market share, strengthen their brand position, improve the corporate image and enhance employee morale. Having such a plan may also lead to increased attraction on the part of stakeholders.

While it has been recommended that you be aware of companies that have a well-developed CSR plan, it also would behoove you to promote CSR to targeted partners or stakeholders. By doing so, you can enhance the reputation and success of the event and create a win–win situation for the event and community.

Chapters 3 and 4 have outlined the development phase of the planning model. We now move to Chapter 5 and the event operational planning phase of the model.

CHAPTER QUESTIONS

1 Discuss the impact of volunteers in the field of event management and the need to properly service the volunteers.
2 Describe practices within a volunteer life cycle.
3 Describe a minimum of three strategies outlined in this chapter that are used to reveal areas that require the generation of policy statements that direct personnel involved in an event.
4 What is corporate social responsibility (CSR)?
5 How can CSR be instituted within events, and what value do you place on CSR?

CHAPTER 5

THE EVENT PLANNING MODEL: THE EVENT OPERATIONAL PLANNING PHASE

CHERYL MALLEN

The second phase in the event planning model, the event operational planning phase, encompasses the creation of the written operational plans for the variety of event components. These plans include the guiding instructions for hosting the event. Examples of event components include accommodations, accreditation, ceremonies, communications, drug testing or doping control, food and beverage services, hospitality services, media management, management of officials, participant management, volunteer management, results and awards, spectator services and transportation. Importantly, this chapter details four key mechanisms that aid in operational planning success. These mechanisms include the cultivation of the operational planning network, the creation of logical, sequential, detailed and integrated plans, the inclusion of contingency plans and the activation of a plan-refining process. Finally, the chapter outlines key issues in operational planning and provides practice scenarios.

MECHANISM 1: THE CULTIVATION OF THE OPERATIONAL PLANNING NETWORK

To begin the operational process, an event manager must facilitate the formation of the operational planning network. This network requires an event manager to have the sensitivity to facilitate the assignment of the best possible people, along with the correct number and combination of individuals with planning expertise to meet the event's operational planning requirements. There is no single formula for assigning the network of individuals correctly; each situation is unique. However, if individuals are assigned incorrectly, problems that influence the efficiency of plan development may arise. The task of creating operational plans for each component requires an intricate combination of talented planners who can develop the operational plans for their component as well as coordinate and cooperate with other event component personnel.

A simple exercise will demonstrate the complexity of assigning individuals to tasks. Consider subdividing the members of your class to complete a number of components that could be in a typical traditional or niche event. How would you subdivide the class? What elements would you consider in subdividing the group? There are many ways to assign network members, including dividing individuals into groups that have similar expertise; creating groups that offer a wide variety of expertise, which could broaden the knowledge base; or creating groups that are devised on the basis of whether they work well together. Individuals could be placed in groups on the basis of their personal interest in the component. There is not one particular way to subdivide the group that can be applied to every situation. It is important for an event manager to develop an understanding and sensitivity to the elements of assigning individual members of the network according to the particular context.

Individuals assigned to each event operational planning component make up a node. A node may be further subdivided into constituent nodes. For example, those planning the accommodation component can be subdivided into constituent nodes whereby each is responsible for the accommodation plans of a separate part, such as those for the event participants, another for the officials and a third node that manages the accommodations for the organizing committee members. Linkages between constituent nodes foster the interactions required to complete the overall accommodation planning tasks.

The linkages between nodes (including linkages within a component and between components) create a network of multilateral intraorganizational alliances. These linkages determine how members interact to establish plans, manage planning decisions and manage issues or problems. Each linkage is part of the structural design creating a network alliance that can be unique in its application.

The design of the network alliance is crucial to the effectiveness of the development of successful operational plans. There are many influences that impact the design of a network alliance. To illustrate examples of some of the influences, the characteristics found within contingency

70

theory, complexity theory and agency theory can be applied to a network design.

Application of contingency theory

Contingency theory indicates that there is no single correct way to structure the alliance linkages between the planning nodes. This is because, as contingency theory states, the search for one correct structure is simply not appropriate in our world, as no one system of organization that "is superior to all others in all cases" can be found (Owen, 2001, p. 399). The structure of each operational planning alliance must be efficiently designed for the specific needs of each event.

An application of this characteristic of contingency theory during the event operational phase implies that an operational network design that worked for a previous event may not work for any other event. So what guides the design of each network in the operational planning phase?

Wijngaard and de Vries (2006) suggest that it is the authority and responsibility assigned with the tasks that determine a configuration or structure. This structure establishes expected behaviours of the event operational network members and the event planners who guide the network design. This implies that an event manager needs to be sensitive to the event context in order to effectively configure the multilateral positions – the role of the members, the power, approvals, subdivisions and overall autonomy – required for event operational planning. A combination of organic structures (whereby members have the authority to make decisions concerning their component) and hierarchical structures may be needed for the complex event environment. There is no one predetermined structural design that has been deemed best for operational planning for the event components. An event manager needs to be open to different intraorganizational network designs which may be needed for the various event components.

Application of complexity theory

Complexity theory is also applicable in the event operational phase. Complexity theory indicates that a basic condition of our contemporary environment is that it is in a pivotal state (Doherty & Delener, 2001). This means that the environmental conditions include levels of "uncertainty, diversity and instability" (Stacey, 1996, p. 349). A stable state in the environment is not achievable because "the world is primarily made of dissipative structures" (Keirsey, 2003, p. 4). Dissipative structures involve a constant evolution of structures as they are being pulled apart and refitted by several forces, and this means one cannot be expected to be in a state of "equilibrium" (p. 4). Complexity in the environment includes the evolving nature of structures, which means we cannot expect to work in an environment devoid of change.

An application of the characteristics of complexity theory indicates that an event manager must efficiently design the operational network alliance to make it adaptable for conditions of change. An understanding that change is expected implies that once the network alliance is designed and instituted, the work of the designer is not finished. The network must be managed to cope with new or changing conditions.

A state of equilibrium cannot be expected within the event operational network. Change may involve the movement of network members within the nodes, the replacement of some members or the reconfiguration of how the nodes interact. Multilateral intraorganizational network alliances are made over time, and adaptations must also be made continuously to ensure that the design meets the flexibility demands for developing operational plans to stage an event. This requirement can be a constant and time-consuming task for an event manager.

Application of agency theory

Agency theory is concerned with two key issues that are applicable to the operational planning phase. Both issues are concerned with ensuring the cooperation of planning efforts. The first issue involves "the desires or goals of the principal and agent conflict [as] . . . it is difficult or expensive for the principal to verify what the agent is actually doing" (Eisenhardt, 1989, p. 57). An application of this issue means that the operational planning network needs to (1) ensure all parties understand their expected behaviour while in the operational planning phase, (2) encourage the group to work toward the collective goals and objectives, (3) work toward efficient group progress, and (4) ensure excellent communication among the network members concerning the operational planning progress. If excellent communication is not facilitated between network members, the result can be difficulty in understanding or verifying the progress being

72

made by the multiple members in the network that are completing the operational planning. Further, the second issue in agency theory involves "risk sharing that arises when the principal and agent have different attitudes toward risk" (p. 58). An application of this issue means that the network members must manage operating planning risk elements, such as the timing of the completion of operational plans, and be concerned with the impact of critical time periods.

MECHANISM 2: GENERATING WRITTEN OPERATIONAL PLANS

The event operational network members are assigned the task of generating the written operational plans that constitute guiding instructions for staging each component within an event. This task compels the members of the operational network to produce the directions for the delivery of the event (Wijngaard & de Vries, 2006). These written operational plans establish the goals and directions for managing all functions for staging the event. Generally, multiple operational plans are created in tandem. All members of an operational network within each node are required to have the expertise needed to meet the scope of responsibility for the planning function. This scope includes designing the written format for the operational plan and creating logical, sequential, detailed and integrated plans.

The written event operational plan: establishing a design format

To begin the task of recording the step-by-step instructions for the operational plan, a format is needed in order to achieve consistency and control (Wijngaard & de Vries, 2006). This format guides how all written operational plans are to be laid out. Multiple formats have been used for sport, recreation and tourism events. There is no one correct format that could be used. The general rule for selecting a format is to ensure that all requirements of the plan can be expressed. These requirements can include a number of items, such as:

- an executive summary;
- the goals and objectives;
- the timing of each planned activity;
- a detailed list of planned tasks;
- the authority for each planned element;

- event diagrams illustrating activity sites and the placement of key event items.

Any format selected must take into account the complexity and fluidity of event operational planning, along with the requirements of what must be recorded within a specific plan to ensure the elements are communicated in an easy-to-use manner. See examples of design formats in the example operational plans to be found at the end of this chapter.

Logical operational planning

During the creation of the written operational plans for the event, all members of the operational planning network must learn to determine and record the individual activities or tasks necessary to complete their particular component. *Operational planning includes the deliberate creation of suppositions, assumptions and conclusions for the development of a coherent and logical step-by-step written list of reasoned event activities to stage a successful event.* The process requires a "thinking through" process that is not a simple activity. This is because a concentration on each element within the component and the delineation of each logical step and the recording of the steps is a complex and time-consuming task. Goals can be established to aid members as they "think through" the logistical requirements.

Why the provisions of operational planning lists that follow are not included
Many events that have been held previously have information that provides lists or outlines of event activities. This reference information may provide guidance for developing logical operational plans for an event. However, the reference information is contextually specific and does not take into consideration the numerous nuances that exist within other events. The information is tied to the structure of the operational network, the components and detailed actions that were designed for that event. Reference information is valuable only for gaining common knowledge about an event. The reference material does not replace an event manager's responsibility for thinking through each activity and developing advanced knowledge for the specific facility and activities of the current event. There are no shortcuts to the thinking-through process for excellent – event-specific – operational plans.

74

Sequential operational planning

Each operational plan needs to itemize the event tasks in an ordered and reasoned sequence. The most common method used to achieve this end involves using the concept of time. For example, an operational plan can be subdivided to record all of the tasks that must be completed three, six or 12 months prior to an event, as well as the activities during the week prior to the event and a minute-by-minute list of tasks for each day of the event. As a parallel activity, separate sequential plans can be created to outline the specific items needed for the venue (such as rod and drape, tables, chairs), including the time and site at which they are required.

To aid in the development of sequential operational plans, the concept of *weaving* is used. Weaving involves conceptually thinking through all of the requirements for one element of an event at a time. For example, a network member can conceive and record the tasks necessary to complete the media management operational plans by conceptually weaving the potential requirements of one media member from the moment of arrival at the event parking lot until they depart. This weaving process is followed repeatedly to develop the multiple logical and sequential steps that must be recorded in the operational plan. A planner can *weave forwards* or *weave backwards*.

Weaving forwards involves recording elements as they will happen, in a progressive, unfolding process. In contrast, weaving backwards requires conceptually thinking of the end product and then backtracking to determine the step-by-step activities that were completed in order to achieve that end product.

It does not matter whether a planner conceptually thinks through the planning requirements by weaving forwards or weaving backwards. The aim is to develop a process that aids in determining the sequential steps to stage the event.

Detailed operational planning

The amount of detail required in an operational plan differs from event to event and can be a difficult decision for an event manager. The plans need to be written in a clear format to ensure other members in the network can read and understand them, and be guided to complete the tasks as outlined. The plan must provide clarity, limit emerging questions and reduce the potential for incorrect interpretations concerning the actions needed to produce the event. A detailed account of each task is necessary, but the difficulty lies in determining the appropriate threshold for detail. How much detail is required?

There are three threshold levels of detail in operational planning. Each level requires a different amount of detail in the written record concerning each event task. The three levels are referred to as level 1, level 2 and level 3 planning. The higher the threshold level, the greater the detail provided within the operational plan.

Level 1 planning provides the lowest level of planning detail. A level 1 plan exhibits a minimal level of detail to explain each task. Level 1 planning is open to questions concerning clarity of the event tasks and does not provide a detailed step-by-step list of directions to avoid misinterpretations should others enact the plan. Consequently, level 1 planning is open to the interpretations of those completing the implementation of the plans, and these interpretations may alter the planned activities.

Level 2 planning requires a higher, or medium, amount of planning detail. This level of planning provides general clarity and offers more detailed step-by-step directions to enact the plan. Level 2 planning answers the majority of questions one would have if implementing the plan. However, the plan is still open to some interpretations that may alter the planned activities.

Level 3 planning demands the highest level of detail. The level 3 plan provides clear instructions and includes the intimate requirements to complete the tasks. Level 3 planning is open to a limited number of questions and potential plan deviations, as minute details for the completion of each task have been provided.

An event manager must facilitate an understanding of the sensitivities of the detail required for a particular event to the members of the operational planning network. There is a subtle difference between providing instructions and offering too much detail to the point where the network members do not read the plans. Select a simple task and consider at which point you could be given too much detailed instruction that would impair your ability to complete the task.

Next, integrating the multiple plans for the various event components is necessary.

Integrated operational planning

The development of each component operational plan begins as a separate entity, but a key to successful event management is the integration of the multiple detailed plans. Integration of event elements, interlacing or inter-twining them, creates multiple coherent, cohesive and smoothly flowing plans for the overall event.

An example of integration for an accommodation plan is the interlacing of elements from the transportation plan within the accommodation plan. This integration can help to coordinate elements such as the transportation drop-off and pick-up sites at the accommodation venue. The integration can also ensure that transportation coincides with the accommodation check-in time arrangements. Integrating elements from the accreditation plan can also assist in the distribution of accreditation and room assignments all in one coordinated effort.

A successful integration process is reliant upon a key operational factor. This factor is the *establishment of integration exchange opportunities* for the operational network members. The integration process must be designed to provide an adequate number of exchange opportunities on a regular basis and must be adaptable to allow intermittent integration exchanges to meet the integration workflow requirements. Generally, there is a large amount of planning detail, and the integration process is complex (Matusik, 2002). An event manager facilitates an integration process and ensures that multiple exchange opportunities are arranged, if required. Common strategies for integration can include messages, bulletins, announcements, charts, drawings, diagrams, sketches, maps and reports. A particularly key strategy for integration is to set up production meetings between the members from different components. These meetings provide opportunities to discuss and coordinate items that are important to more than one component. *Network theory* indicates that operational network members can exchange planning data without the use of a hierarchy. The success of an event is, however, contingent upon the extent to which the event manager can facilitate the transfer of operational data across the planning nodes. The flow of the operational planning knowledge is con-tingent on the structure and strategies established to disseminate the transfer.

Another mechanism that aids the development of excellent event opera-tional plans is the inclusion of contingency operational plans. Contingency operational plans are developed simultaneously with the event operational plans.

MECHANISM 3: THE INCLUSION OF CONTINGENCY PLANS

To enhance planning preparedness, contingency plans involve two key elements. The first is to conceive potential deviations from the operational plan that could occur. The second is to predetermine action steps to reduce the chance of the deviation or, should it occur, to manage each deviation. The outcome of contingency planning is a backup plan.

Contingency planning can help to develop a greater level of preparation for any event. However, contingency planning cannot ensure that all deviations will be foreseen. There will usually be unexpected deviations from the operational plans, owing to the complex nature of events. The more contingency situations predicted and planned for, the more time the operational planning members provide to the network members to manage deviations that were not predetermined.

Generally, to begin contingency planning, a contingency meeting is held. The objective of a contingency meeting is to host an open forum for operational network members to express their ideas concerning potential deviations from the plan that could occur. Each event component or sub-component hosts a contingency meeting to discuss the potential plan deviations for that specific component. Examples of contingency issues include concerns about equipment malfunction, should a hot-water pipe unexpectedly burst or should a protest on a social issue be staged at the venue on the day of your event.

Facilitating a contingency meeting requires an event manager to keep members on the task of determining deviation ideas and to prepare a written record of these ideas (and not move into how to manage each deviation). Contingency meetings allow members to be creative about what could potentially go wrong at an event. It is important to facilitate the meeting to allow the ideas to flow and defer the assessment of practicality concerning a potential deviation until the next step of contingency planning.

After a contingency meeting, the next step is to determine which of the deviations suggested will be managed prior to the event. The operational network members develop action steps for coping with each deviation

78

should it occur. Contingency action steps are created in the weeks and months after the initial contingency planning meetings have been completed. Each contingency issue can be integrated within the operational plan or can be added as a supplementary or contingency operational plan.

MECHANISM 4: THE ACTIVATION OF A PLAN-REFINING PROCESS WITH PRODUCTION MEETINGS

Once a logical, sequential, detailed integrated operational plan has been developed, along with the contingency plans, it must be refined for use. One method of refining it involves hosting a meeting with key representatives from each component and facilitating a production meeting for fine-tuning the plans. In this meeting, the representatives review the integrated plans and refine the details into a coordinated and efficient effort.

The refining process is intended to add detail to the plan and eliminate any questions that may arise when the plan is implemented. An example of a refining process was illustrated by the 2002 Salt Lake Olympics Organizing Committee (SLOC). This committee instituted a peer review process as a refining technique along with what the committee members called an "Executive Roadmap" (Bowen, 2006). The peer review process included an exchange of operational plans for consideration by others within the event operational network. Reviewers searched for gaps in the detail provided in the operational plan, ensured clarity in the planning statements and determined any arising questions when reading the operational plans. The roadmap consisted of an executive summary of the key timelines that needed to be met and was used for quick reference. Skilled event planners completed the refining process to meet the goal of planning excellence.

CONTEMPORARY ISSUES IN THE EVENT OPERATIONAL PHASE

There are three key issues in contemporary event operational planning. These issues include time, communication and an environment of cooperation for coordinating operational plans.

Time is an issue for an event manger. Event management involves struggling to facilitate the completion of all operational plans within the time frame available. Time impacts the level of planning detail that can be completed, the contingency plans developed and the refining process. An event manager must be continuously cognizant of the pace of planning and facilitate the completion of operational plans within a set time frame.

Communication is vitally important in event management. Facilitating excellent communication is the role of the event manager. This role involves ensuring that the operational network exchange opportunities are utilized and encouraging interactions between nodes in the operational network. Encouraging greater communication is vital to the outcome of the event.

Facilitating an environment of *cooperation for coordinating* operational plans can be the greatest challenge an event manager faces. According to Grant (2001), the foundational issues in operations include problems of cooperation and coordination. Cooperation problems stem from the variety of personalities involved in the operational network. Coordination problems stem from the skills, abilities and knowledge of the operational network members that are required to integrate the plans.

In addition, coordination issues that are due to the advancing virtual or dispersed work environment emerge. This environment allows you to work from anywhere in the world with the use of communication technology. Coordinating activities from off site requires additional communication and demands clarity within the communications.

PRACTICE TO ADVANCE YOUR OPERATIONAL SKILL DEVELOPMENT

To aid in your skill development, attached at the end of this chapter are operational planning scenario practice assignments and example operational plans. Complete the scenario assignments, but first review the example operational plans to aid in your understanding of the planning requirements. During this review, be sure to consider raising questions about the stated actions should the plans be implemented.

Practice operational planning

The best way to develop operational planning skills is to understand the planning process and to practise operational planning. At the end of this chapter, there are a number of figures.

80

Figure 5.1 provides a scenario concerning an event media conference and is a practice assignment for you to complete.

Figure 5.2 provides an example operational plan for event volunteer management by Iain Sime. Instructions are provided for you; read the planning instructions and make judgments and interpretations concerning what has to be completed and how it is to be done. Any questions arising during this review will provide you with more knowledge as to the level of planning detail that is required.

Figures 5.3, 5.4 and 5.5 are planning frameworks developed for an event that is staged annually, but in different venues. They are guides, but do not replace the need to think through the requirements for the particular venue. They are offered to provide an overview of the type of planning detail needed in event management.

Figure 5.6 provides an excellent example of a completed operational plan that was devised for the National Collegiate Athletic Association (NCAA) Men's Basketball Championship, Round 2, San Jose, California: The Hospitality Component, by Lauren Thompson.

After reviewing the operational plans in Figures 5.1 to 5.6, select an event and component (such as the accommodation or transportation) and start practising operational planning.

CONCLUSION

In the second phase in the planning model, the operational planning phase, network members complete operational plans that include timed activities for each event component. The strength of an event operational plan is determined by the logical and sequential process, the amount of planning detail provided, the integration forged between the planned components, the extra preparedness based on the contingency plans and the process of refining the plans prior to their use. The facilitating of quality operational plans can be developed with practice. The concept of quality in event operational planning is discussed further in Chapter 9, "Facilitating quality in event management," after the event planning phases have been presented. Overall, the operational plans are created in preparation for the next phase in the planning model, the implementation, monitoring and management phase.

1   What are the characteristics of contingency theory, complexity theory, network theory and agency theory and how do these characteristics guide an event manager in the event operational planning phase?

2   Describe the difference between level 1, level 2 and level 3 planning.

3   What do contingency plans provide, and why are they important in event management?

4   What is a plan refining process and how does it assist an event manager?

5   Describe three key issues in the event operational planning phase and then outline how an event manager can act to overcome these issues.

Complete the following practice assignment using the following process:

1   Select an event (you will be completing operational plans for a media conference for this event).
2   Read the assignment scenario below and then develop two to three planning objectives for the media conference.
3   Think through the requirements and generate an operational plan for the media conference (see the guiding framework provided below).
4   Develop contingency plans (for a minimum of five event contingency issues) and place these at the end of the operational plan.
5   Record the process to be used to refine the operational plan.

The assignment scenario

You are responsible for managing the media conference for a major tourism event (an event of your choice). This media conference is to be held mid-morning, one day prior to the launch of the event, and is to be held at a major hotel in the downtown area of your city or town. Create a written operational plan for managing the key elements to complete the media conference. Be sure to include the invitations for four key media outlets to attend, including one medium from each of the following types: newspaper, radio, television and web-based media. Further, the operational details must include setting up the media conference room or area in the hotel, managing the media as they arrive, checking credentials, providing accreditation, providing the media conference activities and a media question period. Remember that the operational plan must include all communication requirements (for example, communicating to the venue staff the requirements for tables, chairs, microphones, platforms, rod and drape, the hanging of signage and security). Build into the plan the speakers representing the event, along with the media opportunities such as personal interviews and photo opportunities. Assume you have the funding to support all of your activities. *The chart below is only a starting point*. Expand the operational planning details as you think through the requirements.

C. Mallen

Planning Objectives:
Objective 1:
Objective 2:

DATE	ITEM	WHO IS RESPONSIBLE?
Eight months prior to event	**Media personnel preparations:** What will be in place for: – Media policies, procedures and processes (consider television, radio, print, social and online media) – Media accommodation preparations – Provision of media shuttles – Provision of media accreditation – Media television production truck management – Media parking (including space for media production trucks) – Media venue requirements – In-house electrical requirements for media	Media Coordinator and Volunteers A, B and C
Six months prior to event	**Pre-event media release:** – Media release contents – Distribution plans for media release	
Five months prior to event	**Media information package** – Contents (consider accreditation, media centre, shuttle, site details, parking, team practices, competition details, environmental sustainability plans, and a contact for further information)	
Four months prior to event	**Design of media centre** – Media centre requirements – Media centre volunteer requirements – Media security plans – Media food and beverage provision – Media signage (consider signage to be placed inside and outside of the media centre and how the signage will be held in place) – Media check-in process	

Three months prior to event	***Assignment of media space*** – Consider television booths, radio booths, on-line and social media space, photographer sites and camera positions and seats that must not be filled due to camera positions)
Three months prior to event	***Volunteer management:*** – Determine pre-event volunteer requirements – Event volunteer roles (specific duties) – Communication system
One month prior to event	***Contingency plan development:*** Contingency A: Contingency B: Contingency C: Contingency D: Contingency E:

Figure 5.1 Operational plan: practice assignment

Instructions for reviewing the four example operational plans

Operational plans are generated by an individual or group of individuals – but are generally implemented by a large group of volunteers who were not involved in the operational planning development. Thus, it is imperative that the operational plans clearly outline what is to be completed. This is difficult, as everyone can read the operational plans as instructions and make judgments and interpretations concerning what has to be completed.

Read the following operational plans as if you will be responsible for organizing the volunteers at a local league basketball championship game.

While reading, record any questions that arise, based on the planning instructions provided.

Think through the requirements to answer your arising questions and record any additional operational planning details necessary to provide instructions for these questions.

84

Planning objectives:

Objective 1: To conduct a well-organized volunteer recruiting and training program to fully support the event.

Objective 2: To manage volunteers well, so that they are interested in returning to volunteer at future events.

Time frame	Activity responsible	Person
Six months prior to event	**_Volunteer recruiting_** _Volunteer orientation session timeframe:_ • Establish volunteer orientation session date, time at event site _Develop and post volunteer recruitment information on event website and send to local team websites for posting:_ – Website posting to include: • event name • event dates • how to apply to volunteer • request volunteer name, address, email, telephone number, cell phone number, previous volunteer or work experience • a checklist of volunteer opportunities & an overview of tasks • minimum age requirements • deadline date for applications • shirt size (men's/women's – small, medium, large or extra large) • mandatory volunteer orientation session date/time information • volunteer shirts as uniform to be provided – shirts to be provided at volunteer session; volunteers to wear black pants and comfortable shoes • complimentary ticket policy for volunteers • contact site for further information on the event and volunteer roles _Word-of-mouth volunteer recruitment activities:_ • Develop a business-card-style information sheet indicating volunteers needed for event • Include on card: event name, dates and website for further information • Distribute business cards at league basketball games to potential volunteers	Volunteer Coordinator and Volunteer Committee members

Twitter and Facebook – call for volunteers (and other sites your group utilizes

- Direct all potential volunteers to the website

Develop newspaper volunteer recruitment posting:

- Develop local newspaper ad(s) to attract volunteers (include event name, dates, and how to apply via the website

Five months prior to event	**Volunteer orientation session preparation**	Venue Manager and Volunteer Coordinator and two Volunteer Committee members assigned to orientation session and Accreditation Coordinator
	Work with the venue coordinator to put all details into place for the volunteer orientation session, including:	

- Date and time confirmed
- Venue room finalized; space based on number of people to be in attendance
- Venue entrance gate to be used by volunteers finalized
- Plan venue tour
- Generate a volunteer placement list with the name of the volunteer assigned to each role; have a copy at the volunteer orientation session as a sign-in process; manage any volunteers not in attendance
- Arrange for volunteer parking for orientation session
- Work with the Accreditation/Credentials Committee to arrange for accreditation passes to be developed and distributed at the orientation session
- Ensure volunteer room has a whiteboard (and markers) along with a bulletin board (and tacks)
- Design training session to review each volunteer position
- Order wireless microphone
- Order volunteer golf shirts (gain pre-approval from event committee for colour and logo prior to order)
- Volunteer media manager and volunteers to develop media package for distribution at event (hard copy and online copy)
- Entertainment volunteers to obtain prizes for tossing into the crowd and for entertainment prizes
- Arrange for parking passes to distribute to volunteers at the orientation session (determine number of passes required and the distribution process)
- Prepare to discuss the emergency protocols and generate written overview sheets for distribution
- Arrange for the volunteer communication system

	(a number of cell phones) and be prepared to explain how a volunteer signs out and returns to the system (i.e. number of cell phones) and prepare a list of all cell phone numbers and the name and title of each person in possession of one of the event phones	
Four and a half months prior to event	**Order for Volunteer Room** • Room to be set up by 8 am on Date: ____ • Coat racks × 3 (to hold 20 coats per rack) • Eight tables (10/rounds; white tablecloths) positioned in two rows of four in room for volunteers • Ten chairs at each table for a total of 80 chairs • Arrange for two security staff to be stationed just outside the Volunteer Room doorway for the orientation session and the event date(s) • Order volunteer golf shirts (based on sizes from volunteer applications) and establish distribution process) • Arrange for food and beverages for Volunteer Orientation Session (to be available 45 minutes prior to start of orientation session for 60 people; to include coffee/tea/orange juice/apple juice; four kinds of muffins and bread sticks; fruit tray and vegetable tray • Arrange for tables for food and beverages: three 3' × 8' tables, white table cloths, basketball centrepiece (× 3), tables placed on north wall • Generate a diagram showing where tables, coat racks, food, etc. are to be positioned within the Volunteer Room	Volunteer Coordinator and Venue Manager
Three months prior to event	**Volunteer selection and confirmation** • Review volunteer applications and selection pool of volunteers • Select six "rover" volunteers who will learn all roles and be able to fill in whenever necessary • Subdivide list between event committee members and ensure all volunteers are called • Establish an overall checklist to confirm each volunteer's participation/confirmation and their attendance at the mandatory volunteer orientation session • Send all volunteers an email confirming their role, agreement to participate and the details concerning the mandatory volunteer orientation session date, time, site, specific room, parking arrangements, the	Volunteer Coordinator and all Volunteer Committee members

fact that coffee, tea, etc. are to be provided and event contact name/contact information

- Prepare for a number of volunteer selection issues, such as:

    i. If more than enough interested volunteers are available, how you will respond to those not getting a role at the event
    ii. Keeping a reserve group of volunteers in case they are needed as replacements

Three weeks prior to event	***Volunteer orientation session*** Date: Time: Venue: Room: Attendance required from ____ to ____pm *Set-up:* • Room to be set up two to three hours prior to orientation session (see set-up requirements in preparations above) • Place at each seat an information card welcoming all volunteers to the volunteer upcoming appreciation night; card to include the date, time and site; agenda for the orientation session • Place emergency protocols sheet at each seat • Ensure the Accreditation Committee is set up to begin taking headshots and adding required information for the printed and laminated accreditation passes 1 hour prior to orientation session; lanyards to be available; distribution process pre-established • Ensure security staff in place 45 minutes prior to orientation session • Meet and greet all volunteers as they arrive *Orientation agenda:* 1 Welcome and introductions (ask all volunteers to sign in next to their name on the volunteer sheet) 2 Review of volunteer roles (see list below) 3 Volunteer communication system explained 4 Emergency protocols discussed (provided in writing) 5 Review process for volunteer breaks during event 6 Facility tour 7 Dress code and distribution of volunteer golf shirts 8 Accreditation distribution 9 Parking pass distribution	Event Volunteer Coordinator and Venue Manager and Event Accreditation Coordinator and volunteers

88

10 Discuss volunteer complimentary tickets; how to order and pick up their tickets
11 Discuss the Volunteer Appreciation Night

Examples of volunteer roles to be reviewed:

Anthem singer – informed of timing, confirm introduction for public address (PA), where they are to walk/stand, direction to face, bilingual version anthem required, where they go after anthem, pre-event technical check time and site on event day

Team hosts – one per team; to ensure teams know their assigned warm-up and game schedules, etc.

Statistics Managers – to gather pre-event team statistics, to distribute statistics to media and PA announcer at preassigned intervals throughout the event

Game Sheet Manager – to manage the completion of the official game sheet for each team within a predetermined timeframe; information distributed to Media Manager

Media Manager and volunteers – to meet and greet media in attendance, to develop and distribute a media package, to develop event statistics and distribute them in a timely fashion to media at preassigned intervals throughout the event in print form and via the website; to aid media in their arrangements to interview coaches and players

Volunteer security – to ensure only those with the correct accreditation have access to the volunteer room, the team rooms, the media room, etc.

Entertainment volunteers – to secure prizes and to design and conduct fan entertainment during team timeouts/between quarters and during half-time; to work directly with the public address (PA) announcer to ensure promotions are announced

Communication Managers: If two-way radios are available, then the volunteers should be shown how to use them. If there are not enough radios for each volunteer, then just assign the radios to the volunteers who you determine need them the most

i. Make sure volunteers stay in constant contact with one another as well as yourself
ii. If any problems occur, make sure they are communicated to one another right away

	Process for volunteer orientation for those missing the preparation session: • Place a copy of the volunteer orientation information on the website • Confirm attendance of volunteers who did not attend the volunteer orientation session and then direct them to the website orientation information site • Answer any questions the volunteers have accordingly	
Two weeks prior to event	**Volunteer Management Contingency Plan Development** *Generate "What if scenarios" and the response for each situation:* • What if a volunteer doesn't show up? – Train three "floater volunteers" who are prepared to do any of a list of multiple volunteer jobs • What if a volunteer unexpectedly brings their young child with them? – If you can do the event without their help, then you could inform them that their child cannot attend – If you have a spot where the child could stay supervised, then they can leave their child supervised while the event is going on • What if they lose their accreditation or volunteer golf shirt? – Make sure to keep extra shirts and accreditations on hand in case they are forgotten – If there is more than one type of accreditation, then make sure you have some extra of each type	
Eight days prior to event	**Volunteer reminder notices** • Send out an email reminding all volunteers about the event, including the date, time and their role and the fact that the orientation information has been posted on the website for their review/ reminders • Update them on any new information regarding the event	Volunteer Coordinator

90

Five days prior to event	**_Volunteer Room final preparations_**
	• Prepare to post on Volunteer Room bulletin board an overview of each volunteer position (reference material) – state name of volunteer to complete each task
	• Double-check on the order for tables, chairs, food and beverages, and communication equipment
Four to six hours prior to event	**_Volunteer Room set-up_**
	• Post all job assignment overviews with name of volunteer to complete each job on the bulletin board
	• Set up food and drink in the locker room for volunteers
	• Volunteer Room security to be stationed at the entrance of the room
Two hours prior to event	**_Final volunteer meeting_** **_(subdivided into their volunteer groups)_**
	• Checklist utilized to show whether all volunteers have arrived
	• If volunteer has not arrived, replace with a "floater volunteer"
	• Distribution of volunteer communication system (sign-out list utilized)
	• Coordinator available in Volunteer Room for any questions and to manage issues
	• Answer arising questions
One and a half hours prior to event	**Anthem technical check**
	• Anthem singer and technical manager to conduct technical check
	• Review with the PA announcer the anthem signer's introduction information to ensure all is correct
	• Be prepared to use a taped anthem should anything go wrong
Event time	**During the event**
	Distribution of volunteer communication system of cell phones
	• List of all contacts and their cell phone numbers provided with phones
	• Utilize checklist of volunteers to ensure that all are in attendance and in position; manage volunteer absentees
	• Monitor volunteer activities; manage arising issues

	Volunteer breaks: – Make sure volunteers get at least one break during the event – Stagger breaks so not all volunteers are on break at once – Limit breaks to 15 minutes – Make sure volunteers keep their radios with them during break in case of an emergency
At end of event	**After the event** *Volunteer communication system collection* ***Say thanks and encourage attendance at Volunteer Appreciation Night***
One week post-event	**Obtain confirmation of attendance for Volunteer Appreciation Night** • Confirm attendance • Establish agenda • Order awards • Establish a Master of Ceremonies for the night • Complete preparations for food and beverages
Four weeks post-event	***Volunteer Appreciation Night*** *Room set-up:* • Set up tables and chairs • Put out drinks and food on a "snack table" • Coat racks available • Music predetermined; have music and speakers ready to go *Master of Ceremonies briefing:* • Written overview of event details (order of speakers) and their timing, along with specific announcements to be made provided to Master of Ceremonies; reviewed/discussed orally *Awards:* • Hand out awards to each of the volunteers

Figure 5.2 Example operational plan 1: event volunteer management (by Iain Sime)

Planning Objectives:

Objective 1: To establish information booths in the event of high traffic areas to offer a high level of service on event and tourism information to all patrons.

Objective 2: To provide an operational planning template to be utilized for events held on an annual basis.

Objective 3: To be prepared with excellent communication systems in order to manage "unusual" information requests.

Pre-event determinations	*Information booth locations*

	• Location of booths (at arenas and all key hotels)
	   • Consider booths in lobby of hotels and high traffic areas of the venues
	• Only needed in VIP hotels (i.e. players, media, officials, etc.)
	   • Number of booths per location
	      • Hotels had one booth
	      • Event venues had two information booths

Information booth set-up – materials required	*Materials needed for each information booth*

	• 1 × 6 or 8 foot table (tablecloth)
	• 2 chairs
	   • Supplies needed at each information centre
	      • Maps of area for distribution
	      • Entertainment/attraction brochures
	      • Pocket schedules
	      • Game day promotional schedule
	      • Arena venue guide
	         • Seating chart, location of concessions, location of merchandising, other pertinent information
	      • Restaurant/bar guide
	         • Address, phone number, hours of operation, directions from arenas
	      • Tournament schedule
	         • Pocket schedules
	   • Free fan guide
	      • Including team information (team stats, coaches, etc.)
	      • Roster sheet was not added in the 2011 free fan guide and this would have made the crowd very happy; they did not like having to purchase the extra roster sheet
	   • Create a daily news brochure
	      • Stories of the games the day before
	      • Events for the day
	      • Special daily promotions
	      • Player features

- Stat sheets from the game/day before
- Team info (stats, players, coaches, etc.)
- Suggest the addition of a trivia section in the free fan guide
  - Trivia could be on:
    - Coaching staff backgrounds
    - Drafting situation of players
    - Quirky information
    - Tournament historical records
    - Arena history
    - Past tournament locations
    - Medal records
    - National body information
- Sign identifying table as Information Services
- Computer – with internet access
- Communication radio/walkie-talkie (with headset so no one else can hear "issues" being discussed)
  - Where to store/recharge radio at the end of the night
- Access to an electrical plug at the table

Pre-event information guide development	**Information guide creation**
	- Can be used as reference material for information booth volunteers
	- Focus on tournament-specific information, including:
	- Tournament promotions
	- What is going on concerning other activities, such as the fan fest, Hockey Hall of Fame exhibit, etc.
	- Any unique or interesting events during the period of the tournament
	- New Year's Eve celebrations, other games, etc.
	- Merchandise locations
	- International merchandise, shopping centres, etc.
	- Directions to locations from arenas
	- Transportation systems
	- Bus, monorail, train, taxi, etc.
	- Price per ride
	- Media/officials' shuttles
	- Location of pick-up and drop-off times
	- Place to pass time between games but near arenas
	- Location of ATMs in arena
	- How and where to purchase tickets and sell tickets
	- Tournament policies
	- Point system
	- Play-off rules
	- Overtime rules
	- Include game scripts for all games
	- This will allow volunteers to answer questions regarding intermission activities

	• Include sheet of paper to list all questions that could not be answered by booth attendees • Schedule of locations, shifts and volunteer names for entire tournament • Contact information for all information booth attendees • Name and cell phone number

Information services – volunteer roles	***Information guide creators***
	(Six needed prior to the tournament, but can also be used as Information Booth Attendees)
	
	• Research local area in the following areas:
	  • Tournament-specific promotions
	    • Fan fest, etc.
	  • Any unique or interesting events during the period of the tournament
	    • New Year's Eve celebrations, ski resorts, etc.
	  • Merchandise locations
	    • International merchandise, shopping centres, etc.
	  • Transportation systems
	    • Bus, monorail, train, taxi, etc.
	    • Media/officials' shuttles
	
	Information booth attendees
	(Two volunteers per shift – booth to be open 1 hour prior to the first game time and close 30 min. after last game)
	
	• Booths should always have one general volunteer and one local volunteer
	
	General volunteers (1 per booth for each shift)
	
	• Be knowledgeable about information guide
	• Knowledge of area is asset
	• 25 general volunteers needed
	
	Local volunteers (1 per booth for each shift)
	
	• Must be resident of the area
	• Knowledge of the area is essential
	  • Restaurants, bars, transportation system, distances and travel times, etc.
	• 25 local volunteers needed

Information services volunteer training – pre-training determinants	***Pre-training handouts***
	• Online shift availability form
	  • Create schedule of games with all possible shifts
	  • Make it easy for the volunteers to "check off" which shifts they can work
	  • 2011 tournament used www.leaguetoolbox.com
	    • Assisted with scheduling

	• Each volunteer was able to see each shift and check their availability
	• Can go back and change availability
	• Have all volunteers provide their contact information during the tournament
	    • This information will be included in the information booklet to allow contact between all information services volunteers
	       • After the tournament, all personal information will be destroyed
	• Volunteer role and responsibility outline
	    • Detail volunteer responsibilities, who they report to, how to contact that person
	    • Specify that all volunteers must be available for a minimum of 20 hours for the duration of the tournament
	       • This is to ensure people do not volunteer for one shift in order to get a tournament uniform
	• Volunteer uniform information
	    • Need all volunteers to select their clothing size (establish a website to manage this activity)
	    • Detail the colour of pants and shoe style the volunteers should wear

During training sessions	***Training session inclusions***
	
	• Site tour
	    • Areas of importance in venues
	       • Check-in room
	       • Media room
	       • Shuttle pick-up area
	       • Location of information booths
	       • Dispatch centre location
	       • General layout of the building and seating area
	• Check-in process overview
	    • Specify how many hours before each shift the volunteers should arrive
	    • Specify which exterior door to enter
	    • Show where the photos will be taken for credentials
	    • Show where to receive credentials and meal voucher
	       • Credentials must be visible at all times when inside venue
	       • Volunteers only receive meal voucher if they work a 6+ hour shift
	• FAQs handout
	    • Create a list of frequently asked questions from last year's tournament
	    • Give each volunteer a copy and tell them to read the questions and know the answers as they relate to the city and related area

	• Other topics to include:
	  • Introductions of important people
	    • People who will be available to the information services volunteers
	    • How to contact these people
	  • Information booths
	    • Who will set up the booth at the beginning of the tournament
	    • How it will be left at the end of the night
	    • What materials should be on each table at all times
	    • How to get materials replenished before, during and after a shift
	    • How to contact each department (i.e. dispatch centre, venue services, media staff, etc.)
	  • Hand out uniforms
	    • Re-detail uniform code (i.e. colour of pants and style of shoes)
	  • Hand out work schedules
	    • Games the volunteer will work and the time of the shift
	  • Hand out first-shift parking passes
	    • During each shift's check-in, the volunteers will receive a new parking pass
	    • Parking should be free for all volunteers

Post-training session coordination	***Coordination with Accreditation Committee*** • Send Accreditation Committee list of information services volunteer names, contact information and schedules

Issues relating to information services	***Typical issues***
	
	• Common questions asked at the Buffalo tournament:
	  • How can I contact media services, venue services, Transportation Committee, Accreditation Committee, etc.?
	  • What is process for dealing with media requests?
	    • For example, if media outlet requested transportation to a local site 45 min. before game time in order to shoot a video opening, how would this be managed?
	  • What is the proximity of the bus routes, monorails, taxi services and shuttles to the arena?
	  • Can I walk to the arena from the major hotels?
	  • How often do the shuttles leave the hotels?
	  • Who is allowed to ride the shuttles?
	  • Where can I buy international merchandise (especially for countries other than Canada/United States)

97

- Supplies at booth run out
  - Need to have effective communication system in place in order to replenish materials when they are low
  - Information booth materials need to be replenished before the start of each day
  - Information booth attendees need to notify supervisor via radio when supplies are getting low
- Overnight storage of information booth materials
  - There was confusion in Buffalo as to what the volunteers were supposed to do with the information booth materials at the end of the night
- Uniforms
  - There was a lack of uniforms provided to volunteers working at the arena
  - Order a sufficient number of uniforms
    - One for each volunteer and a few extras for emergencies
- Accreditation
  - During the tournament, volunteers had to return their accreditation nightly as the information booth volunteers turned over daily
    - Have the volunteer's photo on their own credential
    - Keep the photo on file but get a newly coloured credential at the beginning of each shift
- Merchandise
  - There was a lack of international merchandise sold in the event venues
    - Order a wide variety of international merchandise
  - The little bit of international merchandise that there was sold out very quickly
    - Order a large quantity of international merchandise
  - The flag was wrong on all merchandise that had every team flag
    - Ensure that all flags are correct before creating merchandise

Information services recommendations	***Volunteers***
	• Have information services and transportation volunteers more familiar with one another, the role they play and how to contact each other
	• Have local volunteers at each booth – specific questions get asked and the volunteer must know the area intimately
	• Have volunteers familiar with venue and tournament format – specifically, the point system and where teams are positioned at any given moment
	• Ensure all volunteers who are working the information

booths attend the training orientation. Set up a secondary training session for those who missed the first training orientation, or consider not utilizing anyone who could not attend the orientation (missing this orientation generally means that they cannot help with questions)
- Ensure the ability for each of the volunteer booths to be able to communicate easily (i.e. via walkie-talkies), and that the volunteers have been trained on the communication system protocols
- Important to know walking distances and times to specific locations

Information booth materials

- Give away roster sheets, especially for low-profile games
  - Not many were purchased, and this would make fans happy
  - Possibly give profits to charity, if roster sheets are not given away

Figure 5.3 Example operational plan 2: event information services management (by Meredith Macdonald and Mike Kitchen)

Goal	To create a program whereby those purchasing event tickets can:
	(a) donate tickets to military families
	(b) donate tickets to pre-established minor hockey teams
	(c) resell the tickets
	A database system is to be established to monitor, track and manage the donation and resale program system
Pre-event implementation	**Why donate?**
	1) Ticket holders' standpoint:
	a. Tax receipts
	b. Free swag
	c. Added value/exclusivity
	d. Goodwill
	e. Share the game (easy way to offload tickets)
	2) Organization standpoint:
	a. Corporate social responsibility
	b. Goodwill

c. Tool to achieve goals (filling all venues for all games)
d. Increased concession revenue
e. Publicity of the event
f. Introduce more people to the game/event

Creation of two (2) donation programs:

1) Military donation and minor hockey team donation
2) Policies of donation programs (who can give, how many can they give, how to give)
3) How are tickets taken from current ticket holders and distributed to lottery winners?

Military donation program:

1) What military arms to partner with?
   a. Local bases

2) Theme of donation program
   a. Ideas:
      i. "Say thanks to the military"
      ii. "Give back to those who give the most"
   b. Who receives donated tickets?
   c. Two tickets per person per game (upon availability) to a member of one of the partnered bases.

3) Tickets:
   a. Tickets are distributed through will-call with proof of identification

Minor hockey donation program:

1) What organizations will tickets be donated to?
   a. Preselected minor hockey teams (players age 12 and under)

2) Theme of donation program
   a. Ideas:
      i. "Make a dream come true"
      ii. "Remember when you were a kid?"
      iii. "How much would this have meant to you?"
      iv. "Give back"

Criteria for distribution	**Communication process:**
	Communicate with military and minor hockey to express qualifying criteria to receive donated ticket packages. Have separate meetings with each donation party to express these policies and regulations
	1) Must have a contact with all involved parties during business hours (leading up to tournament) and through end of last game (during tournament)

C. Mallen

2) Tickets must be distributed according to criteria and regulations outlined during meetings and provided in writing on official letterhead

Suggested criteria:

It is recommended that each game of the tournament be assigned to one participating charitable organization. This process will ensure efficiency in distributing tickets and ensure all distributed tickets are claimed. This will generate the least amount of workload for current staff, while assuring that the donation program upholds its integrity and purpose

Indicated below are the suggested qualify criteria for selection for each program

Military program:

1) Two tickets per person for one game (may only receive tickets for one game during tournament)
2) Must currently be involved with military and served within 18 months prior to December
3) Must be able to attend game if accepting of tickets

Minor hockey program:

1) Must currently be registered with a sanctioned Minor Hockey Association within the province of the event
2) Must be the age of 12 or under as of December 31
3) Must be able to attend game to receive tickets

Ticket distribution

Distribution process:

1) Prior to ticket distribution:
   a. Create partnership with local military bases, local hockey associations
   b. Market the program (interviews, partnerships, public service announcements)

2) Create online donation form:
   a. Donors are to indicate the following:
      i. Game
      ii. Ticket (seat, aisle, section)
      iii. Who to donate to (military, minor hockey)
      iv. Donated by (anonymous, in name of, your name, etc.)
      v. Process:
         1. What happens with tickets?
         2. Where do they go?
         3. Tickets to be marked as donation; no refunds
         4. Information on Military and Minor Hockey
         5. Why donate?
         6. Donation incentives

3) Ticket distribution:
   a. Receiving organization for each game is told the number of tickets they can receive
   b. Organization provides tournament with the number of people who can attend the game. The names of these people are collected and compiled. The names are given to will-call on day of game
   c. Will-call distributes tickets to individuals on list. Individuals are responsible for providing a piece of identification to claim tickets
      i. Note: When tickets are distributed to children, the organization from which these children receive tickets must also provide the name of the child's guardian. The guardian will claim the tickets from will-call

4) During tournament:
   a. It is encouraged that individuals donate tickets 48 hours in advance of games. However, this is not always possible
   b. Have an individual on staff to handle last-minute ticket distribution. These tickets need not go to the assigned organization for that game; however, it should receive priority. In the event that the assigned organization cannot make use of the tickets, it is more important that the tickets are distributed, claimed and used. In this case, donate tickets to another partner charitable organization

Incentive to donate program	*Value*:
	
	Must create value for ticket holders to donate tickets as opposed to selling
	
	1) Explore possibility of issuing tax receipts based on face value of the ticket.
	   a. Encourages tickets holders of more expensive seats to donate. Closes the gap on value between lesser-valued donated tickets
	   b. Process for tax receipts issue to be established
	
	2) Each person who donates tickets receives a thank-you letter following the completion of the tournament. The letter should include:
	   a. Indication of where the tickets were donated
	   b. Results of the program
	   c. Impact of the tournament itself
	   d. Free or severely discounted tickets to a future event
	
	3) Incentive based on number of tickets donated:
	   a. Each set of tickets donated earns the donor another level of incentive:
	      i. 1 pair – access to party for donors and those

102

	receiving donated tickets. (January 1 was an off day for the tournament in Buffalo. This creates an opportunity to increase revenue on the off day) ii. 2 pairs – party, free water bottle iii. Etc.

Staffing	**List of potential jobs:**
	
	1) Creation of website (with Ticketmaster) to allow tickets holders to submit tickets to donation
	2) Monitor and manage tickets that are donated
	3) Liaison between tickets and receiving partner
	4) Marketing of program
	5) Manage the database:
	   a. People who donated tickets (for thank-you and incentive purposes)
	   b. People who receive tickets (for potential future opportunities)
	6) Coordinate and distribute incentives (thank-you letters, tax receipts, potential parties, swag, etc.)
	7) Distribution of tickets (monitor, manage, execute)
	8) Evaluation of program post-event
	
	One individual to coordinate the distribution of all donated tickets

Marketing	**Target market:**
	
	Focus marketing on current ticket holders
	
	1) Focus on reasons to donate:
	   a. Tax receipts
	   b. Incentives (value) to donate
	   c. Goodwill
	
	2) Create theme for program:
	   a. Military
	      i. "Say thanks to the military"
	      ii. "Give back to those who give the most"
	   b. Minor hockey
	      i. "Make a dream come true"
	      ii. "Remember when you were a kid?"
	      iii. How much would this have meant to you"
	      iv. "Give back"
	
	3) Second stage of marketing plan is to reach out to general population
	   a. Use marketing tools 3 and 4 to achieve goal
	
	Marketing tools:
	
	1) Public service announcements

	2) Email to all current ticket holders 3) Broadcast partners 4) Interviews (TV, radio, phone call, etc.)
Database	*Purpose*: Database to be used not only for current tournament but potential for future use in other events put on by Hockey Canada Goal of database is to ensure constant contact with current consumers, with goal of filling all venues for all games Database content collected through: 1) All people who signed up for lottery 2) All people who use resale site 3) All people who use donation site 4) People who receive donated tickets 5) All people who apply to be a volunteer
Implementation	*Process*: Implement process as outlined within program. Follow step-by-step instructions for each section: 1) Establish partnerships needed to set up webpage and complete set-up of the webpage 2) Indicate to package holders the presence of webpage/program and launch webpage 3) Market webpage and donation program to general population 4) Operate and manage webpage and program 5) Evaluate program, assess future viability and improve as needed

Evaluation	*Criteria*:
	Evaluate the following areas:
	
	1) How set-up of page worked:
	   a. Easy to navigate
	   b. Easy to set up
	   c. Feasible
	
	2) Number of tickets donated:
	   a. Did ticket holders donate a worthwhile amount of tickets?
	   b. Military
	   c. Minor hockey
	
	3) Database growth:
	   a. Were there significant additions to database?
	
	4) Did donation incentives provide value?

> 5) How much work was this program for military and Minor Hockey Association?
> 6) How cooperative were the donation partners?
> 7) Future viability?
>   a. Success
>   b. Failure
>   c. Future recommendation

Figure 5.4 Example operational plan 3: event ticket donation and resale program management (by Ian Phillips and Matt Hill)

Transport command centre	***Set-up required for command centre office*** Tables (2 tables, 8′) Tablecloths (2; white) Chairs (3–4 chairs) Internet access Computer (minimum 1; preferably 2 laptops) Electrical outlets Electrical power bars as surge protectors for laptops Whiteboards (2) and whiteboard markers ***Site for vehicles at command centre*** Size of room needed (to hold 1–3 people) Location (need a place where transport vehicles can be parked at night; and where volunteer drivers can park their vehicles while working as transport drivers) Ease of access (easy access to vehicles and for vehicles to begin their routes) Proximity to other key areas/offices Security needed at this site at all times
Command centre volunteer responsibilities	***Administration requirements at command centre*** **Volunteers at command centre** Two volunteers needed at command centre at all times (3–4 hours prior to games until 1.5 hours after last game) to manage all communication and administrative activities including the following: **Design and manage the vehicle sign-in sheet:** • All drivers must sign in and be assigned a vehicle, route and time period **Design and manage the driver log:** • Record of mileage and gas levels

Manage special pick-up requests:
- Need to be recorded in a special request log
  - Needs to be determined who is allowed to make a special request. VIP? Official? Media?
  - Need to determine the process for assigning drivers for special requests

Receipt tracking sheet:
- Drivers need to fill tank and be refunded; possibly give each driver $100 in advance
- A cash box or safe should be used in order to keep all money safe
- Cash on hand will be needed in order to pay drivers for transport expenses
  - Only one person should keep track of this so that there is no confusion and no money goes missing
  - Determine whether drivers can be reimbursed immediately after their shift

Driver records – Photocopies of "G" driver's licence from all drivers:
- Copy provided to:_____
- Deadline date:____
- Confidentiality of records to be established (who has access; when will they be shredded?)
- Determine if drivers will need a copy of proof of insurance

Communication requirements at command centre

Walkie-talkies:
- Create list of those to be on walkie-talkies:
  - Dispatch
  - All drivers
  - Info services booths
  - Host event coordinator
  - Team hosts
- **Order walkies-talkies**
  - 24 needed for transportation
  - extra batteries – order 1 per walkie talkie
  - chargers – order enough to ensure all walkie talkies are charged overnight
  - headsets – 1 per walkie talkie
- **Headsets** are recommended so that the general public doesn't hear what is going on over the walkie-talkies
- **Protocols** for walkie-talkie use to be established and provided to drivers verbally and in writing (for reference)

OR, instead of walkie-talkies:

Suggest the use of a system of cell phones
Need to establish a list of names and cell numbers and make sure all that need a list has one
Determine payment for cell phone use prior to the event

Transport members that need to be included in the cell phone system include:

- Command centre
- Team bus drivers
- Team hosts
- Shuttle drivers
- Host event coordinator
- Police officers/station

Consider including information services (as they are the point people for providing the information)

Whiteboards (2):

- One board to state the following information:
  - Team vans with the host
  - Vehicle number
  - Host's name
  - Route that they are on
- The other board to state the following:
  - Each team
  - Hotel they were staying at
  - Hotel phone number
  - Practice and game schedule
  - Locations for team's games and practices

Schedules:

- Game schedule should be posed in command centre for quick reference
- Media shuttle schedule should be posted in the command centre for quick reference

Team transportation: team buses

Outsource team bus requirements to bus company:

- Size of vehicle (52-seat bus)
- 1 bus needed for each team
- # of days required
- Mileage pre-determined
  - (i.e. can bus be used for team tours of the region?)
- Insurance requirements

Team bus rules to be provided to teams (in writing):

- When the bus will be provided to each team (i.e. the bus picks up the team at the airport upon their arrival)
- Where the bus can take teams (i.e. arrangements they need to make should they take the bus to tour the region)
- If the team wants to come in early, they will be required to pay for the extra days for which they will need the bus
  - Payments for extra days using the bus should be made in advance so that no team can leave without paying

Bus driver package should include:

- Team game schedule

	• Team practice schedule
	• Locations of games and practices
	• Contacts in case of emergency for:
	  • Command centre
	  • Team host
	  • Host event coordinator

Shuttle transportation	**Shuttle vehicle rentals:**
	• Size of shuttle vehicles to be determined
	  • used 15-seaters for game officials
	  • 7-seat mini vans for media shuttles
	• Number of shuttle vehicles to be determined
	  • 4 shuttles for games officials
	  • 5 media shuttles out at a time before games plus a 55-passenger bus
	
	Note: games with expected high attendance may require more shuttles to be out at one time
	
	Note: if the 55-passenger bus was to carry fewer than 10 people, what adaptations would be required in the shuttle rental and schedule?
	
	• Dates to be available
	• Insurance required
	• Minimum age of drivers
	• Driver's licence needed to drive a shuttle bus of this size
	
	Shuttle route:
	• Route to be determined (from each hotel selected to the competition site)
	  – Alternative routes to be predetermined
	• How often will the shuttle arrive at any one site?
	
	Shuttle volunteer drivers:
	• Volunteers to be secured (need one for each shuttle and # on call should they need to be replaced for any reason)
	• Process established to check their driver's licence status (and copy kept on file)
	• What type of form will shuttle drivers have to sign prior to starting their role (i.e. guaranteeing that they have a valid driver's licence and are eligible by law to drive the size of vehicle selected, etc.)?
	
	Shuttle rules:
	• Who has access to the shuttle service? (i.e. shuttles are for VIPs, media and game officials who do not want to utilize their own vehicles)
	• What identification is required to access the shuttle service?
	  • Any individual using the shuttle should have proper accreditation

- What communication system is available to access the shuttle service to manage issues?
  - All drivers, command centre and info services booths should have walkie-talkies to communicate any issues
- List of accredited individuals allowed to use the shuttle system needs to be set in stone so that it is clear who can and can't use the shuttle

Note: This is a process that needs to be managed, as some people will be added each day or at the last minute. Updated copies of the accredited individuals allowed to use the shuttle need to be provided to each site

Note: Some game officials prefer to have the vehicle to themselves rather than sharing it with other accredited individuals. Need to determine whether this will be allowed or if they will be required to share

Provision of event information to be posted in each shuttle vehicle includes:
- Game schedule
- Shuttle schedule

Transportation volunteers: training

Driver training
- Date:
- Time:
- Site:
- Attendees: all drivers

Conduct a shuttle volunteer driver training session to provide an overview of the event:
- Give out game schedules and practice schedules
- Discuss sign-in and out requirements for the drivers to obtain a shuttle vehicle
- Review the shuttle rules (see rules stated above)
- Provide contact information
- Discuss communication system
- Discuss emergency procedures and distribute emergency report form
- Outline logistics for routes/dates/requirements
- Provide information on volunteer training uniforms, volunteer accreditation and volunteer meals

Communication training for transport volunteers
- Create and distribute list of key contact names/information
- Where/when to get walkie-talkie
- Walkie talkie protocol (how do they contact dispatch? What is the proper wording and terminology to use over the radio?)

Logistics training for transport volunteers
- Emergency management (process provided in writing)
  - Forms to report incidents
- Route/dates/time requirements
  - Walk-through of exactly where shuttle drivers will pick up and drop off people. These exact locations will ensure consistency
  - If the pick-up and drop-off locations change at any time, a plan needs to be put in place to communicate with all drivers to inform them of the change
  - What accredited individuals they are allowed to pick up
  - Maps given to all drivers in case they need to change route

What if driver could not attend training session?
- Is there an alternative training session?
- Will they receive instructions upon arrival for first shift?
- Will they still be allowed to volunteer?
- Can someone train them on the spot?
- What is the liability if they did not go through the proper training session?

Note: Recommended that info services volunteers are also involved in this training so that they have the same info and transportation and can provide accurate info to anyone approaching their booths

Transport volunteer uniforms
- Sizes of uniforms for each volunteer should be determined during volunteer application process
- Uniforms can be picked up at the training session
- If an individual does not attend the training session, alternative arrangements will need to be made for that individual to pick up the uniform

Transport volunteer accreditation
- Accreditation passes can be picked up by all members upon arrival for their first shift
- There should be an individual in the command centre responsible for distributing accreditation passes to all transport volunteers
- Drivers should be on site at least one hour before their first shift in order to get their accreditation

Transport volunteer meals
- Meal vouchers to be given only to volunteers who have worked double shifts (eight-hour shifts)
- There should be an individual in the command centre responsible for distributing meal vouchers to specified volunteers
- Meal vouchers should not be left unattended in order to control how many are distributed

Transportation issues in coordination:	
1 Coordination between transport personnel and other event components	Be sure team interpreter/host has transportation information and a contact number to use to manage any transport issues
2 Shuttle breakdowns	Establish a consistent process to manage any shuttle mechanical issues
3 Interpreters	Establish a system to be able to gain access to a particular interpreter at any time during the event
4 Police escorts and road blocks	Meet with the local police department concerning: • Police escorts – team buses were escorted by police from the hotel to the arena • Road blocks – team bus and shuttle drivers need to be made aware of what roads will be blocked off and when these roads will be blocked so that they can adjust their route accordingly • Ensure that all officers have the same information regarding escorts and road blocks

Transportation Incident Report Form

Name:

Position:

Date:

Time:

Location:

Explanation of Incident:

Figure 5.5 Example operational plan 4: event transportation management (by Matt Darte)

The following chart offers an example of an event operational plan. This particular plan outlines examples of the operational details for the hospitality functions for an elite National Collegiate Athletic Association (NCAA) Men's Basketball Championship, Round 2, held in San Jose, California. The event had a four-day schedule, Wednesday to Saturday. A total of three games were held during the four days (two games on Thursday and one on Saturday). Four teams participated, with two being eliminated after Thursday's games. Wednesday and Friday were practice days. At the conclusion of the four days, the winning team moved to the next stage of the tournament, to be held at a different facility. An American university served as the host for this event, using a professional sport level facility as the venue.

As the Hospitality Coordinator for this event, I have created an operational planning chart to provide you with an example of the types of responsibilities that are included when preparing to stage hospitality areas and coordinating all elements using volunteer assistance. The general duties of the overall hospitality committee included, but were not limited to, creating and fulfilling all catering contracts for the event for athletes, coaches, official evaluators, officials, staff, volunteers and the basketball committee representatives for lunches, dinners, beverages and snacks. This required hospitality plans to be staged at the event venue and the host hotel.

As you review the chart below, position yourself as the individual responsible for implementing each detail listed. Record any arising questions as you consider how you are to implement the plan. Develop additional level 3 detail for the plan. How would you advance and adapt this plan if you were responsible? Also, you must be prepared prior to any task being implemented. How would you adapt your personal operational plan to ensure you have prepared all items in advance?

Time Frame	Task	Responsibility
Three months prior	Budget development: Obtain the budget for the hospitality committee from the host university – Develop a budget overview chart to personally keep track of your hospitality spending – Continuously develop the budget details to have a realistic picture of the budget at all times	Facilitated by the event Hospitality Coordinator
	Hospitality preparation: Create an overview of all of the hospitality areas to be set up in the competition venue, the potential capacity, constituents to cater to, food/beverage requirements for patrons and volunteers, and equipment requirements – Include: staff/media buffet, locker rooms, officials' rooms, official evaluators' room, basketball committee room, back room/press conference area, media refreshment area and breakfast/evening hospitality room at the host hotel	Event Hospitality Coordinator

- Include: constituent to cater to athletes, coaches, officials, official evaluators, media, host university staff, volunteers and basketball committee

Competition Venue Facility Manager meeting: Meet the host venue's Facility Manager and Event Coordinators with host university staff - Go on a site visit and become familiar with the venue - Determine: the hospitality food and beverage areas, all set-up details, storage areas available, including size and access process - Obtain diagrams of the facility and create a specific site-map of all event hospitality areas - Develop a written timeline and list of hospitality preparation or set-up details	Event Hospitality Coordinator and Competition Venue Facility Manager
Confirmations: Confirm set-up areas with the host university staff by: - Communicating with the facility manager the site-map timeline and details	Event Hospitality Coordinator
Competition venue food services meeting: Arrange meeting with the facility's Food Services Manager - Prepare for meeting by creating an outline of the different areas for hospitality services, the amount of people to cater to and the type of food/beverage to be served for discussion - Obtain the already existent sponsorship contacts and the list of products that will be provided that apply to the hospitality component of the event - Attend meeting and discuss the catering options based on the event budget and the type and number of people for catering service - Also discuss event beverage sponsors, who will provide certain products to be served - Determine the appropriate area and time for product drop-off - Develop potential catering contracts (determine approval process for approving and signing contracts) - Confirm catering contracts at venue with the host university staff. - Communicate with the facility's Food Services Manager the final food/beverage requirements for the venue catering contracts. Notify them that the delivery times will be communicated at	Event Hospitality Coordinator and Competition Venue Food Services Manager

	a later date once game and practice times are established	
	Host hotel meeting: Arrange meeting with host hotel to discuss hotel hospitality area and menu options/contracts for the daily media breakfast and evening drinks and snacks – Attend meeting with the host hotel and determine the area for media hospitality and the hours of operation, and establish the food and beverage contracts. Food and beverages should be served in a buffet-style format. During the evening hospitality time, a server will be required to serve alcoholic beverages. All of the details should be agreed upon in light of the hospitality committee's budget – Confirm hotel catering contracts with the host university staff – Communicate with the host hotel the final food/beverage requirements for the catering contracts	Event Hospitality Coordinator and Host Hotel Food Services Representative
	Coordinate sponsor hospitality details: – Work with the Sponsor Committee to communicate to event sponsors the details for hospitality product time and drop-off at the venue and host hotel	Event Hospitality Coordinator and the Sponsor Committee
Two months prior	*Hospitality volunteer development:* Obtain the tentative schedule for event game and practice times from the host university – Determine the hospitality areas where volunteer staff will be needed – Determine the number of volunteer staff required to fulfill the duties of the hospitality areas – Determine the potential shift times for the volunteer positions based on the tentative schedule for game and practice times – Communicate the staffing requirements to the staffing coordinator. Ensure to include extra bodies to help cover positions in case of drop outs or no shows. The Staffing Coordinator will be responsible for volunteer recruitment and assignment	Hospitality Coordinator and Staffing Coordinator
	Hospitality signage: Determine all signage needs for the hospitality areas	Hospitality Coordinator and Signage Committee

	– Provide diagram of all signage placement in the venue and host hotel – Communicate to the host university the signage required and its placement (including date and time requirements)	
One month prior	*Volunteer assignment:* Obtain the list of contacts who will be volunteering for the hospitality component from the Staffing Coordinator – Determine the appropriate hospitality volunteer shifts for each of the four days of the tournament – Assign the volunteers in the contact list to daily hospitality shifts – Prepare a daily schedule of events, individual schedules, and list of responsibilities and duties to be included in the volunteer training packages for the hospitality committee to distribute at volunteer training. Also include the venue site map of the hospitality areas – Submit the hospitality committee documents for the volunteer training packages to the Staffing Coordinator and determine the volunteer training dates. The Staffing Coordinator will make up all of the training packages and call each volunteer to inform them of their training times – Create volunteer training agenda for the volunteer training night. Following the main presentation, volunteers will be broken up into committees for 30 minutes for specialized training and a venue walk-through	Hospitality Coordinator and Staffing Coordinator
Two weeks prior	*Volunteer hospitality training:* – Attend volunteer training sessions – Conduct a specific training session to communicate all of the hospitality committee details to the assigned volunteers – Conduct a walk-through of the venue and point out where all of the hospitality areas are as well as the beverage storage area to be used if beverages are running low before new delivery times – Show the volunteers where the proper entrances and exits are and where radios (if necessary) and credentials can be picked up – Ensure time is allocated for a question–answer period – For those hospitality volunteers unable to attend the training, ensure that arrangements	Hospitality Coordinator and Staffing Coordinator

are made for them to pick up their training package and uniform and communicate any essential information from the training session

Credentials or accreditation:
- Arrange for the creation of credentials or accreditation for the Hospitality Coordinator and all of the hospitality volunteers for the competition venue and host hotel. The credentials indicate the name and access areas the person is allowed to enter
- Arrange for the distribution of credentials for the hospitality coordinator and hospitality volunteers
- Distribute information to all volunteers concerning their access, entrance areas for the competition venue and host hotel and their credential access allowance
- Understand the system for replacing credentials should anyone lose or forget their credentials

Hospitality Coordinator and Credentialing Coordinator

Confirmations:
- Confirm all game and practice times with the host university
- Confirm and adjust the catering and staffing details, if needed
- Contact the Sponsor Committee and ensure food/beverage event sponsors' product and delivery times are confirmed and exact delivery site and contact names are provided. Ensure all deliveries will take place the day before the event begins. Keep an overview of contact names and numbers to call should deliveries be delayed
- Confirm with facility manager the set-up areas and where signage is to be hung (and how it is to be fastened)
- Confirm signage has arrived at facility from the Signage Committee to the venue and delivered to the facility manager
- Confirm with the Food Services Manager at host hotel: the catering contracts, all menu items, including breakfast and evening catering requirements, delivery times, clean-up times, sponsor product use and placement, the signage to be placed at the hotel directing patrons to the hospitality area and the signage in the hospitality area to be hung by the event volunteers
- Receive a copy of all finalized contracts from the venue and host hotel and review details again

Hospitality Coordinator

	Event daily review meetings: – Arrange a meeting time and location with the host university venue and Host Hotel Facility Managers for each morning of the event to ensure all hospitality details are reviewed and are correct	Hospitality Coordinator, Competition Venue Facility Manager, and the Host Hotel Facility Manager
Day before the event	*Final Preparations:* – Arrive at venue and conduct a venue walk-through to oversee that all hospitality areas are in the proper spots and are set up correctly, and that all of the necessary signage is present – Ensure all sponsor product has been delivered and stored at the proper location – Check into the hotel – Conduct a walk-through of the host hotel hospitality areas and ensure all are correctly set up and signage is up	Hospitality Coordinator
Day 1: practice day	*Event day activities*	
6:30 am	– Arrive at host hotel hospitality area. Be sure to have credentials on hand – Ensure that all breakfast set-ups are complete and that the proper food is out for the buffet and signage is out properly – Speak with the hotel representative in charge and retrieve an extension number to call if any food and beverage is running low	Hospitality Coordinator and Volunteer A
7:00 am–10:00 am	– Greet all media guests into the breakfast room – Check for proper credentials upon each person's entry	Volunteer A
8:00 am	– Go to the competition venue; be sure to have credentials on hand – Conduct walk-through of the competition venue hospitality areas to ensure all areas are set up correctly – Conduct a final volunteer briefing session	Hospitality Coordinator
8:30 am	– Meet with the competition venue Food Services Manager to confirm all daily catering details	Hospitality Coordinator and Competition

		Venue Food Services Manager
8:45 am	– Report to media refreshment area and go through your checklist to ensure that all food, beverage and supplies (cups, napkins, bowls, tablecloths, cloths to wipe up spills, and so on) have been delivered to the media refreshment area – Ensure tables are set –1 table for beverage distribution and the other for snacks to be distributed	Volunteers B, C, D and Hospitality Coordinator
8:30 am– 5:00 pm	– Main duty is to be a floater and conduct regular checks on every hospitality area to ensure its smooth functioning as well as to fulfill any special requests and manage volunteers	Hospitality Coordinator
9:00 am	– Work areas and courtside areas open to the media	Competition Venue Facility Manager
9:00 am– 5:00 pm	– Work in the media refreshment area – drinks should be poured for the media by the volunteers in order to save product – Ensure that the area is kept tidy at all times – The food services staff will be making regular deliveries. However, if product is running low, communicate to either the coordinator or one of the food service staff. If necessary, use stock from the storage area – The janitorial staff to complete regular clean-up as scheduled. However, if their services are required at other times, communicate to either the coordinator or one of the janitorial staff directly – Volunteers at the media refreshment area will take turns eating lunch and take breaks as scheduled, ensuring that the area is never unattended	Volunteers B, C, D
10:00 am	– Arrive at venue; be sure credentials are on hand – Gather beverages from storage areas and fill two coolers in each locker room with drinks and ice (one water and one a sponsored replenishment drink). Ensure different flavours of the replenishment drink are present. The	Volunteer E

118

	coolers and buckets of ice will already be placed in the locker rooms by the food services staff	
10:00 am–4:30 pm	– Conduct regularly scheduled check of the locker rooms to ensure coolers remain stocked with fresh ice throughout the duration of the day. Note: do not enter the locker rooms if they are occupied by the teams	Volunteer E
10:30 am	– Team entrance opens	Competition Venue Facility Manager
10:30 am	– Ensure that the Basketball Committee room is set up and that their meals, beverages and snacks are all in place	Volunteer F
11:00 am–2:00 pm	– Ensure that the Basketball Committee room stays tidy and meal food stays hot and fresh – The food services staff will be doing regular deliveries; however, if product is running low, communicate to either the coordinator or one of the food service staff	Volunteer F
11:00 am–4:30 pm	– Ensure that the Basketball Committee room stays tidy and snacks and beverages stay stocked – The food services staff will be making regular deliveries. However, if product is running low, communicate to either the coordinator or one of the food service staff. If necessary, use stock from the storage area	Volunteer F
11:00 am	– Facility opens to the public	
11:00 am	– Arrive at venue and obtain credential – Ensure that the media/staff buffet area is set up and that the correct food, beverages and supplies are in place according to the catering contracts – Put up the "Staff Only" buffet sign in the staff/media buffet area	Volunteer G
11:30 am–12:30 pm	– Check the buffet area to ensure it is ready and then communicate over the radio that the staff buffet is ready and for all coordinators to send their volunteers for their meal when they are able to get away	Hospitality Coordinator and Volunteer G

	– Staff buffet takes place – Ensure the area remains tidy and stocked and that no bottles leave the area. All drinks must be poured into cups – The food services staff will be making regular deliveries. However, if product is running low, communicate to either the coordinator or one of the food service staff – The janitorial staff will be doing regular clean-up. However, if their services are required, communicate to either the coordinator or one of the janitorial staff	
12:00 noon– 12:50 pm	Team #1 practises	
12:30 pm– 2:00 pm	– Ensure the "Media Buffet" sign is up in the staff/media buffet area – Welcome the media personnel into the buffet area – Check for proper credentials at the door – Watch for any person without proper media credentials and keep them out of the area – Ensure the area remains tidy and stocked and that no bottles leave the area. All drinks must be poured into cups	Volunteer G
12:30 pm	– Ensure the delivery and proper set-up of Team #1's box lunches into their locker room is on time	Volunteer E
12:30 pm	– Ensure that the area for the press conferences is set up and the beverages and supplies are stocked	Volunteer F
1:00 pm– 1:50 pm	Team #2 practises	
1:00 pm– 3:30 pm	– Press conferences take place – Ensure the area remains tidy and stocked	Volunteer F
1:30 pm	– Ensure the delivery and proper set-up of Team #2's box lunches into their locker room is on time	Volunteer E
2:10 pm– 3:00 pm	Team #3 practises	
2:40 pm	– Ensure the delivery and proper set-up of	

	Team #3's box lunches into their locker room is on time	Volunteer E
3:10 pm–4:00 pm	Team #4 practises	
3:40 pm	– Ensure the delivery and proper set-up of Team #4's box lunches into their locker room	Volunteer E
4:30 pm	– Arrive at hotel hospitality area and ensure that the proper snacks and beverages are set up and a server is present for the cash bar	Volunteer A
5:00 pm–8:00 pm	– Greet all media guests into the hospitality room – Check for proper credentials upon each person's entry	Volunteer A
5:30 pm	– Ensure all hospitality areas are tidy and any necessary products or supplies are put away – Confirm all shift times for the following day	All volunteers and Hospitality Coordinator
Day 2: Game Day		
6:30 am	– Arrive at hotel hospitality area – Ensure that all breakfast set-ups are complete and the proper food is out for the buffet	Volunteer A
7:00 am–10:00 am	– Greet all media guests into the breakfast room – Check for proper credentials upon each person's entry	Volunteer A
8:00am	– Arrive at venue – Conduct walk-through of the venue to ensure all hospitality areas are set up correctly	Hospitality Coordinator
8:15 am	– Meet with the food services manager to confirm all daily catering details	Hospitality Coordinator
8:30 am–11:00 pm	– The main duty is to be a floater and conduct regular checks on every hospitality area to ensure its smooth functioning as well as to fulfill any special requests	Hospitality Coordinator
8:30 am	– Arrive at venue – Gather beverages from storage areas and fill two coolers in each locker room with drinks and ice. The coolers and buckets of ice will already	Volunteer E

	have been placed in the locker rooms by the food services staff	
8:30 am– 9:30 pm	– Ensure the locker room coolers remain stocked with fresh ice throughout the duration of the day. Ensure regular checks are made of the coolers; however, do not enter the locker rooms if they are occupied by the teams	Volunteer E
9:00 am	– Team entrance opens	
9:30 am	– Arrive at venue. – Ensure that all food, beverages and supplies (cups, napkins, bowls, tablecloths, and so on) have been delivered to the media refreshment area – Set up both tables neatly. One table should be used for beverages and the other for snacks	Volunteers B, C, D
10:00 am– 11 pm	– Work the media refreshment area. Drinks should be poured for the media by the volunteers in order to save product – Ensure the area is kept tidy at all times – The food services staff will be making regular deliveries. However, if product is running low, communicate to either the coordinator or one of the food services staff. If necessary, use stock from the storage area – The janitorial staff will be doing regular clean-ups. However, if their services are required, communicate to either the coordinator or one of the janitorial staff – Volunteers at the media refreshment area will take turns eating lunch, dinner and taking breaks, ensuring that the area never remains unattended	Volunteers B, C, D
10:00 am	– Backstage work areas open to the media	
10:00 am– 1:50 pm	– Closed practices (Teams 1–4)	
10:30 am	– Arrive at venue – Ensure that the Basketball Committee room is set up and that their meals, beverages and snacks are all in place	Volunteer F
11:00 am– 2:00 pm	– Ensure the Basketball Committee room remains tidy and meals stay hot and fresh – The food services staff will be making regular	Volunteer F

122

	deliveries. However, if product is running low, communicate to either the coordinator or one of the food services staff	
11:00 am–7:00 am	– Ensure the Basketball Committee room remains tidy and snacks and beverages stay stocked – The food services staff will be making regular deliveries. However, if product is running low, communicate to either the coordinator or one of the food services staff	Volunteer F
12:00 noon	– Arrive at competition venue – Ensure that the media/staff buffet is set up and that the correct food, beverages and supplies are in place according to the contracts	Volunteer G
	– Put up the "Staff Only" buffet sign – Confirm with the facility manager the proper spot for delivery of pizza at 5:00 pm – Obtain a credit card from the host university staff to order pizza for the volunteers – Call a local pizza restaurant and pre-order 50 large pizzas of various kinds to be delivered to the venue for 5:00 pm. Ensure to communicate the location for drop-off and the credit card information for payment – Communicate the details of the pizza delivery to the volunteer running the staff/media buffet area, as this will be the area used for dinner – Communicate the details of the pizza dinner to the food services staff. Beverages will be required in the staff/media buffet area by 4:30 pm	Hospitality Coordinator
12:30 pm–1:30 pm	– Check the buffet area to ensure it is ready and then communicate over the radio that the staff buffet is ready and for all coordinators to send their volunteers when possible – Staff buffet takes place	Hospitality Coordinator
	– Ensure the area remains tidy and stocked and that no bottles leave the area. All drinks must be poured into cups – The food services staff will be making regular deliveries. However if product is running low, communicate to either the coordinator or one of the food services staff – The janitorial staff will be doing regular clean-ups. However, if their services are required, communicate to either the coordinator or one of the janitorial staff	Volunteer G

Time	Tasks	Responsible
1:30 pm–4:00 pm	– Welcome the media personnel into the buffet area – Check for proper credentials and turn away any person who does not have the proper media credential – Ensure the area stays tidy and stocked and that no one leaves the area with bottles. All drinks must go into cups	Volunteer G
2:30 pm	– Ensure that the official evaluators' room is set up and the correct snacks and beverages are present – Ensure that the officials' room is set up and the correct snacks and beverages are present – Ensure that the cheerleading warm-up area is stocked with snacks and beverages	Volunteer F
3:00 pm–10:00 pm	– Ensure the official evaluators' room stays tidy and stocked with snacks and beverages – Ensure the officials' room stays tidy and stocked with snacks and beverages – Ensure the cheerleading warm-up area remains tidy and stocked with snacks and beverages – The food services staff will be making regular deliveries. However, if product is running low in the cheerleading warm-up area, communicate to either the coordinator or one of the food services staff. If necessary, use stock from the storage area	Volunteer F
3:00 pm	The doors open to the public	
4:00 pm	– Call the pizza restaurant to confirm delivery of 50 large pizzas at 5:00 pm – Gather three hospitality volunteers to meet at the delivery location to help bring in the pizzas	Hospitality Coordinator
4:30 pm	Game #1	
5:00 pm	– Report to the pizza delivery location – Bring the pizzas into the staff/media buffet area and set them up buffet-style, separating the different kinds – Ensure the beverages have been set up in the staff/media area	Hospitality Coordinator and three Hospitality Volunteers
	– Hang up the "Staff Only" sign in the staff/media buffet area	Volunteer G

124

5:15 pm	– Communicate over the radio that the pizza is ready and for all coordinators to send their volunteers when possible	Hospitality Coordinator
5:30 pm	– Ensure the box lunches have been delivered into the official evaluators' room – Ensure the box lunches have been delivered into the officials' room	Volunteer F
6:00 pm	– Ensure the box lunches have been delivered to the Game #1 team locker rooms – Ensure the holding area for the press conferences is set up and the beverages and supplies are stocked	Volunteer E
6:30 pm– 10:30 pm	– Press conferences take place – Ensure the holding area remains tidy and stocked with beverages	Volunteer F
7:00 pm	Game #2	
7:30 pm	– Pizza dinner ends – Put any leftover pizzas into the volunteer room	Volunteer G
9:00 pm	– Arrive at hotel hospitality area and ensure the proper snacks and beverages are set up and a server is present for the cash bar	Volunteer A
9:30 pm– 12:00 noon	– Greet all media guests in the hospitality room – Check for proper credentials upon each person's entry	Volunteer A
9:30 pm	– Ensure the box lunches have been delivered to the Game #2 team locker rooms	Volunteer E
11:00 pm	– Ensure all hospitality areas are tidy and any necessary products are put away – Confirm shift times for the following day	All volunteers and coordinator
Day 3: practice day	Follow the same logical steps as were used on Day 1, based on the following daily schedule: 10:30 am: Backstage work areas open to the media 12:00 noon: Team entrance opens 1:00 pm–2:30 pm: Team #1 closed practice 3:00 pm–4:30 pm: Team #2 closed practice 1:30 pm–4:30 pm: Press conferences/interviews	

Day 4: game day	Follow the same steps used on Day 2 based on the following daily schedule:
	10:00 am: Team entrance opens 11:00 am: Backstage work areas open to the media 11:00 am–11:50 am: Team #1 closed practice 12:00 noon–12:50 pm: Team #2 closed practice 4:00 pm: Game 6:00 pm–8:00 pm: Press conferences/interviews

Note:*During any down time in their assigned areas, the hospitality volunteers were asked to help cover other hospitality areas. On occasion during their down time, the volunteers had permission to watch the basketball games or practices.

Figure 5.6 Example of an operational plan for the National Collegiate Athletic Association (NCAA) Men's Basketball Championship, round 2, San Jose, California: the hospitality component (by Lauren Thompson)

CHAPTER 6

THE EVENT PLANNING MODEL: THE EVENT IMPLEMENTATION, MONITORING AND MANAGEMENT PHASE

LORNE J. ADAMS

This chapter emphasizes the role of the event manager in making the operational plan work when it counts most: at the event itself. While many may be aware of the detail within the operational plan, no one knows it as well as you, the event manager. That is why you will be called upon to facilitate the work of the people who implement the plan, monitor the activities as well as manage and provide guidance concerning the unforeseen problems that arise. How you manage all of this will determine not only the success of the event but your success as a quality manager.

A lot will be asked of you as the event unfolds. Understanding yourself and your role is critical to the success of the event. You will not be a dispassionate observer; you will be totally immersed in the event and all it entails. You will also bring your unique set of skills and abilities, predispositions and biases with you. They are as much a part of the event as the people and systems you are attempting to manage.

IMPLEMENTATION: EXECUTING THE PLAN

Implementation involves the execution of the plan by moving the planned operational concepts and processes from the members who completed the planning to a myriad of event staff and volunteers who are tasked with executing the plan (Buchanan & O'Connell, 2006). Facilitating the implementation of the operational plans does not take place in a passive world; it is purpose driven, goal oriented and dynamic, as we live in a unique change-based time (Mallen, 2006), and the forces of change demand that we react to and manage the repercussions of that change. In this environment, implementation is not easy. The first step entails coordinating and getting all of the people implementing the plan on the same page.

DISSEMINATING IMPLEMENTATION REQUIREMENTS AND PRODUCTION MEETINGS

The group or team responsible for implementing the plan will be much broader than that which created the plan. They need an opportunity to hear, understand and assimilate the plan in their unique area of responsibility and in the larger context of the overall plan. *Production meetings* are held to provide this opportunity. There are several key elements required in the art of hosting production meetings. These meetings include a variety of event invitees who are involved in the integral act of implementing the event operational plans. These meetings need to have a pre-established detailed agenda; to offer supplementary materials that ensure understandings of goals and objectives of the organization, as well as of the event; to delineate the specific roles and responsibilities; and to offer facility tours to ensure that all of those implementing the event plans know the facility.

Who is involved in these meetings? In some cases, when the event is small, it is possible to involve everyone in the production meeting. However, as the size and complexity of the event increase, it becomes progressively less practical and possible to involve everyone. Your plan should have determined managers for each event component. It is essential that these people are in attendance. They in turn will be responsible for holding implementation meetings with the staff and volunteers who make up the network members associated with their unique area of responsibility.

What does hosting an implementation meeting entail? To begin with, a detailed agenda needs to be developed. This will help you prescribe an adequate amount of time for the meeting and an agenda. You want to maximize the use of people's time and keep them focused. A detailed agenda with some general guidelines allotting time for each item helps to maintain attendees' focus and will allow a flow to occur in the meeting.

Be considerate of people's time: be sure to send the agenda out early enough for participants to review and analyze the material. The exact timing is a subjective judgment. If you send it too early, you risk having it set aside and forgotten. If you send it too late, people may still be reviewing materials as the meeting unfolds, which will lead to needless discussion and can derail a meeting quite quickly. As a rule of thumb, 7–10 days of advance notice is a reasonable time frame for many people.

Supplementary materials should also be provided with the agenda. These include the written operational plans. Once again, as these are the people who are going to train others and keep them on track, a high level of detail is required here. Throughout the plan, each member's personal responsibilities should be highlighted in some way. The highlighting can be done as simply as by the use of bold text or a coloured highlighter. Producing such a personalized plan for each member takes time, but it provides focus. Also, the addition of an executive summary can minimize questions and providing an organizational flowchart will help delineate responsibilities and establish a context for each node involved in the plan. Finally, a diagram of the facility with detailed and accurate instructions will help those concerned understand locations and the placement of equipment. A pictorial representation of this kind will save a lot of oral explanations that can be misinterpreted.

When members attend production meetings, never assume that everyone has read the material provided in advance. People do not intend to derail a meeting, nor do they deliberately attempt to hold up the process by shirking their responsibility to review the material. However, they may have busy, complex lives, and sometimes even the well-intentioned have to deal with issues not associated with your event, no matter how important it may seem to you. It is your responsibility as the facilitator to provide an oral review to ensure that everyone understands the written operational plans and the specific tasks for which they are responsible.

Production meetings provide opportunities to ensure that each member implementing the plan understands the goals and objectives of the event. They must also know their responsibilities, including required actions. Creating specific responsibilities limits the possibility of someone thinking that someone else is responsible for a particular task, and thereby increases accountability.

It is also important that team members understand the interrelatedness of their role with other elements of the plan. They need to see how what they are doing contributes to the larger plan and that what they are doing is valued. When it becomes clear that what they are doing is not an end in itself but an important part of a much larger whole, commitment and motivation are enhanced.

In addition to providing written materials and discussing them at the production meeting, giving team members a tour of the facility or facilities to discuss elements on-site in the context of the operational plan is essential. During a tour, managers of each event component may be able to assess specific needs or problems, such as access to electrical outlets, sound system, running water, internet access and so on.

At the end of production meeting(s) and facility tour(s), component managers and the constituent managers within each component should be aware of the specific goals of the event, their unique responsibilities and how they fit into the overall plan. They should also be familiar with the venue(s) and be prepared to motivate and train those who will report to them. Their questions should have been answered and, if you have done a good job, they will be excited about getting started.

MONITORING THE DYNAMIC AND FLUID OPERATIONAL ENVIRONMENT

During implementation, you as the facilitator need to focus on the details of the plan using a "zoom lens." Two key areas to focus on are the monitoring of timing and progress. For example, you need to monitor whether enough time has been allotted for getting essential materials to the venue in a timely manner so that people are not sitting around waiting to do their work. Also, have you allocated enough time for set-up and to test the equipment? If people need to be at two or more venues at specific times, is there enough travelling time available for them? Monitoring involves questioning to determine whether people are attending to the task so that the plan can be successfully implemented in the time scheduled.

It is important that you, as a facilitator, see and be seen by the event staff and volunteers. You should employ an operating principle that involves "the five Ps of implementation." Use your *presence* and *profile* to support *positive* and *productive performance.* Presence is the concept of management by walking around. When you are present, it is easier for dialogue to occur. Implementers can ask you questions, and you in turn can question them. This will reduce ambiguity in the first instance, and in addition provide implementers with the sense that what they are doing is important and a worthwhile contribution. Your presence also reinforces your perception of attention to detail. Ultimately, you will have a working knowledge of all phases of the plan.

Your presence also raises the profile of the specific components. If a task is deemed important enough for you to visit its implementers, it raises the value of their unit to the people completing the task. Like it or not, as an event manager you have a profile, and you can use that profile in positive, productive ways. When you have taken the time to visit, and to ask and respond to questions, a subtle process of accountability has been introduced. If you have addressed the concerns of the front-line workers, have listened to their suggestions and provided your vision of the project or event, people will be more committed to doing the work, and doing it well. They are people, and you are seen as a person, not an object. If workers have the sense that everyone concerned is important to the eventual success of the project, they will be more committed to ensuring that success with their productive performance.

MANAGING OPERATIONAL PLAN IMPLEMENTATION

It is your responsibility as the event manager to facilitate the management of deviations from the operational plan that may happen for any reason. Doing so will be a tough task. According to Wijngaard and de Vries (2006), tacit knowledge is required to make judgments on the precision of performance. Tacit knowledge, you will recall, is related to advancement knowledge. As the text has pointed out, tacit knowledge has been acquired through personal experience. It is the know-how you have acquired over the years as a student, as a volunteer, as an emerging professional. It is that "job sense" that comes from having been there. Schön (1983), in his book *The Reflective Practitioner*, refers to professionals as being able to work "in the indeterminate zones" that their training has not explicitly prepared them for. Doing so requires an application of knowledge. Several tips (adapted from "How to stay on course," 2006) can aid you to keep implementation on track:

- Determine deviations from the operational plans through a variety of mechanisms, such as periodic progress reviews, anecdotal reports and direct observation.
- Create a climate in which people are not afraid to report implementations in a timely way, including arising problems and issues.
- Do not wait for progress reports; be out on the front lines of implementation, observing and asking questions.
- Every implementation plan contains risks – some unforeseeable.

Create a contingency plan for all foreseeable issues and be prepared with a strategy to assess and manage unforeseeable issues.

Once you have noted that there is a deviation from the plan, you will need knowledge and the ability to develop a strategy for bringing things back on track. A skilled and knowledgeable event manager is needed to handle issues, to create a decision-making process and complete the adaptations to ensure that the planned activities conform to timelines and acceptable levels of completeness. The decisions on how to manage issues must be aligned with the overall objectives and priorities of the event. You will need to determine ahead of time the process to be used, who will be involved, a strategy to resolve conflict and an implementation stage; you will also have to be mindful of time constraints and the need to act quickly.

Overcome foreseeable failure when managing deviations from the plan

You need to be conscious of the fact that managing deviations from the operational plan can invoke a predictable response that can result in a negative impact for the event. You need to overcome this predictability to improve your decision-making abilities during event implementation. This predictability was revealed by Dörner (1996) as he outlined in great detail how well-intentioned, intelligent people can experience difficulty in complex, dynamic systems. He developed a game with a hypothetical population and simulated the real-world environment, and found participants responded in a consistent and patterned manner.

His research indicated that participants tended to *act without prior analysis of the situation* – that is, they accepted things at face value without much consideration of prior events or history that were germane to sound decision making. The lack of an immediately obvious negative effect of an action deluded them into thinking that their decision had solved the problem. Participants *failed to anticipate side effects and the long-term consequences of a particular course of action*. In addition, participants *failed to take into account the lag time between action and consequences* and were forced to react quickly at a future point as a consequence of their prior decision. This "domino effect" was repeated in the simulations and in most cases compounded the problem or created new problems that needed to be handled with increasing urgency. In his terms, problems

132

increased exponentially, not in a linear fashion, and created a catastrophic conclusion. In his words, participants demonstrated "an inadequate understanding of exponential development and an inability to see that a process that develops exponentially will, once it has begun, race to its conclusion with incredible speed" (p. 33). Dörner (1996) concluded: "People court failure in predictable ways" (p. 10).

When you consider that events are run under strict time constraints, Dörner's (1996) work is worth remembering. Certainly, no one intends to fail, nor would you actively court that outcome. However, if you do not understand yourself or the system (event) you are dealing with, the possibility exists that your desired outcome will not be achieved. In addition, when you are called upon to make decisions, it is worth noting that decision making is not a single activity, something that takes place at a particular time. Decision making is best described as a process, one that takes place over time and is "replete with personal nuance and institutional history" (Garvin and Roberto, 2001, p. 1).

It would behoove you to go back and look at the material on complexity theory, contingency theory and systems theory presented earlier in this text. Knowledge of theories will help you make the decisions that will need to be made during the implementation of an event. In addition, consider how you will analyze situations (including taking into consideration the history, side effects and consequences of actions).

Predetermine the decision-making team and process

When you are managing deviations from the written operational plan, the decision-making team must be predetermined. Basically, you are answering the questions, who's in and why? There is no magic formula, or guidelines for answering these two questions. There will be key players that your advancement knowledge will make obvious. Certainly, anyone who will be directly impacted should be considered.

The process that the decision-making team works within must be predetermined:

- Who gets brought into the issue?
- How are they informed?
- How much time is needed to assemble or obtain a decision?

- How quickly must the decision be disseminated?
- Is there a need for a dispersed decision process (teleconference)?
- How will the decision-making process unfold (consensus, simple majority, majority, advisory to an ultimate decision maker)?
- How will conflicts in the decision-making process be handled?

As I have already indicated, any response to a plan deviation needs to relate to the vision and goals of the event. Mintzberg, Raisinghani and Theoret (1976) described a process model as a situation in which the goals are clear but the methods of attaining them require decision making. These researchers indicate that decision making in a process model includes an environment in which "the entire process is highly dynamic, with many factors changing the tempo and direction of the decision process" (p. 263). In a process model, the decision-making process has historically been divided into three areas, including *identification*, *development* and *selection* (Mintzberg et al., 1976). Identification provides the recognition of the situation and communication through the system that a decision is required. Development involves the search for options as solutions. Selection includes the evaluation of options and the finalization of the chosen decision for implementation.

Once a decision is reached, a decision-making implementation process must be followed. This process determines how decisions will be implemented.

- Who will implement the decision?
- What processes will be put in place to ensure that the decision is being acted upon?
- What monitoring will be put in place to ensure that the decision is achieving its desired outcome?

The process of implementing decisions must be facilitated for efficient and effective application of decisions. To help to achieve this state, programmed decisions are created.

Programmed and non-programmed decisions

As you have spent many hours developing the plan for your event, you will have asked yourself the question, "What if . . .?" on many occasions. In

134

event management, a large portion of decision making in the operational network is prescribed and automatically implemented at a designated time. The prescribed decisions are stated in the contingency operational plans. When the situation(s) arises, the decisions are enacted. These decisions are considered to be programmed or pre-established.

In contrast, there will be situations when the decision making is not programmed. During these situations, the communication system that was pre-established becomes vitally important to achieve operational network membership negotiation, coordination, decision making and cooperation, and for the integration of actions within the overall operational plan. According to Wijngaard and de Vries (2006), when completing operating plans outside of the programmed decisions, a pattern of decision making and work functionality is established that requires support from the system. Facilitating the communication system is a priority in managing non-programmed decisions.

INHERENT IMPLEMENTATION, MONITORING AND MANAGEMENT ISSUES IN OPERATIONAL NETWORK PRACTICE

In operations management, be sure to allow staff and volunteers to "contribute significantly to the performance of the system" (Wijngaard & de Vries, 2006, p. 408). These event members are positioned within the planning and control framework to implement tasks and manage arising issues and problems. These members thus need some level of autonomy. Yet "this autonomy adds also to the unpredictability and ambiguity of the system of control" (p. 395). This is because although the planning and control elements eliminate as many potential situations as possible, they "can never be complete; there are too many tacit elements in the situation to control" (p. 405).

Clearly, operational implementation performance cannot be fully controlled, and the concept of control may even be a misnomer in a dynamic and fluid environment. However, as an event manager you will be looking for *scope control*. Scope control asks that people stay within the confines of the project and do not add or introduce elements that are not part of the overall plan. While we attempt to control as much as we can and operate within the parameters of the plan, "basically the system is not 'closed'. That is, the system is open to all kinds of unexpected influencers" (Wijngaard & de Vries, 2006, p. 395).

If planning and control frameworks can never provide full control, then the system is open to providing inadequate planning and control (Konijnendijk, 1994). This inadequacy includes ambiguity, which in turn provides opportunities for individual interpretations of planned tasks (Wijngaard & de Vries, 2006). Without the possibility of full control, the planning and control frameworks can offer what Wijngaard and de Vries call "perceived control" (p. 405) and a baseline from which deviations can be determined. Thus, full control is not possible and the event environment will involve the facilitating of arising issues.

Maintaining control is a complex issue in events, but regardless, it is your job to ensure the required level of quality in the control aspect of the event. In addition, it is your task as a facilitator to self-manage your stress levels well when attempting to obtain some semblance of control over the event implementation aspects. Knowledge of strategies for doing so should be studied by watching those in the field.

Issue: operational plan detail and implementation performance

If the operational plans are not detailed in nature, or if circumstances arise that require deviations from the operational plans, then there is a necessity for a degree of operational freedom, and the need for decision making increases. In order for members to be effective in their decision making, the operational network members implementing the plan need "a good understanding of the system to control, the specifics of the actual situation, as well as of the underlying rationale of the planning and control framework" (Wijngaard & de Vries, 2006, p. 398). In addition, the operational network members adapting the plan need a solid understanding of the event goals and expected outcomes.

If the operational plans are detailed in nature, the operational network need only initiate the steps as prescribed. A detailed plan limits the degree of decision making and operational change or freedom to make changes.

Issue: implementation knowledge and performance

One of the issues that may impact implementation performance is the knowledge level of the operational team members. You will need to ascertain whether the implementation network members understand and have

136

a working knowledge of the overall event requirements and objectives. Obviously, you can't administer a test to ensure that they do have the requisite understanding, but they should be given a number of opportunities and forums to facilitate this objective.

An initial way to help ascertain whether the level of knowledge has been transferred to the implementation network members is simply to check the attendance records in the minutes of production meetings. For instance:

■ Have the members attended the meetings regularly so they can learn the requirements and the objectives?
■ If they have missed meetings, what steps have they taken to obtain the information provided? What steps have you taken to assist those who have missed access to the information?

Another issue that arises is the implementation team members' knowledge concerning their role(s). As the event manager, you might think this a good time to look in the mirror and ask yourself questions, such as the following:

■ How well did I facilitate the process to ensure every member understands their role?
■ Did I make assumptions because of my own deep familiarity with what is required?
■ Did I use language that was clear and understandable?
■ Was a time frame allotted to every task, and was it realistic?
■ Was the integration process completed?

The answers to these questions illustrate the complexities within the role of event facilitation.

Issue: deviations from the plan

There are any numbers of reasons why an activity may not be completed as planned. Some of the issues that may contribute to that outcome will now be highlighted. One of the most obvious problems is that one or more operational team members adapt the role or the event in light of their own level of understanding, or lack thereof. Further, sometimes people take it upon themselves to alter the activity for reasons known only to them; perhaps prior experience: "it's the way it's 'always' been done"; "it's not the way we used to do it"; "I can make it better"; and so on.

One of the main contributing factors to activities not being completed as planned is the communication system and the communication skills of the members. In addition, communication is a key factor in the capacity of the intraorganizational network members to function as a team. Communication assists in the level of cooperation present to complete tasks. Your role is to facilitate the communication process to ensure that general communication problems are overcome. These problems can worsen if information is withheld, if information is available to only a select few or if decisions that affect a particular role or task are not communicated.

Issue: implementation conflict

Conflict may not be inevitable, but any time you bring a group together to work toward a common goal, the potential exists for conflict to occur. "Ironically, one of the important characteristics of a well structured team – diversity of thinking, backgrounds and skills – is itself a potential source of conflict" (Keeping on track, 2004, p. 8). One of the purposes of bringing people together is to examine options, to engage in critical thinking and collaborative thinking, and, ultimately, to embark on the best course of action. Obviously, this kind of focus can engender great debate; people can have widely divergent thinking. As meetings unfold, there may come a time when, in trying to decide between two alternative positions, people become entrenched in one camp or another. The longer this goes on, the greater the likelihood conflict will result. Garvin and Roberto (2001) point out that conflict comes in two forms: cognitive conflict and affective conflict.

Cognitive conflict is the kind of healthy debate that is focused on the task at hand. It is substantive in nature, open to other alternatives and ultimately is designed to solve problems. The exchanges can be quite intense, but they are not personal; they are about the exchange of ideas with the ultimate goal of coming up with the best possible plan.

Affective conflict, on the other hand, is personal. It may arise from a clash of personalities, a visceral dislike for someone or a defensive reaction to criticism. When you have interpersonal conflict, people are less likely to cooperate, to listen to new ideas, to move the project forward. They may become entrenched in a particular position, as noted above, and are less accepting if a decision is made that is at odds with their firmly held stance.

To promote cognitive conflict and to reduce affective conflict, Garvin and Roberto (2001) provide a framework comprising the "three Cs" of effective decision making: *conflict*, *consideration* and *closure*. As they point out, each of them needs to be handled carefully. The conflict portion has been outlined already, but bears repeating. As an event manager, you should aim to facilitate as much cognitive conflict as possible while at the same time minimizing affective conflict.

The second "C," consideration, is a fairly simple concept but one that in practice is often ignored. As I have pointed out, when there are two sides to an issue, one side will be chosen and the other set aside. Obviously, then, some people are going to have to support and implement a course of action that they did not, at one point in time, prefer.

The concept of consideration is sometimes referred to as due diligence or procedural justice. At its heart, it refers to a sense of fairness. It is a far different thing to be heard, to express your views and ideas, than it is to be considered. "Considered" indicates that your ideas have been listened to carefully, been weighed in the context of what must be done and that your ideas are clearly understood.

Consideration requires a climate in which members listen actively, ask questions, take notes, ask for explanations, are patient during explanations of positions and keep personal positions to themselves. At all costs, avoid looking as if you already have made up your mind.

Consideration also means that once you have decided, you communicate what the final choice is and why it is the best course of action. Making reference to the input you have received and how it impacted your choice will go a long way to providing acceptance.

Providing closure is also a balancing act. Debate cannot go on incessantly, but nor should it be halted prematurely. In many cases, the event itself will dictate the time frame in which a decision is to be rendered, but even if that is the case, there is a need for closure. It is a skilful facilitator who knows when to "call the question." The skilled know when enough information has been gathered, when repetitiveness is apparent and when to avoid the trap of paralysis by analysis.

Issue: implementation communication

Throughout this text, you will find both explicit and implicit exhortations to communicate frequently and effectively. Effective communication at every stage is essential for an event manager. So much has been written about communication that it is beyond the scope of this text. However, we encourage you to constantly work on the development of your communication skills. Be an active listener and all that it entails, including eye contact, bridging, paraphrasing, body language, asking the right questions, being non-judgmental, not personalizing issues, and so on.

Finally, be generous with your praise. Publicly acknowledge the accomplishments and successes of those who are carrying out the plan. Additional suggestions for facilitating the Implementation, Monitoring and Management Phase of the Planning Model are offered by Scott McRoberts at the end of this chapter.

CONCLUSION

Clearly, a lot is expected of an event manager in facilitating the event implementation phase, and your skills will be tested. Event managers need to understand themselves and the complex systems that are part of any event. It is also quite clear that careful preplanning and well-articulated goals and processes are essential in achieving a successful event.

You need to be aware that decisions you make will have both short-term and long-term effects on the eventual success of the event. Event managers have the ultimate responsibility of monitoring and managing the implementation effort. You will be called upon to use direct observation and tacit knowledge. As you will be responsible for keeping the operational plan on track, you are also responsible for putting in place the processes for implementing it, monitoring it and ensuring that deviations are managed. Be cognizant of the two different types of conflict that were discussed (cognitive and affective) during your facilitation activities. Also, remember the importance of improving your communication skills.

We now move to the next phase of the event planning model, the evaluation phase. This phase actually begins in the development phase and advances through each phase of the model; however, we will discuss this phase overall in the next chapter.

CHAPTER QUESTIONS

1   Describe a production meeting (including why the meeting is held, who participates in the meeting and what is accomplished at the meeting).
2   What are two key areas of focus when monitoring an event?
3   Describe the five Ps of implementation.
4   What can you do to overcome foreseeable failure when managing the implementation of events?
5   There are inherent issues when implementing an event. What are those issues and how do they influence an event?

Facilitating communication

The facilitation of an effective communication process is crucial if an event is to run properly. Experience indicates that the majority of communication issues arise in the first hours following the opening of an event. The result can often be mass confusion over the communication lines (such as radios, walkie-talkies, or clear coms) established for an event. From my experience at a National Collegiate Athletic Association (NCAA) Men's Basketball Championship and the San Francisco International Children's Games, where over 400 volunteers and 100 staff were involved in each event, at least a third of the operational network members need to be connected to the communication system radios. Therefore, an event manager must facilitate the proper use of the communication system as a key element in helping to resolve situations in a fast and timely manner. In addition, the proper use of the communication system aids to keep the airways clear in case of an emergency.

Facilitating motivation and direction

Sport, recreation and tourism events that last for longer than one day require an event manager to facilitate a high level of morale and energy throughout the members of the operational network, and this can be a challenge. You may be aware of the phrase "It's all about the first impression." However, in event management the reverse is also the case: the last impression of the event is also vitally important to participants, spectators, sponsors and all partners. It is important for the event manager to consistently facilitate the interactions with network members staging the event to maintain the professionalism from the first to the last day of the event.

One way to facilitate a high level of motivation is to constantly show a presence. The event manager must be available and responsive to network members' issues. This responsiveness involves facilitating the care and concern of each member for a fair and effective process for providing breaks or rotating positions. It is also the event manager's role to provide a sense of appreciation throughout the event. A simple comment such as "Good job!" can mean a lot to a member.

Facilitating appropriate direction to operational network members during the staging of an event is also an important role for an event manager. The following are a few strategies for facilitating direction with a process for continuous dialogue to aid production.

After an initial briefing meeting prior to the start of an event, a daily production meeting can be held. This meeting can be offered at the end of the event day or held in the early hours each morning of the event. It is important that this meeting be facilitated to stay on the agenda topics and to be conducted in a short time period (such as in one hour).

Another process can be a debriefing page posted for members to review. This provides members with an overview of changes and can confirm activities as well as be presented as an inspirational and upbeat message to aid morale.

Whatever process is used, it is important that an event manager facilitates event changes with the operational network members and eliminates the occurrence of repeated problems. An event is conducted in an environment of change and interpretations that can lead to issues or problems. A process for continuous dialogue needs to be established and facilitated to allow key personnel the opportunity to collectively provide input on the current state of the implementation, monitoring and management of an event and to provide positive suggestions for moving the event forward.

Facilitating through credentialling issues

A key challenge in event management involves the credentialling or accreditation process at an event. This can be a large issue if an event anticipates a significant media presence. The following are suggestions for alleviating credentialling issues:

Facilitate a process to develop an understanding of the number of individuals who may attend but have not registered for a credential or accreditation pass and a system for managing these individuals upon their arrival. It is important to have a plan in place as well as personnel to deal with this issue. It is also important to monitor the process and to adapt to be able to provide additional personnel should they be needed or to reassign members should there be only a few unregistered individuals arriving.

There will be credentials that have misspelled names or provide the wrong access within the event venue. Having a credential machine on site with a dedicated and qualified person to operate the machine will help resolve these issues in a timely manner.

Subdivide all credentials alphabetically and spread out the distribution sites of each group of alphabetical credentials to make the process efficient without a lot of congestion.

Facilitating personality issues

It is important for an event manager to facilitate the management of common situations that arise due to the personalities of the members within the operational network. There are three common issues that every event manager should be cognizant of and be prepared to manage: the fan versus the worker scenario, personality conflicts and the need to rotate members to other positions for the purpose of advancing their experience.

The *fan versus worker scenario* is common in the majority of events. Volunteers apply for a role in an event because they have an interest in the product. This situation can produce one of two potential outcomes. The first outcome is a terrific operational volunteer who, because of their interest in the event, maintains professionalism and attention to their position or duties. The second outcome is a member who becomes a spectator and is looking for access to participants, autographs and perks, which means they do not pay attention to their position or duties. It is important for an event manager to establish, communicate and facilitate the rules for participation at the outset and create a zero tolerance policy for infractions. These infractions are witnessed in all types of events and can have an adverse effect on the motivation, direction and professionalism of others involved in the event.

Personality conflicts abound in event management. It is important for an event manager to position members within their strengths and to manage personality conflicts as they arise. Long hours at an event can lead to short fuses or people becoming impatient with others they are working with. Other conflicts arise from individuals who think tasks should be completed in a particular manner that differs from what is in the operational plan. Facility managers must be cognizant of these types of situations and facilitate the efficient and effective management of the conflicts in a timely manner. One way to establish a process that aids in alleviating such conflicts is to rotate members within a series of positions.

Facilitating a *rotation of members* between a series of event positions is a good way to meet the needs of members who ask to expand their experiences and develop their skills, to help keep members alert during events that are staged over many days as well as to alleviate personality conflicts. A process that does not impede the outcome of a successful event must be developed to offer the opportunity to "shuffle" event operational members to a new post or a series of new posts. It is important that event managers be cautious while doing this, as they must first provide the training to cover the new duties and must involve the members in the production meetings that update the members. In addition, the member must be flexible, and sufficiently competent to manage a changing environment of tasks.

Learning the strengths of the members is difficult, especially when there are potentially hundreds of members involved in staging an event. In some situations there may be members who are better suited to positions that require continued interaction with people, whether celebrities, event members or consumers. Having an upbeat and positive member who can think on their feet will only reflect positively on the event as a whole. Furthermore, you may be able to determine whether an individual is better suited to one specific task, one that may not involve decision making. Therefore, rotating members is a difficult activity to facilitate and, once begun, it requires constant monitoring and management. If facilitated effectively, a rotating process can leave event members happier and more experienced in the end.

Overall, the role of the event manager is very complex. The environment is forever changing. It is important that the event manager facilitates the event implementation, monitoring and management activities to ensure the vision of the event is accomplished. Therefore, the vision must be conveyed to all event operational members, and they must be reminded of the vision throughout the staging of the event, especially as common implementation issues are being managed.

Remember, an important person in the entire process is the event manager. This means you must facilitate your own process to maintain control of your emotions, remain calm, be positive and present a positive perspective while managing all implementation issues. This includes presenting an attitude that situations can be solved positively, in a timely manner, with demonstrated professionalism and confidence. The manner in which an event manager conducts themselves strongly influences the operational network members and ultimately the outcome of the event.

An important element for an event manager is to enjoy the facilitation process and to see the fruition of well-prepared tasks or activities happen over many tireless nights. Relaxation techniques aid an event manager to worry about only the elements they can control and to have an overall perspective of the event so as to be able to determine which these elements are.

Figure 6.1 Suggestions for facilitating the implementation, monitoring and management phase of the planning model (by Scott McRoberts)

CHAPTER 7

THE EVENT PLANNING MODEL: THE EVENT EVALUATION AND RENEWAL PHASE

SCOTT FORRESTER AND LORNE J. ADAMS

This chapter focuses on the evaluation and renewal phase of the event planning model. The goal in this phase is to equip the event manager with the necessary knowledge to evaluate the event effectively and make data-driven decisions regarding renewing the event. This chapter discusses the background knowledge in evaluation and renewal for the event manager and the decisions required before evaluating. It is important to note that preparation for the evaluation and renewal phase begins in the development phase of the planning model and continues through all of the phases.

BACKGROUND KNOWLEDGE FOR THE EVENT MANAGER

Earlier, in Chapter 2, the author defined common knowledge as basic foundational knowledge. In order for event managers to be able to successfully facilitate the evaluation phase of event planning, they need to develop a foundational level of understanding with respect to both the concept and the application of evaluation. Managers need to understand what evaluation is, why evaluation is necessary and how evaluation is different from research or assessment. They need to know the key evaluation questions, general steps in evaluating the event, and decisions required by the event manager in order to successfully facilitate the process of conducting event evaluations.

How many times have you attended an event when someone presented you with a questionnaire or survey as the event is coming to a close and asked you to take the time to fill it out? How many times have you been asked, as a participant, for your feedback while an event is taking place? Have you ever been asked for feedback relating to an event that took place days or weeks ago? While some may regard these requests as petty annoyances, such requests are part of your responsibility as an event manager. The need to gather information about many aspects of your event is crucial on many levels.

Evaluation is something that many might perceive as a culminating activity; indeed, sometimes it is even approached as an afterthought. However, the skilled event manager knows that thinking about evaluation should begin at the earliest stages of planning and continue well past the day the event finishes.

Evaluation, in general terms, is what you engage in to determine how well an event has succeeded in achieving its purpose. In order to ascertain this, the event manager will have to collect a lot of information, from many sources, in order to make decisions about improving the event and ultimately whether the event could or should be conducted again in the future. The question now becomes "What do I evaluate?" In an ideal world, the correct answer would be simply to evaluate everything. However, that may not be realistic as there can be many costs associated with a comprehensive and thorough evaluation. Once again, you will have to decide, depending on available resources, including financial, human and technical, the degree of evaluation needed for your particular event. Obviously, the bigger the event, the more stakeholders and the more participants and staff, the higher the level of evaluation required.

Henderson and Bialeschki (2002) indicate that three components are necessary in order to conduct evaluations. The first necessary component is the *purpose*, the second is the *data* and the third involves *decisions*. The purpose refers to why the evaluation is being undertaken in the first place, or what, specifically, about the event is being evaluated.

Identifying the purpose of the evaluation involves establishing evaluation questions that determine the framework in which to evaluate the event. As Henderson and Bialeschki (2002) suggest, "it is essential to clearly identify what questions are to be addressed or what criteria to evaluate before data are collected for an evaluation or research project" (p. 18). "Data" refers to the information that will be systematically collected in order to address the purpose. Last, the decision-making component involves determining the "significance," "value" or "worth" of the event, based on the analysis of the information (data) collected in relation to the purpose of the evaluation. These decisions come in the form of conclusions, interpretations stemming from the data analysis, as well as recommendations: proposed courses of action regarding what needs to be done or could be done, based on the conclusions. These findings often suggest how the data might be applied in practice and subsequently inform the renewal phase of event planning.

EVALUATION CONSIDERATIONS

A review of the evaluation literature indicates that there are two main types of tools available to you as an evaluator. Those are quantitative methods and qualitative methods. As part of formal evaluation methods, both types of evaluation are useful for events. While there are many texts devoted to delineating their differences, a rule of thumb is that *quantitative methods* are numerically based (such as the number of attendees, revenue raised, tickets sold, etc.), while *qualitative methods* are opinion based (such as how much you enjoyed the event, what your experience was like).

In addition, as an event manager you might wish to take advantage of two different types of evaluation, *formative* and *summative* evaluation. These types of evaluation can be differentiated on the basis of their timing. Formative evaluation takes place while the event is ongoing and tends to be process oriented. Summative evaluation typically takes place after an event has concluded and tends to examine whether or not the event achieved its goals and objectives. The advantage of formative evaluations is that they can take place at any time and allow for changes to take place as the event unfolds, and perhaps before something becomes a problem. For example, in formative evaluation we could ascertain whether or not volunteers are satisfied with their position, and whether or not they are getting the support they require (Gotlieb, 2011). Summative evaluation as a post-event process allows the event manager to make judgment decisions about whether or not the goals and objectives have been met. For some, this type of evaluation allows for accountability to be assessed and to make decisions about whether or not an event should be renewed. In short, it allows you to identify what worked, what did not work and what needs to be improved.

It has been pointed out that evaluation has very often been done as an afterthought, or at least in a haphazard manner. The wise event manager includes thinking about evaluation right from the pre-planning stage.

A useful exercise that is done pre-event can be very helpful when it comes time for event analysis. SWOT analysis is a useful tool that can help you identify and analyze the event: S = strengths, W = weaknesses, O = opportunities and T = threats.

Strengths are parts of your event and organizational structure that will aid you to achieve your goals and objectives. Examples might include an experienced organizing committee, adequate and well-trained volunteers, and community support.

Weaknesses are features of your event and organizational structure that might get in the way of achieving your goals and objectives. Examples might include turnover in staffing, inexperienced volunteers, lack of sponsorship and limited media availability.

Opportunities are external factors that contribute to achieving your goals and objectives. Examples might include the novelty of the event, the lack of other, competing events, community engagement and economic impact.

Threats are external factors (sometimes out of your control) that can hinder you in achieving your goals and objectives. Examples could include bad weather, poor infrastructure, competition at the particular time of year (such as a number of golf tournaments being held in the same time frame) and a lack of community support.

Including a SWOT analysis as part of your pre-event planning will allow you to document all of the components of your analysis. This research will then be very valuable later when it is time to evaluate your event. To some degree, it will provide a baseline against which you can evaluate. Further, creating this type of analysis report may help you with other aspects of planning the event such as obtaining sponsorships or community buy-in.

In addition to doing a SWOT analysis, in a previous chapter we have pointed out the importance of creating goals and objectives in the context of a mission statement. These goals and objectives become a critical piece in terms of evaluation. Setting goals and objectives for an event is easier said than done. Dudley (2009) has indicated that "goals and objectives provide a central anchor or reference point for conducting most evaluations" (p. 138). While Dudley's work was oriented to intervention in social work, he has pointed to some pertinent questions about goals that can be easily contextualized for event management. These questions include (2009, p. 38):

- What are the goals of the program (event)?
- Are measurable objectives crafted for each of these goals?
- Are the goals and objectives logically linked to clients' problems and unmet needs, and to underlying causes?
- Is there a logical link between the goals and objectives and how the program is implemented to reach these goals?

It is not hard to extrapolate Dudley's questions to the event management milieu, and to appreciate their contribution to creating and evaluating an event. The more care invested in the beginning stages of planning, the easier it will be to create an evaluation strategy that will allow for decisions to be made. "Measurable goals are critical to any successful program. . . . They are important because they provide . . . a direction to pursue and an outcome to reach" (Dudley, 2009, p. 140).

Why is evaluation necessary?

Evaluating the event is a necessary step in the event planning model so that data-based decisions can be made regarding the merit, worth, value or significance of the event, which then allows the event manager to make informed decisions regarding the disposition of the event. The event manager can also use evaluations to justify the allocation of resources, scrutinize the competing interests and analyze the finite budgets that most events operate under. Results from evaluations that are well thought out and carefully and systematically executed are essential to sound decision making. Event managers are increasingly being held accountable for numerous aspects relating to the production of an event, such as human resource and volunteer management and security, to name a couple. In general, regardless of what aspect of the event is being evaluated, the purpose of evaluating the event is to measure the effectiveness of the event in terms of meeting its stated goals and objectives and to measure the quality of the performance of the event such as whether or not the event was profitable. Henderson and Bialeschki (2002) in their summary of evaluation identified five key purposes:

1 *Determine accountability.* Determining accountability involves establishing the extent to which the allocation of resources, revenue and expenses, marketing, promotion and sponsorship efforts, activities and processes "effectively and efficiently accomplish the purposes for which an [event] was developed" (Henderson & Bialeschki, p. 25).

2   *Assess goals and objectives.* Events can be evaluated in terms of whether or not the goals and objectives for the event were met. Such an evaluation may also help determine the appropriateness of the stated goals and objectives, and assist the event manager in deciding whether they need to be modified for future events.
3   *Ascertain outcomes and impact.* The extent to which festivals, conferences, conventions or local, regional, national or international sporting events have encouraged tourism can be measured by the economic impact of the event through examining the direct and indirect financial benefits through tourist expenditures on a local economy. Or the event manager may wish to determine the impact that a local festival has on the quality of life in a community.
4   *Identify keys to success and failure.* Evaluating the event may also serve the purpose of identifying what worked well and why, what didn't work well, why it didn't work well and how it could be avoided or improved upon in the future.
5   *Improve and set a future course of action.* Evaluations can also help identify ways in which particular aspects of an event can be improved, as well as assist in the process of making decisions regarding the implementation, continuation, expansion or termination of an event.

In addition to these five key purposes, evaluation can also identify and solve problems, help the event manager find ways to improve management, determine the worth of the event or its programs, measure success or failure, identify costs and benefits, identify and measure impacts, satisfy sponsors and authorities or help the event gain acceptance or credibility or support (Getz, 1997). Another summary, this one by Chelimsky (1997), outlines three key functions of evaluation. The first is the development or the provision of evaluative help to strengthen the event and to improve event performance. The second is accountability, or the measurement of results or efficiency, which provides information to decision makers. The third key function is knowledge, or the acquisition of a deeper understanding surrounding the factors and processes underpinning the event and contributing to either its success or its failure. Regardless of the specific purpose, evaluation is a key component in the event planning model.

Differentiating between evaluation, research and assessment

Before proceeding further, it is important that the event manager is able to distinguish between similar but different terms in order to be able to effectively facilitate the event evaluation process. The terms "assessment," "evaluation" and "research" are often mistakenly used interchangeably. While there are similarities between the three terms with respect to the systematic methods used to collect data, their purpose and outcomes are very different.

Assessment is oriented toward practice and can be defined as "any effort to gather, analyze, and interpret evidence that describes institutional, departmental, divisional, or program effectiveness" (Schuh & Upcraft, 1998, p. 3). *Evaluation* has been defined as the systematic collection and analysis of data in order to make judgments regarding the value or worth of a particular aspect of an event. While assessment and evaluation may share similar systematic methods of collecting and/or analyzing data, assessments have a *descriptive* purpose, while Schuh and Upcraft observe that "evaluation is any effort to use this evidence to improve effectiveness" (p. 3). Evaluation moves beyond just a descriptive function and is used to make decisions regarding the value, worth or improvement of some aspect of an event.

Meanwhile, *research* is generally defined as a systematic inquiry designed to establish facts and principles, generate and test hypotheses, test or generate theory, contribute to a body of knowledge or develop a deeper understanding of a particular phenomenon, the results of which may or may not be generalizable. Erwin (1993) differentiates between research and evaluation in that "research may contribute new knowledge, but it may not suggest that programs need improvements or are functioning well" (p. 231), and similarly, Schuh and Upcraft (1998) observe that research "may or may not have anything to do with determining effectiveness or bringing about change" (p. 3).

When an event manager is making decisions concerning the evaluation of an event, it is important that they are able to distinguish between what constitutes research and what is necessary to complete an effective evaluation of an event. Subsequently, that information can be utilized in the renewal phase of the event planning model.

Key questions that evaluations can answer

In addition to ascertaining whether or not the event was successful in achieving its goals and objectives, there are a number of other questions that evaluations can answer. Evaluation questions typically fall into one of five recognizable types according to the issues that they address (Rossi, Lipsey & Freeman, 2004):

1 *Questions about the need for the event* (needs assessment). Needs assessments are often used as a first step in determining the initial ability to host an event or when designing a new event or restructuring an established event.
2 *Questions about event conceptualization or design* (evaluating program/event theory). Evaluating the conceptualization or design of an event involves explicitly stating in written or graphic form the theory guiding the event and then measuring how appropriate it is. This is most essential when planning brand new events and when pilot-testing events in their early stages.
3 *Questions about event operations, implementation and service delivery* (evaluating event processes). Process evaluation provides information for monitoring a specific procedure or strategy as it is being implemented, so that what works can be preserved and what doesn't can be eliminated.
4 *Questions about the outcomes and impact of the event* (impact evaluation). Impact evaluation examines both the intended and the unintended impacts of the event.
5 *Questions about event cost and cost-effectiveness* (evaluating efficiency). Evaluating event efficiency involves examining the benefits of the event in relation to the costs incurred by the event. Cost–benefit analysis can be used to evaluate the relationship between event costs and outcomes or impacts (benefits) by assigning monetary values to both costs and outcomes or impacts. Cost-effectiveness analysis also uses event costs and outcomes but examines them in terms of the costs per unit of outcome achieved.

FACILITATING THE PROCESS OF EVALUATING THE EVENT

In order to effectively facilitate and manage the event evaluation process, there are a number of questions that the event manager has to consider

S. Forrester and L. J. Adams

before undertaking such an endeavour. The following questions are adapted from McDavid and Hawthorn (2006) in order to better fit within the context of evaluating events.

Key questions to ask

What type of event is it, and where is the event in terms of the program life cycle?

Is it a traditional or a niche event? If traditional, what type of sport (see the overview of traditional events in Chapter 1), and staged for what reasons (recreational, competitive and/or tourism) and at what level (local, regional, provincial/state, national or international)? Or what type of niche event is it (festival, banquet, conference, convention, stampede or other type of show)? Also, if niche, what is the history of the event, how did it evolve and is the event growing, remaining stable or declining? Regardless of whether or not the event is traditional or niche, the event manager should consider where the event is in relation to its life cycle. That is, has the event lost its impact or freshness; does it appear to have gone flat or lost its appeal?

Who are the key stakeholders of the evaluation?

"Stakeholders" refers to all individuals, groups or organizations having a significant interest in how well an event operates. For example, those with decision-making authority over various aspects of the event, sponsors, administrators, personnel, participants, clients, visitors, political decision makers, members of governing bodies, community leaders or intended beneficiaries all have a vested interest in the event. As most evaluations are typically user driven, the event manager should identify early in the process the stakeholders and consider their information needs when designing the evaluation project.

What are the questions or issues driving the evaluation?

What is the goal or purpose of the evaluation? McDavid and Hawthorn (2006) recommend that before evaluating the event, event managers should know: who wants the evaluation done and why, whether there are any hidden agendas or concealed reasons why they want the event to be evaluated and what are the main issues that the evaluation should address (need, event design, event operations and delivery, outcomes and impact, cost and efficiency). While different stakeholders will have varying views and agendas, it is important that the event manager is aware of these groups and views when designing the event evaluation, in order to avoid contaminating the data.

What resources are available to evaluate the event?

Most resources are typically dedicated to the production of an event; there is generally a scarcity of resources available to evaluate that event. When planning the event evaluation, the event manager should consider what resources will be required in order to evaluate the event effectively. These resources could be related to money, time, personnel, necessary expertise required, organizational support or any other resources that the event manager will need.

Have any evaluations been conducted in prior years?

Evaluation projects are different each time they are conducted. In order to reflect the uniqueness of the situation and the particularity of what is being evaluated, event managers can take advantage of evaluations of similar events in other settings, or evaluations conducted in prior years. Rather than simply accept evaluations that have been previously conducted, the event manager should take into consideration the following questions: What issues did the evaluation address? What was evaluated, and how similar is it to what is currently being evaluated? Who conducted the evaluation? Who were the stakeholders? How credible is the evaluation? What measures were used, and what aspects are applicable to the current evaluation effort?

What kind of environment does the event operate in?

You will recall that complexity theory suggests that organizations adapt to their environment by creating event structures that are not overly complex and are also contingent upon the contextual factors of the environment. Questions relating to size of the event, competition with other events, available resources or the degree of formalization, complexity or centralization in the event structure all need to be taken into consideration when preparing to evaluate.

What research design strategies are suitable?

While the details of different quantitative or qualitative research designs are beyond the scope of this chapter, "an important consideration for practitioners is to know the strengths and weaknesses of different designs so that combinations of designs can be chosen that complement each other" (McDavid & Hawthorn, 2006, p. 30).

154

What appropriate sources of evidence are available?

What sources of evidence (data) are available that are appropriate given the evaluation issues, the event structure and the environment in which the event operates? Given the research design of the evaluation project as well as the approach to evaluating the event, what data should be collected in order to address the evaluation questions? Event managers should consider whether there are any existing data that can be used to serve their evaluation purposes, as well as whether quantitative or qualitative data will best meet the needs of the evaluation effort.

What evaluation approach seems appropriate?

The event manager will most likely not be able to answer this until they have a foundational understanding of the strengths and limitations of different evaluation approaches.

Should the evaluation be conducted at all?

After reviewing the previous issues, the event manager must still decide whether or not to evaluate the event. While it is a step in the event planning model outlined in Chapter 3 of this book, "it is possible that after having looked at the mix of evaluation issues, resource constraints, organizational and political issues, research design, and measurement constraints, the [event] evaluator . . . recommends that no evaluation be done at this time" (McDavid & Hawthorn, 2006, p. 32). There is no sense in wasting the significant amounts of money, time and resources needed to evaluate the event if the results of the evaluation are not going to be used.

GENERAL STEPS IN EVALUATING THE EVENT

So far, this chapter has defined evaluation, explained why it is necessary and elaborated on its purpose. We have differentiated between evaluation, research and assessment, and we have identified several key questions that evaluation studies are designed to address. Further, an overview of a number of questions that the event manager has to consider before undertaking such an endeavour has been provided.

If the event manager decides to proceed with the evaluation, the following five steps are common to most evaluation projects:

1   Determine what is being evaluated and specify the evaluation questions.

2 Identify sources of evidence; develop appropriate measures and data collection strategies.
3 Collect and analyze the data.
4 Prepare and disseminate the evaluation report.
5 Make decisions regarding the improvement of the event and modify as necessary.

In order to complete the fifth step or to make recommendations regarding the improvement of the event and to modify or renew the event as necessary, a number of decisions must be made. These decisions are outlined in the next section.

DECISIONS REQUIRED BY THE EVENT MANAGER BEFORE EVALUATING

In order for event managers to be able to successfully facilitate this phase of event planning, there are a number of elements that must be determined regarding evaluation. The evaluation should be conducted in the context of a theoretical framework and might include the following: informal versus formal evaluations, formative versus summative evaluation, what to evaluate, quantitative or qualitative approaches to evaluation, and dealing with political, ethical and moral evaluation issues.

THE ROLE OF THEORY IN EVALUATING EVENTS

Earlier in this chapter, research was differentiated from evaluation. It was stated that research is conducted to develop or test theory, whereas evaluations are conducted in order to make decisions about the value or worth of something. While evaluations are not intended to develop or test theory, theory can be used to guide the evaluation project and determine what is being evaluated. When evaluating an event, it is important to view the event from a systems theory perspective. Recall that systems theory suggests that event structures can be created and managed (as well as evaluated) by understanding the inputs, throughputs and outputs required to deliver the event. While it may not be feasible to evaluate all the resources (inputs), activities (throughputs) and outcomes (outputs) of the event, it is important to view the event from a systems perspective.

156

Process theory involves using the overall event plan to describe the assumptions and expectations about how the event is supposed to operate. These assumptions and expectations should be examined before evaluating the event in order to determine whether or not the expectations for the event were met and whether aspects of the event operated as they were supposed to.

Contingency theory can also help event managers realize that the choice of organizational structures and control systems depends on, or is contingent on, characteristics of the external environment in which the event operates (Jones, George & Langton, 2005). That is why no two evaluation studies are identical. Even if the event has not changed dramatically from previous years, aspects of the external environment most likely have. These changes in turn influence the operation of the event and need to be accounted for when evaluating the event from year to year. So, while evaluation projects are not designed to develop or test theory, systems theory, process theory and contingency theory can help event managers develop a deeper understanding of the event and help them focus on what aspects of the event to evaluate.

WHAT TO EVALUATE?

Before deciding whether to conduct a formative or summative evaluation, the event manager needs to determine what exactly is being evaluated. Henderson and Bialeschki (2002) discuss "five Ps of evaluation" in relation to what aspects of an event could be evaluated: *personnel*, *policies*, *places*, *programs* and *participant outcomes*. They further suggest that programs can be evaluated on the basis of inputs, activities or outputs of the event. The inputs are the resources used to implement the event. Activities are the organizational processes within the event, and outcomes include such considerations as the economic impact of an event.

McDavid and Hawthorn (2006) observe that evaluating program effectiveness is the most common reason for conducting evaluations. They also suggest several other aspects of events that can be evaluated, such as event efficiency (including a cost–benefit analysis of the event), the cost-effectiveness of the event or how well the event was implemented. Event managers should be aware that basically any aspect of an event can be evaluated, including the development and implementation of the event plan, outfitting of the venue, ticketing and accreditation, security, communications, information and signage, transportation, parking, and so on. Before making any decisions with respect to evaluation approaches or data collection strategies, the event manager must clearly determine what aspect of the event is being evaluated, why it is being evaluated and the criteria to be used to evaluate it.

APPROACHES TO EVENT EVALUATION

Goal-based approach

Although two main types of evaluation, formative and summative, have previously been distinguished based on the timing and intended uses of the evaluation numerous evaluation models have been developed over the years. Among the first was the goal-based model developed by Tyler (Isaac & Michael, 1981) in the 1930s. The purpose of this goal-based, goal-attainment (Henderson & Bialeschki, 2002) or evaluation-by-objectives (Worthen, Sanders & Fitzpatrick, 1997) approach is to determine whether or not the event is achieving its goals and objectives. In this approach, goals and objectives are used as the criteria by which the event is evaluated. Goals are a broad statement about what is to be accomplished (Rossman & Schlatter, 2003), whereas objectives are specific statements that describe how the goal will be accomplished. Goal-based evaluation can be used with either outcome or organizational objectives. Outcome objectives examine the impacts or effects of the event on individual behaviours in one of four behavioural domains: cognitive (such as thinking, knowledge), affective (such as feeling, attitudes), psychomotor (such as movement, acting) or social (such as how people relate to each other). Organizational objectives refer to internal processes within the event and relate to both the operation of the event and the amount of effort to be expended in the delivery of the event. In order for this approach to be effective, the goals and objectives for the event have to be well formulated. As Rossman and Schlatter recommend, objectives should be: specific, clear and concrete for understanding, measurable for objective assessment, pragmatic (attainable and realistic) and useful for making programming decisions.

Goal-based evaluation is one of the most common approaches used for evaluating an event, its advantage being the objectivity that this approach provides for establishing accountability. The drawback to using a goal-

158

based approach is that the event needs to have well-formulated goals and objectives.

Goal-free approach

In response to a criticism of goal-based approaches to evaluation, namely that they do not take unintended outcomes into consideration, Scriven (1972) developed the goal-free approach. This approach seeks to discover and judge effects, outcomes and impacts of the event without considering what they should be. When facilitating the use of this approach, the event manager should begin with no predetermined idea of what might be found. The overall purpose of the approach is to find out what is happening with the event. According to Henderson and Bialeschki (2002), in this approach the evaluator will

> usually talk to people, identify program elements, overview the program, discover purposes and concerns, conceptualize issues and problems, identify qualitative and/or quantitative data that needs to be collected, select methods and techniques to use including the possibility of case studies, collect the data, match data and the issues of audiences, and prepare for the delivery of the report.
>
> (p. 72)

The advantage of this approach is that it examines actual effects of the event (regardless of whether or not they were intended) and allows for in-depth analysis, usually through the collection of qualitative data. Its drawback is that it can be very time-consuming, and some effects may be difficult to measure.

Responsive approach

In response to criticisms that evaluations were not being tailored to the needs of stakeholders, Stake (1975) developed the responsive model of evaluation. This approach stresses the importance of being "responsive to realities in the program and to the reactions, concerns, and issues of participants rather than being preordinate with evaluation plans, relying on preconceptions and formal plans and objectives of the program"

(Worthen et al., 1997, p. 159). Stake suggested that an evaluation is responsive if it "orients more directly to program activities than to program intents; responds to audience requirements for information; and if the different value-perspectives present are referred to in reporting the success and failure of the program" (p. 14). The purpose, framework and focus of a responsive evaluation "emerge from interactions with constituents, and those interactions and observations result in progressive focusing on issues" (Worthen et al., 1997, p. 160).

When taking a responsive approach, the event manager must continuously interact with individuals from various stakeholder groups. The manager needs to determine what information is needed and must present it in a way that will result in understanding.

Empowerment evaluation

Fetterman, Kaftarian and Wandersman (1996) developed the empowerment evaluation model. This model uses evaluation concepts, techniques and findings to foster improvement and self-determination. The focus of empowerment evaluation is on programs. It is designed to help program participants evaluate themselves and their programs in order to improve practice and foster self-determination. The evaluator–stakeholder relationship is more participatory and collaborative than Stake's responsive evaluation. As a result, evaluators taking this approach work toward building the capacity of the participating stakeholders to conduct evaluations of their own. This approach enables managers to use the results from evaluations for advocacy and change and to experience some sense of control over the event being evaluated. The process of empowerment evaluation "is not only directed at producing informative and useful findings but also at enhancing the self-development and political influence of the participants" (Rossi et al., 1999, p. 58).

The content, input, process and product (CIPP) model: a systems approach to evaluation

The CIPP model (Stufflebeam, 1971) is intended to provide a basis for making decisions within a systems analysis of planned change. The CIPP model defines evaluation as the process of delineating, obtaining and

S. Forrester and L. J. Adams

providing useful information for judging decision alternatives. This definition, in effect, incorporates three basic points. First, evaluation is a continuous, systematic process. Second, this process includes three pivotal steps: the first is stating questions requiring answers and specifying information to be obtained; the second is acquiring relevant data; and the third is providing the resulting information as it becomes available to potential decision makers. The manager can then consider and interpret information in relation to its impact upon decision alternatives that can modify or improve the event. Third, evaluation supports the process of decision making by allowing the selection of an alternative and by following up on the consequences of a decision.

The CIPP model of evaluation is concerned with four types of decisions: planning decisions, which influence selection of goals and objectives; structuring decisions, which ascertain optimal strategies and procedural designs for achieving the objectives that have been derived from planning decisions; implementing decisions, which afford the means for carrying out and improving upon the execution of already selected designs, methods or strategies; and recycling decisions, which determine whether to continue, change or terminate an activity, or even the event itself. In addition, there are four respective kinds of evaluation: context, input, process and product – hence the abbreviation CIPP.

Context evaluation yields information regarding the extent to which discrepancies exist between what is and what is desired relative to certain value expectations, areas of concern, difficulties and opportunities in order that goals and objectives may be formulated. *Input evaluation* provides information about strong and weak points of alternative strategies, and designs for the realization of specified objectives. *Process evaluation* provides information for monitoring a chosen procedure or strategy as it is being implemented so that its strong points can be preserved and its weak points eliminated. *Product evaluation* furnishes information to ascertain whether the strategies, procedures or methods being implemented to attain these objectives should be terminated, modified or continued in their present form.

Event managers can use the CIPP model of evaluation as a framework for ensuring a complete and comprehensive evaluation of any event or aspect of an event. Utilizing the CIPP model as a guideline, event managers can evaluate not just the outcome of the event but the entire planning process, the event itself and the intended and unintended outcomes of the event.

The CIPP model is designed to evaluate the selection of goals and objectives, optimal strategies or program designs for achieving these objectives, methods to improve the execution of already selected program designs, methods or strategies, and whether to continue, modify or terminate the event or aspects of it.

The professional judgment approach

Should the event manager feel that they do not have the necessary expertise required to facilitate the event evaluation, one option, and another approach, would be to hire an outside professional consultant. If a high degree of objectivity is required, or if the evaluation requires expertise beyond that of the event manager, then they may want to consider hiring an external expert. One case in which an outside expert might be brought in is if the event manager is interested in undertaking some sort of economic evaluation of the event. Hiring a professional consultant means that the event manager does not need to spend as much time evaluating the event, and it is generally easier for the organization. In addition, the event manager obtains the results from a neutral, external expert. This adds a degree of objectivity to the evaluation process, which may be important where there are political issues surrounding the event. On the other hand, hiring an expert can be expensive, and also the external consultant needs to have a degree of familiarity with the event, which may reduce the pool of experts that a manager has to choose from.

The decision regarding which evaluation approach to use should be based on the purpose of the evaluation as well as what is being evaluated. If experts and standards exist, *professional judgment* might be best. If goals and measurable objectives exist for a program, evaluating by using those goals and objectives (*goal attainment*) as the foundation will be best. If one is interested in finding out what is happening without comparing to established goals, the *goal-free approach* may be superior. If the event manager is interested in evaluating one component of the event in relation to the inputs, throughputs, and outputs, then a systems approach such as the *CIPP model* will enable them to choose the elements to examine in relation to the broad purpose of the event.

Regardless of the approach taken, event managers should also ensure that the evaluation is responsive to stakeholders. Evaluation reports are utilized for making decisions concerning how to improve the event, and

162

decisions about whether to continue, modify or terminate the event or aspects of it. The process of generating the reports will help clients or participants evaluate themselves and their events.

POLITICAL, ETHICAL AND MORAL DECISIONS IN EVENT EVALUATION

There are many issues that arise during the course of conducting an evaluation, and event managers should be aware of political, legal, ethical and/or moral issues that they could be confronted with when facilitating the event evaluation process. Given that multiple stakeholders are involved, all having differing views and/or agendas, evaluation by its very nature is political. Henderson and Bialeschki (2002) make several suggestions that, if event managers adhere to them, should make the evaluation process less political. The first suggestion is to have a thorough understanding of the organization or event, including its history, development and evolution, who the key stakeholders are, who the decision makers are and all facets of the operation of the event. Second, event managers should articulate a clear purpose to all stakeholders, and this purpose should drive the evaluation and be at the forefront during the evaluation process. Last, any conclusions or recommendations that event managers make as a result of the evaluation should be based on evidence: that is, the data that were collected during the evaluation process. Subsequently, judgments regarding the value or worth of the event must be linked back to the purpose of the evaluation and be supported by data. In addition to these suggestions, Worthen et al. (1997) recommend knowing the answers to the following questions in order to have a thorough appreciation of any political issues surrounding the event:

- Which individuals or groups have power, and who would have the most to gain or lose from the evaluation depending on the results? Have these parties endorsed the evaluation and agreed to cooperate?
- How is the evaluator expected to relate to different stakeholders? As an impartial outsider? Advocate? Consultant or subcontractor? Assistant?
- From which stakeholders is cooperation essential? Have they agreed to cooperate and provide full access to the data?
- Which stakeholders have a vested interest in the results of the evaluation?

- Who will need to be informed during the evaluation about plans, procedures, progress, changes and findings?

Ethical issues typically deal with what is right or wrong and how individuals responsible for facilitating the event evaluation should make thoughtful decisions based on principles. The Interagency Advisory Panel on Research Ethics (PRE) and the American Psychological Association (APA) have established ethical principles that event managers should use to guide event evaluations. Several of the more applicable principles involve a respect for human dignity, free and informed consent, vulnerable persons, privacy and confidentiality, and being able to balance harms and benefits. *Respect for human dignity* aspires to protect the interests of individuals and forms the basis of the subsequent ethical obligations. *Respect for free and informed consent* requires that evaluators must acknowledge that individuals have the right to choose whether or not to participate in the evaluation and have the right to make free and informed decisions. *Respect for vulnerable persons* requires event managers to take extra precautions in order to protect the interests of individuals with a diminished competence and/or decision-making capacity, thus making them vulnerable. *Respect for privacy and confidentiality* means that the information collected during the evaluation process holds the expectation of privacy. Furthermore, information revealed by participants in the evaluation process should not have distinctive or recognizable features in order to maintain the anonymity of individuals. *Balancing harms and benefits* requires that event managers avoid, prevent or minimize harm to individuals while maximizing the benefits of the evaluation. Overall, the foreseeable harms should not outweigh anticipated benefits of the evaluation project; if they do, it should not be undertaken.

In addition to political and ethical issues, event managers may also be confronted with a number of moral issues when facilitating the evaluation of an event. For example, Henderson and Bialeschki (2002) suggest a moral obligation to conduct the best evaluation one can. This is accomplished by being rigorous with their evaluation approach, sampling and data collection strategies and reporting the results in a timely fashion so that they can be used to make improvements to the event. Further, being honest about what worked well and what didn't during the evaluation process is essential. Evaluators should not discount any results that may seem insignificant, or fail to disclose negative results arising from the evaluation process.

164

CONCLUSION

This chapter has focused on providing the event manager with the background knowledge to successfully facilitate the evaluation phase of event planning. Evaluation was defined as the systematic collection and analysis of data in order to make judgments regarding the value or worth of a particular aspect of an event, and distinctions were made between the terms *evaluation*, *research* and *assessment*. The chapter also explained why evaluation is necessary and identified several key evaluation questions. Five general steps to be taken when evaluating an event were detailed. Last, the chapter outlined a number of decisions required by the event manager in order to successfully facilitate the process of conducting event evaluations.

CHAPTER QUESTIONS

1   Why is evaluation necessary in event management?
2   What questions does the event manager have to consider before evaluating an event?
3   What are the five key evaluation questions, according to Rossi et al. (1999)?
4   What are the five steps common to most evaluation projects?
5   List and describe six approaches to evaluating an event.

CHAPTER 8

SAFEGUARDING THE NATURAL ENVIRONMENT IN EVENT MANAGEMENT

CHRIS CHARD AND MATT DOLF

"There is no business to be done on a dead planet" (Hollender & Breen, 2010, p. 114).

This chapter focuses on the roles and responsibilities of event managers in producing a quality event while simultaneously considering the impacts of events on the environment. The call to manage events in a more environmentally sustainable manner will surely be amplified in the years to come, as there is increasing pressure to (1) reduce direct harm caused to the environment, (2) satisfy ethical interests of stakeholders (both internal and external), (3) integrate risk management, (4) communicate in a credible manner, (5) ensure that events can operate in a safe and healthy environment, and (6) meet new legal requirements.

In this chapter we will look at sustainability. Specifically, we will focus on environmental sustainability (ES) and consider why ES is important in event management. Next we will outline the various roles and responsibilities for event managers in designing events in a more sustainable way. Finally, we will introduce environmental impact assessment methods for events and specifically outline three approaches: life cycle assessment (LCA), carbon footprints and ecological footprints.

WHAT IS ENVIRONMENTAL SUSTAINABILITY?

In this chapter, we shall follow the well-established definition of environmental sustainability by the United Nations Brundtland Report (United Nations, 1987). This report sets out ES as the capacity of an organization to safeguard the natural environment by "meeting the needs of the present generation without compromising the ability of future generations to meet their own needs" (p. 1). Clearly, this definition offers elements of choice, as both the present and the future must be considered in any organizational decision making. Entwined in these "now" or "later" considerations, sustainability requires that organizations evolve and broaden the metrics to assess long-term success.

The terminology is evolving, too. Robinson (2004) argues that while "sustainable development" is more commonly used by private-sector and government organizations, the term "sustainability" is gaining widespread use among NGOs and academics. This is because the word "development" is tied to growth, whereas sustainability refers to the concept of preservation, or absolute limits. Robinson suggests that sustainability is seen more as a "value change" and sustainable development as a "technical fix." Although the terms *sustainability* and *sustainable development* are often used synonymously in practice, along with other common references such as "corporate social responsibility" and "triple bottom line," the philosophical distinctions are important. There is a growing consensus that achieving gross domestic product (GDP) growth while at the same time shrinking resource use is extremely difficult (UNEP, 2011). Event managers need to be cognizant of the challenge to achieve financial growth on the one hand, and on the other to improve quality of life through lower resource use and lower environmental impacts.

ASSIGNMENT A: EVENT DECISION MAKING FOR ENVIRONMENTAL SUSTAINABILITY

Suppose you are a manager of an annual golf event that is the cornerstone fundraising vehicle for your charitable organization. The tournament has been held at the same nearby golf course for the past six years. While no contracts exist, there is a "general understanding" that the tournament will be held at the same golf course for the coming year; your volunteers and staff have operated under this assumption in all planning. Two months before the event, however, you are approached by the general manager (GM) of a new private course located 50 minutes north of your town. The GM offers financial incentives to move the event to that course; the proposal would increase net revenues from the event by 50%. As you contemplate the change of venue, other considerations spring to mind, such as the increased travel needed for volunteers, staff and participants to attend the event, the longer hours for volunteers, the impact that the loss of the event could have on the local golf course, and negative image issues arising from deserting the local golf course at the last minute. Lastly, the GM tells you the new club is experiencing a host of environmental challenges with pesticide use and water run-off to the local pond.

The financial benefit of changing golf courses is evident, but how will you weigh that against the other social and environmental issues?

As can be seen from the scenario above, decision-making frameworks based entirely on the "bottom line" take into account only the financial consequences of actions and are insufficient for contextualizing social and environmental considerations. Fundamentally, sustainability is about managing three Ps: people, planet and profit! Figure 8.1 provides a visual representation of sustainability in action; here, understanding the interactions between economic, social and environmental contexts forces managers to recalibrate their thinking, managerial decisions and organizational assessment.

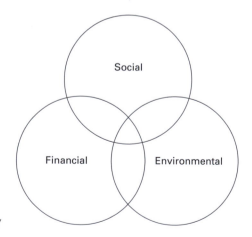

Figure 8.1
The three overlapping spheres of sustainability

168

C. Chard and M. Dolf

THE TRIPLE TOP LINE AND THE TRIPLE BOTTOM LINE

The "Triple Top Line" and "Triple Bottom Line" are each examples of paradigms that embrace a wider scope to organizational management and assessment. In traditional business accounting, the top line relates to incoming revenue for an organization, while the bottom line is what is left of this revenue after expenses have been accounted for. Similarly, the Triple Top Line moves "accountability to the beginning of the design process" (McDonough & Braungart, 2002, p. 252) by encompassing financial, social and environmental concerns. Essentially, the Triple Top Line focuses the event manager's lens on every aspect of planning for an event. For example, knowing that a youth soccer tournament will generate $150,000 in revenue is not enough; we should know "how" the $150,000 is to be generated, socially and environmentally. Likewise, the Triple Bottom Line assesses the "bottom line" results of an event: how did the event perform? Again, consideration is given to the three sustainability measures. For example, considering our youth soccer event, if the event manager shows $28,000 in net profit, financially the tournament is deemed a success. However, if environmental degradation and social injustices occurred to achieve these fiscal gains, a Triple Bottom Line approach would take these deficiencies into account.

McDonough and Braungart (2002) note that frameworks such as these are great tools for integrating sustainability into the business agenda by balancing traditional economic goals with social and environmental concerns. The key word here is *balance*. Of vital importance when interpreting Figure 8.1 is the need for *all* of the spheres to be strong. A common misconception concerning sustainable management is that it is *only* focused on environmental concerns. That is simply not true! ES at the expense of economic viability is in itself unsustainable. Randjelovic, O'Rourke and Orsato (2003) address this point, noting the "need to develop competences . . .which can create economic value *and* reduce environmental impacts/risks" (p. 251).

Hannah Jones, Nike's sustainability chief, addresses the concept of organizational sustainability by noting the desire at Nike to produce ROI[2]. This term is used to describe the company's commitment to increasing value for shareholders, a traditional perspective, while simultaneously enhancing value, socially and environmentally, for the multitude of organizational stakeholders. The thought process at Nike is that ES does not, and should not, come at the expense of increasing shareholder value.

"We can do well and do good at the same time," said Jones (Hollender & Breen, 2010, p. 121).

WHY IS ENVIRONMENTAL SUSTAINABILITY IMPORTANT IN EVENT MANAGEMENT?

Barrett and Scott (2001) note that every organization, small to large, must consider environmental issues such as transportation, personal and organizational consumption, and waste management. Examples abound concerning "an increasing growth in the consumption of natural resources combined with a corresponding ferocious growth in the volume of waste" (Ingebrigtsen & Jakobsen, 2006, p. 389). The United Nations Environment Programme (2007) report noted clear evidence of environmental change facing the world today. Of particular importance, the report clearly assigns responsibility for these environmental changes to "human activities" (p. 8).

If we accept that the actions of all individuals collectively contribute to environmental change, then surely responsibility to enhance sustainability is the duty of everyone: governments, businesses and citizens. Indeed, it can be argued that every event manager should be held accountable for their actions with respect to sustainability. Here, accountability is defined as "being called to account for one's actions" (Mulgan, 2000, p. 555).

Indeed, where no accountability is taken by any individual party for a shared entity, the outcome may be the deterioration or destruction of said entity. In the case of ES, that entity is a vibrant planet. While this assertion may seem dramatic, Perelman (2003) noted that "in a complex world where the environment is now at the breaking point, the continued experiment with this dangerous system of organization represents a grave risk to everybody and everything" (p. 221). According to Meegan Jones, Australian delegation head of ISO 20121:

> Business as usual within the events industry can't continue. Our industry can't keep producing mountain ranges of rubbish, or leave clouds of CO_2 in legacy. No matter the type of event [it can be hosted] with consideration for sustainability.
>
> (Jones, 2011)

170

ROLES AND RESPONSIBILITIES FOR ENVIRONMENTAL SUSTAINABILITY IN EVENT MANAGEMENT

The United Nations Environment Programme (2010, n.p.) lists a number of ways in which sporting events can impact the natural environment, including:

- development of fragile ecosystems or scarce land;
- noise and light pollution;
- consumption of non-renewable resources;
- consumption of natural resources;
- emission of greenhouse gases;
- ozone layer depletion;
- soil and water pollution from pesticide use;
- soil erosion during construction and from spectators;
- waste generation from construction of facilities and from spectators.

In recognition of the problem, it has been argued that event managers should be responsible for playing their part in protecting the natural environment (Mallen & Chard, 2011). Such responsibility has begun to be embraced by some sport organizations. For example, the environment is now recognized as the "third pillar" of the Olympic Movement, alongside sport and culture (Cantelon & Letters, 2000). Indeed, the Olympic Movement's Agenda 21 report highlights the commitment of the organization to environmental sustainability. Other examples of organizations embracing event management environmental sustainability initiatives in sport can be found, including the "Green Goal" work done by the Fédération Internationale de Football Association (FIFA) on the World Cup (FIFA, 2006), the Football Association's FA Cup initiatives (Collins, Flynn, Munday & Roberts, 2007), the newfound focus on sustainability by the National Football League (NFL) and its flagship Super Bowl event (Scharwath, 2012), the 2010 Commonwealth Games (Sobhana, 2010), and the London 2012 Olympic and Paralympic Summer Games (Tian & Brimblecombe, 2008).

At a micro level, Hums (2010) notes that "students need to know the actions they can take with their events and their facilities to contain the impact of sport on the environment" (p. 5). Thus, it appears that environmental sustainability in event management is gaining support from the university classroom to the Olympic boardroom. At a practical level, the question remains: who is ultimately responsible for ES and how might this responsibility be proactively and effectively managed?

ASSIGNMENT B: ACE CORPORATION TRIATHLON GROUP (ACTG) SUSTAINABILITY OWNERSHIP AND ACCOUNTABILITY

Imagine you are the marketing manager of the Ace Corporation Triathlon Group (ACTG). At a recent managers' meeting, which included the heads of finance, legal, human resources, operations, information and yourself, the mandate from the president of ACTG was to move environmental sustainability to the forefront of the company's event delivery for the coming year. After the meeting, everybody is excited about integrating ES into their division's practices.

At the following managers' meeting, the president asks for an update on the company's sustainability initiatives. Who steps forward to give the breakdown of ACTG's progress on this initiative? If challenges are put forth by the management team that "owns" these event management environmental sustainability initiatives, who will be charged with the task of finding solutions?

While environmental sustainability is certainly in its embryonic stage as regards event management, work has begun to move initiatives forward on the managerial agenda. For example, the Sport Event Environmental Performance Measurement (SE-EPM) model designed by Mallen, Stevens, Adams and McRoberts (2010) provides a comprehensive framework for evaluating a sport event's environmental performance. Key items for consideration within the framework include the following:

- the environmental organization system (environmental policies, environmental management committee, involvement in environmental programs);
- the environmental activities, stakeholder disclosure and relationships (information transfer, disclosure and communications);
- the environmental operational countermeasures (proactive initiatives such as renewable energy sources utilized, recycling, reduction, environmental training);

172

- environmental tracking (whether items such as energy use and waste reduction are being measured).
- indicators and measurement items: inputs and outputs (paper, raw materials, CO_2).

The benefit of a framework such as the SE-EPM is in its utility to guide event managers on ES initiatives. Moreover, a clearly defined rubric to guide assessment on event environmental performance can assist event managers in making individuals accountable for their assigned ES projects. This type of guideline should serve event managers well in the coming years. Indeed, as the introduction of formal policies such as ISO 20121: Event Sustainability Management Systems (www.iso.org) becomes commonplace, the future of event management and the requirements placed on the event manager will change. Here, the requirement to be compliant around sustainability will be mandatory and policies to ensure observance of set standards will need to be integrated into event planning decisions.

MEASURING TO MANAGE: INTEGRATING ENVIRONMENTAL IMPACT ASSESSMENT OF EVENTS

Even as a growing number of events incorporate qualitative environmental management, few carry out quantitative assessment or modelling (Jones, 2008). Decisions are therefore often based on intuition, visibility and ease of implementation rather than on an empirical understanding of major contributors to environmental harm.

There is a famous management axiom, "You can't manage what you can't measure." In monetary terms, we rely on budgets and accounting procedures when we are making planning decisions and reflecting on the value of goods and services. As we have discussed earlier in this chapter, the environmental and social costs are not fully captured in current financial valuations. For example, the value of water loss from a water-stressed region is not reflected in the price of goods and services. As event managers, we therefore need additional indicators to make decisions about how we organize our events and answer questions such as: What is the biodiversity impact of fertilizers used by our soccer fields? How much will installing solar panels on our stadium reduce the impact of electricity use? Should we build temporary or permanent venues?

It is common to see events target waste reduction and recycled paper as part of their "green" initiatives. But are these the most important things to focus on? Arguably not, since we know that Canada's greenhouse gas emissions in 2010 showed that the impact of waste was 3% compared to 81% for energy (of which 24% was transport) and 8% for agriculture (Government of Canada, 2010). While not ignoring the symbolic importance of the visibility factor of trash and the expectation of fans to see recycling bins, organizers need tools to help them focus on the areas where they can effect the greatest change. This section will discuss the emerging method of life cycle assessment (LCA) and two commonly used environmental metrics applicable to sport events: the carbon footprint and the ecological footprint.

Life cycle assessment

Sport event organizers can take advantage of a multitude of environmental sustainability assessment methods, tools and indicators (Ness, Urbel-Piirsalu, Anderberg & Olsson, 2007), but no internationally accepted agreement exists on how governments, let alone events, should measure and report on impacts. We will focus on LCA as a promising method for measuring environmental impacts over the life of a product or service: from cradle to grave. LCA is being widely adopted by both the public and the private sectors to assess impacts and report on performance, and as a basis for policies and regulations (Finnveden et al., 2009). Specifically, it can be a powerful tool for deciding between alternatives: *does product/solution A or product/solution B have the lower environmental impact?*

According to the International Organization for Standardization (ISO) (2006), which sets out the ISO 14044 (www.iso.org) guidelines and requirements for carrying out an LCA, two of the key features of this method are, first, life cycle stages: raw material acquisition, production, use, end-of-life treatment, recycling and final disposal; and second, phases for carrying out an LCA study: goal and scope definition, inventory analysis, impact assessment, and interpretation. It is useful to understand each phase in a bit more detail (see Figure 8.2):

■ *Goal and scope.* Define the purpose of the study, the system boundaries and the major assumptions.

174

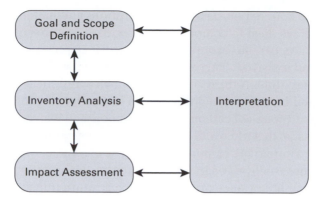

Figure 8.2 The four iterative phases of a life cycle analysis (LCA) study according to ISO 14044

- *Inventory analysis.* Define the inventory of data, environmental inputs (resources) and outputs (emissions, wastes) of the system under study, and the methods for data collection and analysis.
- *Impact assessment:* Translate the inputs and outputs into indicators of potential environmental impact (e.g. human health, climate change, ecosystem quality).
- *Interpretation:* Provide meaning to the results of the inventory and environmental impact assessment relative to the goals of the study.

Thinking with a life cycle perspective encourages both producers and consumers to consider the upstream and downstream impacts in the supply chain. For event management, this means not only understanding the environmental harm caused on-site by factors such as air quality adversely affected by transportation emissions, but also the off-site impacts from purchased food, materials and the generated waste. LCAs are used for a widening range of applications, including business strategy, product and process design, environmental labelling and product declarations. A key strength of LCA is its ability to characterize environmental impacts across multiple damage categories, such as human health, ecosystem quality, climate change and resource depletion (Jolliet et al., 2003). While LCA focuses on environmental impacts, it can be complemented by a broader set of life cycle management (LCM) tools, including life cycle costing (LCC) and social LCA.

There are, however, some considerations with using LCA for event management. First, LCA results should not be used as a basis for comparison unless system boundaries, data sets, assumptions and included processes are the same; we need to compare apples with apples. Second, the complexity of LCAs can be resource-intensive if it requires extensive data collection and expertise. This can be a challenge for events with limited budgets or staff time. A third consideration is communication: while we all understand the value of a dollar, it can be challenging to interpret the importance of 1 tonne of carbon or 1 litre of polluted water. This leads us to a fourth issue, that of how to select between opposing results, such as: which is more important, carbon or water? The answer, of course, depends on many issues, such as geographic location, water scarcity, stakeholder values, placing importance on current versus future impacts, and so on. LCA can be a powerful planning tool for events but brings with it a need for increased expertise, education, stakeholder buy-in and resources to implement it effectively.

Carbon footprint

A carbon footprint measures the global warming potential (synonymous with climate change potential) of a defined activity resulting from associated greenhouse gas emissions over a given time horizon that is usually 100 years (Wright, Kemp & Williams, 2011). The potential impacts of a number of greenhouse gases (some common ones are carbon dioxide, methane and nitrous oxide) have been characterized by the United Nations International Panel on Climate Change into carbon "equivalents" (IPCC, 2007). The unit of measure is therefore the mass of CO_2 equivalents: kilograms of CO_2-eq. The carbon footprint is the most widely used "single" environmental impact category in the sports industry, with a host of mega-events such as Vancouver 2010, London 2012 and the FIFA World Cup 2010 integrating it in their event management strategies. For instance, the United Nations Environment Programme estimated that the global warming impact of the FIFA 2010 World Cup in South Africa totalled over 2 million tons of CO_2-equivalent emissions, with 65% due to international travel, 17% due to national travel and 13% from accommodation energy use (UNEP, n.d.).

Some benefits of applying a carbon footprint approach are that it is a widely used and understood benchmark for environmental impacts; it has also become fairly well known and is therefore easily communicated to the public realm; it has the advantage of being applicable globally, since global

176

warming is not regionalized; and it benefits from a strong consensus in the scientific community on the existence of the problem and on the characterization of impacts (IPCC, 2007). A key drawback of events using a single indicator approach, however, is that it does not provide a full and contextual understanding of other impacts such as water use, land use or resource use (Collins, Jones & Munday, 2009; Weidema, Thrane, Christensen, Schmidt & Løkke, 2008).

Ecological footprint

The ecological footprint method developed by Wackernagel and Rees (1996) puts a focus on the carrying capacity of the earth. By estimating the total human consumption of resources and comparing it to the rate at which the planet can replace them, it can calculate whether our activities are meeting or exceeding its regenerative capacity. The unit of measure is the bioproductive area in hectares required to maintain human consumption. This can also be communicated in terms of the number of Planet Earths required to support our activities. According to a recent World Wildlife Fund *Living Planet Report*, the human population currently exceeds our regenerative capacity by using the equivalent of 1.5 Earths (WWF, 2010).

London 2012, for example, embedded the ecological footprint as a measure for achieving its sustainability platform of a "One Planet Olympics." Collins et al. (2007) applied this assessment framework to measure the impact of the FA Cup Final soccer match in Wales. They were able to show that spectators at the event increased their ecological footprint by seven times, as compared with the daily average for a Welsh citizen.

Whatever environmental impact assessments managers choose to use, it is vital to become literate in the concept of examining impacts with a life cycle approach and across multiple indicators. As new tools develop for the event industry, managers can increase the sophistication level of their assessments and demonstrate increased accountability to their stakeholders.

ASSIGNMENT C: USING A CARBON FOOTPRINT TO MINIMIZE THE ACCOMMODATION IMPACT

You are organizing a baseball tournament for eight teams of 15 people each. You are in the process of selecting a sponsor hotel to house the teams during the seven-day (and seven-night) event. One option, the Dandelion Inn, is certified with a "green hotel" program, partly because its owners have achieved significant reductions in energy use, water use and waste generated compared to the industry average. However, the hotel is located 10 kilometres away from the venue. A second sponsor choice, the Meridian Hotel, is an industry-average hotel and is located only 1 kilometre away. In either case, you need to send a shuttle bus to the hotel twice per day to pick up and drop off the teams. A recent LCA study tells you that the Dandelion Inn has an impact of 6 kg carbon dioxide equivalents (kg CO_2-eq) per person per night and the Meridian Hotel has an impact of 12 kg CO_2-eq per person per night. You also know that the shuttle bus travel impact is 0.050 kg CO_2-eq per person per km.

Hotels	Hotel carbon footprint	Travel carbon footprint	Total carbon footprint
Dandelion Inn	kg CO_2-eq	kg CO_2-eq	kg CO_2-eq
Meridian Hotel	kg CO_2-eq	kg CO_2-eq	kg CO_2-eq

Figure 8.3 Scenario data chart

1 Determine the hotel, travel and total carbon footprints of each option. Which has the lower impact?
2 What other ES considerations are there for an event manager when selecting hotels?
3 How else could you lower the carbon footprint of accommodation?
4 What are the considerations regarding applying carbon as the only environmental impact category?

178

To determine the hotel carbon footprint:

Dandelion: _____ people × _____ nights × $\underline{6}$ kg CO_2-eq/person/night = _____ kg CO_2-eq

Meridian: _____ people × _____ nights × $\underline{12}$ kg CO_2-eq/person/night = _____ kg CO_2-eq

To determine the travel carbon footprint from hotel to venue:

Dandelion: _____ people × _____ km × $\underline{0.050}$ kg CO_2-eq/person/night = _____ kg CO_2-eq

Meridian: _____ people × _____ km × $\underline{0.050}$ kg CO_2-eq/person/night = _____ kg CO_2-eq

Figure 8.4 Guidelines for determining the carbon footprints in Assignment C

CONCLUSION

Alexander (2007) captured the inherent challenge for many managers considering changing business operations to implement ES practices: how to convince those who currently enjoy economic success to enter into a process that could reduce their financial standing? From a similar perspective, Lothe, Myrtveit and Trapani (1999) noted that

> a conflict does not exist when the environmental strategies save on raw materials, reduce government penalties, make waste into positive gross margin products or increase sales because 'green' is marketable. . . . A conflict does exist, however, when the environmental strategies require extra investment.
>
> (pp. 314–315)

The call to manage events in a more environmentally sustainable manner will surely become more urgent in the future. Reducing the direct harm caused to the environment is the responsibility of everyone. Clearly, event managers have a part to play in ES. Indeed, managing events with consideration for each of the three spheres of sustainability should be a priority for every event manager in the future.

1   What is the difference between "sustainability" and "sustainable development"?
2   What are the three perspectives that are used to describe, manage and assess sustainability?
3   "If you cannot measure it, you cannot manage it." Describe how this maxim can be applied to ES initiatives in event management.
4   In your opinion, who, or what department within an organization, should "own" ES?
5   Consider a road race and think of the multiple environmental sustainability initiatives that an event could adopt. Think of at least five other event management environmental sustainability initiatives.

To determine the hotel carbon footprint:

Dandelion Inn: 120 people $\times$ 7 nights $\times$ 6 kg CO_2-eq/person/night = 5,040 kg CO_2-eq

Meridian Hotel: 120 people $\times$ 7 nights $\times$ 12 kg CO_2-eq/person/night = 10,080 kg CO_2-eq

To determine the travel carbon footprint from hotel to venue:

Dandelion Inn: 120 people $\times$ 280 km (10 $\times$ 7 $\times$ 4) $\times$ 0.050 kg CO_2-eq/person/night = 1,680 kg CO_2-eq

Meridian Hotel: 120 people $\times$ 28 km (1 $\times$ 7 $\times$ 4) $\times$ 0.050 kg CO_2-eq/person/night = 168 kg CO_2-eq

Hotel	Hotel carbon footprint	Travel carbon footprint	Total carbon footprint
Dandelion Inn	5,040 kg CO_2-eq	1,680 kg CO_2-eq	6,720 kg CO_2-eq
Meridian Hotel	10,080 kg CO_2-eq	168 kg CO_2-eq	10,248 kg CO_2-eq

Figure 8.5 Answer to the scenario assignment concerning the choice of hotel

180

CHAPTER 9

FACILITATING QUALITY IN EVENT MANAGEMENT

CRAIG HYATT AND CHRIS CHARD

How do you define "quality" with respect to an event manager and their role as a facilitator? In this chapter, we will examine how various theorists have defined quality over time. The theoretical concepts of quality will then be applied to the role of the event manager facilitating the staging of an event. The challenge to define quality for the role of the event manager will be discussed, and quality statements to guide an event manager will be developed.

Every event manager wants to produce a *quality* event. While this seems a fairly simple and straightforward concept, you must remember that most events have at least four different sets of stakeholders: the participant performers or athletes, the staff and volunteers, the sponsors, and the spectators or tourists. Each set of stakeholders can emphasize different criteria when analyzing the quality of the event; defining quality, thus, is complex.

CAN AN EVENT MANAGER MEET ALL OF THE REQUIREMENTS FOR QUALITY?

Each of the event stakeholders can have different needs when it comes to quality requirements. For example, the athletes or performers may judge quality on the basis of the equipment, staging, and amenities in the locker room. To the volunteers, a quality event may involve obtaining experience that advances their personal skills and provides them with event clothing. The sponsors may indicate that quality involves having unlimited product sampling opportunities or being able to mingle with clients in a hospitality area. The spectators may want short lines for quick access into the venue and for food and beverages, and excellent sight lines from their seats. Within each of the four stakeholder groups, quality is a relative concept. Each person involved in an event will have a personally determined idea as to what quality means. This fact challenges event managers. In order for an event manager to know whether they have produced a quality event, understanding definitions of quality, therefore, is a good place to start to manage this challenge.

WHAT IS QUALITY?

For decades, both academic theorists and industry practitioners have attempted to define quality. During the first half of the twentieth century, the service industry was not as prevalent as it is today (especially in the sport, recreation and tourism industries), and the manufacturing and purchasing of durable goods had advanced to be a prominent concern. In that sphere, quality was discussed predominantly in terms of the fabrication of hard goods. During the second half of the last century, there was a gradual shift in our economy's focus from manufacturing to services. The rise of the service industry, including event management, meant a change in how quality was conceptualized. We will consider these two perspectives briefly.

Quality is defined as ruggedness and longevity in the manufacturing industry

Initially, quality was thought of in terms of ruggedness and longevity, and was often expressed in terms of meeting measurable specifications for the size and strength of manufactured parts. This meant that quality was the responsibility of the inspectors who assessed the completed goods prior to leaving a factory – quality controllers. This type of quality process enabled mistakes to be caught and fixed without the consumers ever knowing they had once existed.

Definitions of quality in the service industry

Unlike manufactured goods, services are simultaneously produced and consumed, making it very difficult to catch and fix service mistakes without the consumer's knowledge. In this environment, services often

182

require the knowledgeable input of the consumer to ensure a quality outcome. This means that quality is no longer expressed just in terms of physical specifications; it is now conceived in terms of meeting the expectations of the consumer.

EXPANDED MEANINGS OF QUALITY

Reeves and Bednar (1994), in their study on the evolution of the meaning of quality, concluded that the essence of all the various definitions of quality resulted in only four basic categories: *quality is conformance to specifications*; *quality is excellence*; *quality is value*; and *quality is meeting and/or exceeding customers' expectations*. Yoshida and James (2011) promoted three additional definitions of quality: *aesthetic quality*, *functional quality* and *technical quality*. Each of these seven definitions of quality will now be discussed.

Quality is conformance to specifications

Defining quality as conformance to specifications provides product or service providers, as well as consumers, with a standard that can be agreed upon. Here, "Quality is the degree to which a specific product conforms to a design or specification" (Gilmore cited in Garvin, 1988, p. 41). If the product's quality is called into question, the specifications are examined. If the product meets the specifications, it is of quality. If it does not meet the specifications, it is not.

In 1979, this definition of quality was expanded by corporate executive Philip Crosby when he presented a broader definition that would be applicable when one is not just concerned with a product. He defined quality as "conformance to requirements" (1979, p. 17). Crosby explained that whatever it is that we are examining for quality, including "quality of life," must be broken down into its component parts so that each component part can be specifically defined in such a way as to make it measurable. If each component part is compared to a predetermined measure of acceptability and meets that specification, the entire entity is considered to be of quality. As he stated:

> Those who want to talk about quality of life must define that life in specific terms, such as desirable income, health, pollution

control, political programs and other items that can each be measured. When all criteria are defined and explained, then the measurement of quality of life is possible and practical.

(p. 17)

Thus, over time, the concept of quality as conformance to specifications has expanded to apply not only to products but also to services.

Quality is excellence

Quality conceived as excellence requires something to be as good as it can be. If an alternative is found to be better, yours is no longer thought to be of quality. When Henry Ford introduced his Model T Ford as a "universal car," he said it must have certain attributes (Ford & Crowther, 1922). This first attribute concerned the quality of materials used:

> Quality in material to give service in use. Vanadium steel is the strongest, toughest, and most lasting of steels. It forms the foundation and super-structure of the cars. It is the highest quality steel in this respect in the world, regardless of price.

(p. 68)

While Ford did not define quality, it is obvious from his description that excellence was the determining factor of quality. Ford indicated that quality steel was the best steel available at any price.

Tuchman's definition described quality as excellence. Tuchman indicated that quality

> means investment of the best skill and effort possible to produce the finest and most admirable results possible . . . quality is achieving or reaching for the highest standard against being satisfied with the sloppy or fraudulent . . . it does not allow compromise with the second-rate.

(cited in Reeves & Bednar, 1994, p. 420)

Quality as excellence means being distinguished as exceptional for a product or service.

Quality is value

Quality conceived as value implies that consumers of less-than-perfect products or services can still perceive them as quality if they are positioned financially as providing value. In other words, if you "get what you pay for," then quality transactions involve providing value instead of absolute excellence.

Saad and Siha (2000) emphasized quality as more than just an end result; it is an ongoing "dynamic process of value creation" (p. 1152). An interpretation of this definition of quality was offered by corporate executive Dave Watkins (2006). He indicated that "quality defines how well an enterprise satisfies the performance element in the value equation" (p. 23). He clarified the concept by indicating that the customer defines value (performance relative to cost). Both definitions acknowledge that quality is relative to the price consumers pay for the product or service. Those who pay more want more in return.

Quality is meeting and/or exceeding customers' expectations

Quality has been conceived as meeting and/or exceeding customers' expectations; we have all heard the motto "under-promise, over-deliver." In a manufacturing environment, if the expectation for a set of golf clubs is that it should last for four or five seasons, each summer spent golfing with the same clubs beyond this duration may be seen as a bonus – exceeding expectations. However, when it comes to defining expectations for a service, varied opinions prevail.

Zeithaml, Parasuraman and Berry (1990) noted that "service quality, as perceived by customers, can be defined as the extent of discrepancy between customers' expectations or desires and their perceptions" (p. 19). This definition is of some use when considering the expectations of event attendees. It acknowledges that each patron is unique and may have unique needs or wants that they wish to fulfill by attending your event. It also notes that the onus is on the attendee to decide whether their expectations were fulfilled.

Aesthetic quality

Aesthetic quality focuses on the "interactions between the consumer and the aesthetically pleasing characteristics of the service environment" (Yoshida & James, 2011, p. 21). This type of quality concentrates on the *atmosphere* generated at a sport, recreation or tourism event. This atmosphere encompasses conditions that elicit excitement, participation and/or an appreciation of the appearance. Aesthetic quality can be generated by the provision of high standards in seating and services; the inclusion of participatory activities, such as athlete signing sessions; and consumer tours that allow groups of individuals to walk across a stage or an event location that is of remarkable natural beauty. Aesthetic quality can be expressed in themes that are displayed in designs and decorations to enhance the atmosphere of an event. The crowd experience is an important and foundational characteristic of aesthetic quality.

Functional quality

Functional quality is based on the "interactions between the customer and functional services" (Yoshida & James, 2011, p. 21). Functional quality, thus, is derived from products and services delivering what they are "supposed to deliver." For example, a bicycle with wheels that will not turn does not deliver functional quality. Similarly, from an event perspective, staff and volunteer *services*, including *attitudes* and *behaviours*, are a part of the functional quality; an usher who will not direct attendees to their seats does not deliver functional quality. The staff and volunteer function must also be supported with elements – such as easy access to the seats, the provision of excellent seating space, as well as crowd density – that are conducive to easy movements.

Technical quality

Finally, technical quality is described by Yoshida and James (2011) as consisting of characteristics expressed by *the participants' behaviour* during the practice of their craft. In sport, recreation and tourism events, this includes the participants' individual practical behaviour and their group behaviour between participants and/or between opposing members. Behaviours are guided by rules established for each event, and violations can influence the technical quality perceived by the consumers.

186

A LACK OF GUIDANCE FOR QUALITY IN EVENT MANAGEMENT

Current definitions of quality fall short when it comes to event management. Let's briefly re-examine the basic definitions of quality to explore their shortcomings when they are applied to the role of an event manager. To begin, let's consider the definition of "quality as conformance to specifications" in the context of event management. This definition applies when there are, for example, predetermined specifications in a contract for a stage and lighting or for equipment. However, there are no predetermined, agreed-upon specifications for services. Can you imagine getting everyone involved in an event to agree on what, specifically, constitutes an "entertaining" event? What about trying to agree how long concession lines should be if an event involves tens of thousands of people? Should service still be able to be provided within a minute or two, as some may expect? The specifications for these types of services are not perceived in the same manner by all stakeholders, as they are not predetermined in writing. There is the opportunity for stakeholders to apply their personal idea of specifications. However, even if all of the stakeholders could agree on specifications for many service elements, including entertainment outcomes, the event manager does not have control over all the elements.

When "quality is defined as excellence," there are factors that hinder an event manager from meeting this standard. For instance, resources (financial, human, natural) may not be available to make every component of the event the best it can be. As a result, compromises must be made if, for example, the budget is restrictive. Does this mean that any event that is forced to compromise owing to budgetary restrictions should not be staged, as it will not be a quality event? If it is staged, with certain conciliations, can an event manager ever meet the standard of quality?

When "quality is defined as value," the notion is that the consumer incurred a financial cost for attending the event. In some cases, however, events are free to spectators. Does this mean that a non-paying customer cannot be disappointed? In such cases, can event managers deliver sub-par services because "the event is free"? The answer clearly is no! Even if a spectator incurs no financial cost to watch an event, that person still invested their time and experienced opportunity costs by forgoing other opportunities. Consumers need to know that it is worth the time it takes to attend an event, and that quality will be delivered.

When "quality is defined as meeting and/or exceeding customers' expectations," not all customer expectations are realistic. The old adage "you can't please all of the people all of the time" is something event managers should never forget. For instance, if an event manager facilitates easy parking and venue access, quality food provision, clean restrooms, excellent sight lines and exciting performers but the consumer was hoping there would be free child care, then the evaluation of the event as meeting expectations is based on different expectations. Can a food and beverage service offer enough varied cuisine to meet the tastes of all stakeholders? Not every credit card will be accepted at the box office. If the expectations for an event are personally established, is it realistic to believe an event manager can meet and/or exceed all of the expectations for every stakeholder group? It is our contention that some expectations may be unreasonably high. If an event manager used the definition of quality as meeting and/or exceeding expectations to guide their work, could they ever be successful? Would not some of the many stakeholders always be unhappy? Does this mean the event manager did not produce a quality event?

When quality is defined based on "aesthetic quality," an event manager must create conditions within the operational plan that elicit excitement, participation and/or an appreciation of the environment. Creating such conditions can be done as simply as by decorating a venue. However, generally an event manager does not have control over this aspect of an event; in medium to large events, generally someone skilled in designing the artistry of the event is hired. The event manager does, however, ensure that the operational plans for instituting the event and other areas of aesthetic quality are well planned and executed. Some of these other areas include the need, for example, for high-quality seating, but event managers may not have control over ensuring a high level of these types of services at the facilities. The crowd experience, however, is the foundational characteristic of aesthetic quality.

Event managers do have influence in terms of "functional quality." This type of quality means that they must design training for staff and volunteers that includes service-level expectations. These expectations can include expected staff and volunteer attitudes and behaviours of the highest level. Some aspects of functional quality, however, are beyond event managers' control. Seat access, seating space and crowd density can be dictated by the size, age and type of venue utilized for the event.

Event managers may be guided by a wish for "technical quality," but it is difficult to ensure this type of quality. Technical quality is based on the participants' behaviours displayed during the sport, recreation or tourism event. The event manager may attempt to influence this type of quality by offering briefing sessions with the participants; however, the individuals' practical behaviour and the group behaviour between participants is difficult to control. These behaviours are guided by the rules established for each event. Frequent violations can influence the technical quality perceived by event attendees and other stakeholders.

While the definitions of quality in the literature offer good points, none are truly applicable to all types of events. This certainly does not mean that the quest for quality should be disregarded by the event manager. It simply means that every event manager needs to *create a unique quality statement that can guide their work.*

ISSUES IN CREATING QUALITY STATEMENTS AND DEFINING QUALITY IN EVENT MANAGEMENT

Creating a guiding quality statement for event management is a difficult task. There are many issues that arise as an event manager attempts to define quality specifically for their role and their tasks. One of the parameters concerning quality statements is to concentrate on the items the event manager can control. You cannot promise a level of excellence if management cannot possibly deliver at that level because of circumstances beyond their control. What follows is a list of issues that can directly affect whether or not stakeholders can have their reasonable expectations met. As you will see, many of these issues involve circumstances over which the event manager has little control.

Conflicting stakeholder expectations influence quality perceptions

What happens when one stakeholder group has expectations that are in direct conflict with the expectations of another stakeholder group? Consider the potential tension between event performers and sponsors. The title sponsor may have a hospitality area near the action where its personnel entertain existing or potential clients, or host employees who are being rewarded for achieving excellence in their field. As part of a great experience for its guests, the sponsor may wish performers to be available for autographs, photos, and chatting with the guests. The performers, on the other hand, might want to focus on their tasks and may consider time in the hospitality area to be a distraction. Hence, they may wish to have no obligation to interact with sponsors or guests. Even when contracted to do so, they may provide only a minimal level of service. How is an event manager expected to facilitate a positive outcome from these two contradictory expectations? By promising the elements they can control and making it clear that they cannot deliver certain elements that are outside their control, an event manager can potentially modify a stakeholder's reasonable expectations and facilitate a satisfactory outcome for all parties.

Limited control over inputs influences quality

An event needs inputs. The event manager will need to order supplies from the venue and from outside suppliers. Depending on the nature of the event, you may have to order all of the items for a media conference to be held just prior to the event. For instance, the order may include a platform and tables, along with tablecloths, microphones, chairs for the media, and so on. A technical check is held just prior to the media conference, and all is determined to be working well. However, during the media conference one microphone has technical problems. Does this constitute an event that does not provide quality, or does the manner in which one handles the issue determine whether the event is of quality? If you have a technician on hand to manage the issue or have pre-planned the use of an extra microphone for such a case, will this contribute to making a quality event? The answer is obvious. As has been mentioned before, contingency planning is a paramount concern for an event manager.

Financial constraints influence quality

Most event managers must deal with some financial constraints. Here, event managers might not be able to afford the inputs necessary to meet the reasonable expectations of some stakeholders. For example, spectators may wish to purchase high-end items at your souvenir stand, such as embroidered sweatshirts. However, the cost of ordering these items is high, and, given the time it takes for the garment supplier to fill a large custom order, you must place the order weeks in advance. It is prudent to give the

C. Hyatt and C. Chard

supplier a delivery date a few weeks before the actual event as insurance in case of delays. This might mean that you are paying for these sweatshirts before you have any of the cash flows that you expect to generate during the actual event (same-day ticket sales, sales at the concession stand, sales at the souvenir stand, etc.). Ideally, the event manager would have sponsors pay part of their sponsorship fees well in advance, and to have a budget that takes these advance cash flows into account. These provisions will help ensure that there is sufficient cash flow long before the day the event opens in order that all the quality inputs required can be bought. If, however, in the weeks leading up to the event the actual revenue from sponsorship and advance ticket sales fall short of the projected numbers forecast in the budget, there may not be enough funds available to purchase items such as embroidered sweatshirts. As a result, the event manager may be forced to buy cheaper items (such as silk-screened T-shirts made of a cotton–polyester blend) to stock the souvenir stand. The consequence could be that the lack of premium items creates negative associations with quality for this part of the event in the eyes of some consumers.

How can the event manager avoid this type of negative perception? There are no easy answers. Issues of finance and cash flow plague many businesses and organizations. If financial survival depends on selling sponsorships and tickets in advance of the event, then you, the event manager, must educate the sales staff that sales success in the months and weeks before the event is crucial. As for the bigger picture, all students interested in event management may wish to consider learning all they can about the sales process; the quality of your future event may depend on your ability to sell.

Contingency plans influence quality

No event manager needs to be told that things can go wrong. Managers need to plan ahead to identify potential bumps in the road. This planning is vital and necessitates the development of contingency plans. For example, an experienced event manager might anticipate that the food wholesaler may not deliver the exact product that was ordered. In such a case, a contingency plan may empower the director of concessions to call an alternative wholesaler to arrange the delivery of the necessary product. Creating this kind of contingency plan is fairly straightforward and ensures a quality product. However, not all contingency plans can be implemented in such a straightforward manner. Consider an outdoor event that cannot be held in inclement weather, such as a fireworks show. A simple contingency plan for a fireworks show is to advertise both the specific date (weather permitting) on which the event will be held and the rain date should the show be cancelled owing to bad weather. The problem lies in the unpredictability of bad weather. Imagine that your fireworks show is slated to take place at 21:00 on a Saturday, with the following day listed as the rain date. Starting on the Wednesday prior to the event, the weather forecasts predict evening thunderstorms on the Saturday. You can be sure that the phone will start ringing that Wednesday and throughout the remainder of the week with worried potential attendees asking whether the event will be postponed. Maybe the folks who are calling live a few hours away and plan on leaving home mid-afternoon on the Saturday to do some shopping and enjoy dinner before the fireworks. They do not want to spend many hours in the car and not see fireworks. While you understand their situation, you also know that even if the weather forecast is accurate, an evening thunderstorm might mean rain from 17:30 until 18:30, leaving plenty of time for things to dry out enough for the 21:00 show. Or it could mean rain starting at 23:00, long after the event is over. You also know that for every attendee who could easily attend the event on the rain date, there is one who cannot. Maybe hundreds of tourists have planned a weekend getaway around your event and have hotels booked for Saturday night only, having to return to their home towns during the day on Sunday. If you postpone the fireworks a day or two in advance and it turns out that things are dry enough at 21:00 on Saturday for the show to have been held, the out-of-town tourists will probably conclude that their reasonable expectations were not met. If you wait until the night of the show and decide to postpone, the folks who drove in that day who just as easily could have rescheduled their day trip until the following day will probably conclude that their reasonable expectations were not met. As the event manager, what can you do?

Unfortunately, the nature of weather forecasting often means the event manager must rely on both the data provided and their gut instincts regarding decisions on the event. If in the hours leading up to the event it still looks as though there is a reasonable chance that the event can go ahead as scheduled, the event manager may elect to proceed until the skies open just minutes before the start time. If, however, the noon weather forecast clearly shows a massive slow-moving weather system heading towards the venue, which meteorologists believe will bring six straight hours of heavy rain starting at 19:00, the event manager may announce the postponement of the event at 13:00. In most cases involving inclement weather, the telephones at the event headquarters may ring non-stop before, during and after the event with folks wanting to know whether the event is still proceeding, wanting to know when the decision to cancel (or not) will be made, wanting to know why the decision to postpone the event was not made sooner, wanting to complain that their weekend plans were ruined by the poor decisions of the event staff, etc. The best an event manager can do is to train the staff handling the phones about what to say to the callers and how to say it. If all the staff are briefed on the reasons why decisions to proceed or to postpone are made, they have the opportunity to educate the callers. This education may actually enlighten the caller to the point where they conclude that their expectations for the event might not have been as reasonable as they thought. In such situations, the caller (who questioned the quality of the event when the phone call was first made) may not have that opinion by the time the phone call is over.

Thus, although there are difficulties, an event manager is expected to be able to produce work that is of quality. Therefore, they must be able to define a quality statement to guide their work in the development and implementation of event operational plans.

GENERATE YOUR QUALITY STATEMENT IN EVENT MANAGEMENT

Every event manager who wishes to provide a quality product or service should address the issue by *generating their personal written statement on what quality is based upon* for each event. This quality statement should address the specific definition of quality, and how quality will be delivered and evaluated.

To be sure, there is no "one way" to create a quality statement. A quick internet search reveals a large number of organizations attempting to create quality statements. The quality statement can be as short as two sentences and as long as multiple pages. If a statement is too short, there is a chance that it will be so vague as to be meaningless. If it is too long, it might not be practical enough to serve as a useful guide.

At this time, think of an event that you see yourself managing soon or in the future. Take some time right now to create a quality statement for this event. Consider what the literature offers when defining quality and what elements you can utilize from this literature. Consider also that the event may currently have a mission statement, a vision statement and a statement of values. Your quality statement should be congruent with these other event statements. The difference is that *the quality statement you are developing must guide your work as a facilitator* and needs to be available as a realistic platform with which to evaluate your work throughout and at the end of an event.

Your quality statement needs to seamlessly integrate the facilitation activities that you are personally responsible for as an event manager.

A SAMPLE QUALITY STATEMENT

Imagine a recreational three-on-three basketball tournament that is held annually in a small city. It is organized and managed by a local youth basketball organization that has named it "Rally in the Valley." The tournament is meant to be both a celebration of the game of basketball and a fundraising event for the organization. Temporary outdoor courts are set up throughout a park located in a residential neighbourhood near the city's downtown. Dozens of teams, grouped according to age, sex and skill level, will play games all weekend until winners in each division are determined late on Sunday afternoon. What could a quality statement for Rally in the Valley look like?

QUALITY STATEMENT FOR RALLY IN THE VALLEY

Rally in the Valley is committed to meeting or exceeding the reasonable expectations of all the event's stakeholders, including the players, spectators, sponsors, volunteers and city government. Rally in the Valley management will actively encourage the input of all stakeholder groups for the purpose of mutually determining what constitutes "reasonable expectations." This process will be ongoing, as "reasonable expectations" may change from year to year as the event evolves. A thorough training process to educate the volunteers will be implemented before the event that will empower them to handle routine stakeholder concerns during the event, so that

---

194

reasonable expectations can be met in a timely manner. Rally in the Valley management will be in constant radio contact with the volunteers, should non-routine stakeholder concerns arise during the event. In such cases, management will meet with any concerned stakeholder as soon as possible to rectify the concern. After the event's completion, Rally in the Valley management will make themselves available to meet with concerned stakeholders to rectify any issues regarding meeting their reasonable expectations.

While it is debatable whether or not this quality statement has too much or too little detail, it seems to meet the basic requirements of a quality statement: to define quality and to indicate how quality will be delivered and measured.

To provide further input to guide you in developing a personal quality statement, here are some comments about quality from members in the event management industry. These observations show some of the specific components that drive quality, and, although they are not full quality statements, they offer ideas to consider when generating your personal quality statements for an event.

> With only one chance at a first impression, it is crucial to carefully plan for all possible situations. Planning well thought-out contingencies for situations are often times the difference between a successful event and an event that will no longer be continued.
>
> (Andrew Pittam, Operations Manager, Event Properties International Management Group [IMG] Canada)

> Whatever happens on the field or court will take care of itself. We want the visiting team to be impressed by the way we treat them; beginning from the moment they arrive until their departure from our campus. That is our philosophy that guides the quality in our game operations.
>
> (Tom Calder, Director of Athletics and Recreation, Johns Hopkins University, Division 1 Men's Lacrosse National Collegiate Athletic Association [NCAA] Champions, 2007)

A well-managed event in a clean, modern facility with superior customer service and a product that exceeds expectations will create satisfied customers and ambassadors for your event. A poorly managed event, on the other hand, can negate the effects of all the money you've spent and work you've put into attracting patrons to your event. A poorly managed event that detracts from the fan experience will cost you patrons in the future and limit the ability of your event to grow and flourish.

(John Pesetski, Director of Advertising and Promotions, National Hot Rod Association)

Quality is critical in providing an outstanding experience for our 30,000 participants and enhancing our brand. Collectively we develop a plan which helps us stay focused and on track. Our ultimate goal is for participants to have a positive experience and return to our event year after year.

(Lindsay Crosby, Manager, Run for the Cure, Canadian Breast Cancer Foundation, Toronto)

CONCLUSION

No event manager wants to put in countless hours dedicating their time and energy to staging an event that lacks quality. All of the careful planning leading up to the event must be done with quality in mind. Because of the unique components of each event, managers must define quality in a way that makes sense for their particular situation. To better ensure that their conceptualization of quality is met, they must also institute policies in a quality statement that are meaningful and easy to implement. Managers should also be mindful that other issues, such as conflicting stakeholder expectations, limited control over inputs, financial constraints and contingency planning, can create challenges for anyone wishing to facilitate a quality event. Event management is a complex and challenging field; a personally established statement of quality to guide the facilitation of an event is a key element in succeeding in this industry.

CHAPTER QUESTIONS

1   Describe the characteristics of the seven different definitions of quality (including conformance to specifications, excellence, value, meeting

196

or exceeding customers' expectations, aesthetics, functional quality and technical quality) and show how these definitions can guide event managers.

2   Discuss how stakeholder perceptions, limited control, financial constraints and contingency plans affect the efforts of an event manager striving for quality.

3   Consider a specific sport, recreation or tourism event and generate a guiding quality statement for the event manager. Record the issues that arise as you attempt to create a definitive guiding quality statement.

4   Consider the same event as in the previous question and list three or four items that you think would be expected by the four different stakeholder groups (participants or performers, spectators, sponsors, volunteers and staff) to make the event a high-quality one.

5   Discuss why quality can be an elusive concept in event management and how knowledge of quality can aid you in your work as an event manager.

CHAPTER 10

EVENT BIDDING

CHERYL MALLEN

In this chapter, the process of bidding to procure a sport, recreation or tourism event is presented. Five key elements within the bid process are defined, including a feasibility study, a candidature document, a bid questionnaire, a bid dossier/submission and the bid tour. Importantly, this chapter emphasizes critical factors for successful bids that have been outlined in the literature. This is followed by a presentation and discussion on the proposition that there is one key factor necessary in successful event bidding.

WHAT IS A FEASIBILITY STUDY?

The first key document in a bid process is the feasibility study, which includes an assessment and opinion on the capability of a group to stage or host the particular event. An ability to host involves a determination as to the availability of the necessary resources required to host the event sought. This document records the elements that have been considered and the determination of whether it is feasible to host the event. These elements can include, for example:

- event goals;
- objectives;
- intentions;
- activities;
- the event's history;
- the cultural context (such as the population growth in the area, the consumer spending power and economic development);

- facility and equipment availability (such as parking, seating, accessibility and spatial requirements, including space and the ability of simultaneous activity use);
- resource availability (including competent and experienced human resources);
- venue service access (such as scheduling, ticketing, media, crowd management and security services, the union regulations, zoning regulations for noise, along with health and fire codes);
- technical resources;
- financial resource availability.

Overall, a feasibility study outlines the assessment of the availability of resources to meet the needs for hosting an event, as well as determining whether pursuing the event bid is a practical and reasonable initiative. This means that a feasibility study outlines the plausibility of meeting the bid requirements with the resources available.

WHAT IS A CANDIDATURE DOCUMENT?

The second key document in a bid process is the candidature document. This document is provided by the organization that is accepting the event bids. The candidature document outlines the critical path of deadlines and processes that must be followed for a bid submission to be eligible for consideration. Each deadline must be adhered to by each bid group in order to complete the bid process.

WHAT IS A BID QUESTIONNAIRE?

The third key document in a bid process is a bid questionnaire. This questionnaire is often contained within the candidature document and outlines the list of questions that must be answered in the bid submission. The bid questionnaire provides the format and frames the context for a bid dossier, and must be followed precisely. This framework allows for easy comparisons with other bids being considered by the governing body or organization that is awarding the rights to host the event.

WHAT IS A BID DOSSIER?

The fourth key document in event bidding is a bid dossier or submission. This document follows the framework outlined in the bid questionnaire. The dossier outlines the overall plan, the particular strategies, supporting resources, and supplementary details of the bid. It will also contain testimonials of support. All of these items aim to set the bid submission apart from competitors' bids. Each question listed within the bid questionnaire must be answered within the bid dossier in precisely the order provided for, and be numbered to directly correspond to the number assigned in the bid questionnaire.

One of the best examples of a candidature document and bid questionnaire is provided by the International Olympic Committee and is available for viewing on its website (www.olympic.org). One document to access from this site is the *2014 Candidature Procedure and Questionnaire*. This 265-page document outlines the candidature procedures for the 2014 Olympic Winter Games, including the deadline dates, signatures required, the schedule of payments, guarantees required, the bid questionnaire, presentation layout and requirements, along with an outline for the visit by the evaluation commission and the selection decision process. An Olympic bid questionnaire is subdivided into the 17 themes outlined in Figure 10.1. Each theme is further subdivided into a series of questions that must be answered in the bid dossier.

To advance your knowledge on the process of bidding, it is suggested that you select at least three events that are of interest to you and review their event candidature documents and bid questionnaires. Many of these documents can be located on the World Wide Web. For example, the European Football Championship Final Tournament bid documents can be found at www.uefa.com. You will find a number of bid documents on this site, including the bid regulations and reports on bid dossiers submitted for hosting events. Another website you may want to visit to find bid documents is www.gamesbids.com/eng/. You could also approach festivals, conferences and conventions in your area to obtain their bid documents.

200

Theme	Sample bid questionnaire topic areas to be answered in a bid dossier
Theme 1: Olympic Games concept and legacy	The event vision, impact, legacy, motivation and plans for sustainable development
Theme 2: Political and economic climate and structure	Guarantees provided, government structure, stability, per capita income, inflation rate, referendum results and opinions concerning support
Theme 3: Legal aspects	Stipulation of authority, event exclusivity, trademark protection, official languages
Theme 4: Customs and immigration formalities	Visa regulations, guarantee of entrance for those with Games accreditation, health and vaccination requirements, restrictions on media broadcasts, regulations on imported print media, guide dogs and equipment
Theme 5: Environment and meteorology	Construction agreements and guarantees, protocols to protect the environment, geographical features, environmentally and culturally protected areas, collaborative efforts, plans and systems to manage the environment, the environmental impact, temperatures, humidity, precipitation, wind directions and strength
Theme 6: Finance	Budget template outlining the financial details, including capital investment, cash flow, sponsorship and contributions, ticket sales, licensing, lotteries, disposal of assets, subsidies and other hosting costs
Theme 7: Marketing	Guarantees of a marketing program, domestic sponsorship, ticketing, advertising and advertising controls
Theme 8: Sports and venues	Venue descriptions, competition schedules, technical manuals for meeting competition standards, venue responsibilities and the tendering process and agreements, reporting, monitoring and management plans, workforce and sport experience
Theme 9: Paralympic Games	Plans for financial, security, accommodations, transportation, sport venues, opening and closing ceremonies, finances, accessibility, and so on for hosting the Paralympic Games
Theme 10: Olympic Village	Concept, location, venue design and construction, financing, including guarantees for construction, types of accommodation, distance from competition venues, control of commercial rights, accessibility and post-event use
Theme 11: Medical services and doping control	Plans for meeting the world anti-doping code and the IOC anti-doping rules, guarantees of investment in anti-doping, medical service facilities, public health authorities,

	epidemiological issues in the region and systems for managing Games medical expenses, including serving visiting foreign nationals
Theme 12: Security	Safety and peaceful hosting guarantees, international, national, regional and local government security involvement, analysis of risks concerning fire, crime, traffic, terrorism, and so on, security organizations and intelligence services to be involved and financial planning for security
Theme 13: Accommodation	Hotel room capacity, guarantees on room availability and room rate and other pricing controls, construction guarantees, work timelines and finances, binding contracts, accommodation tables with maps outlining sites and distances
Theme 14: Transportation	Traffic management guarantees, including public and private transport, control centres, distances, airport capability, parking and additional transport infrastructure, training and testing, timelines and authorities
Theme 15: Technology	Guarantees of competent bodies offering communication services, systems and broadcast capabilities for print, radio, television and internet, network support
Theme 16: Media operations	Provision of broadcast centres for print, radio, television, and internet outlets, construction, timelines, financing, media transport and accommodation
Theme 17: Olympism and culture	Protocols, plans for ceremonies including opening, closing and awards ceremonies, provision of intent, location, seating capacity, financing and facilities

Figure 10.1 Themes and topic areas requiring answers in the International Olympic Committee bid questionnaire

WHAT IS A BID TOUR?

A bid tour involves hosting the members of a bid evaluation commission that will make the selection of the winning bid. The opportunity to stage a bid tour generally means that the bid submission has been placed on the shortlist of potential groups that are eligible to host the event. The tour offers an opportunity to present the information outlined in the bid dossier, to tour and highlight the planned ceremonies and facilities, to demonstrate local community and business support for the bid and to promote the reasons why your bid should win the competition to host.

A bid tour involves arranging for the needs of the bid evaluation commission members from the moment of their arrival until their departure. To meet this requirement, an event manager facilitates the adaptation of the event planning model phases to generate operational plans specifically for a bid tour.

To begin, a bid tour follows the phases of the Planning Model. First, the Development phase of the Planning Model is instituted. This involves the facilitation of elements such as the organizational structure for governance of the tour, the policies and volunteer practices, along with the determination of how corporate social responsibility can be incorporated within the tour. Next, the event Operational Planning phase involves the facilitation of the written logical, sequential and detailed operational plans for the bid tour, including the arrangements for components such as transportation, accommodation, entertainment, tours of the facilities and a presentation of the bid to the commission members. Contingency plans and a plan refining process should always be considered within the operational plans. Further, a bid tour involves the Implementation, Monitoring and Management phase as the bid tour moves from the conceptual stage to reality. Finally, the Evaluation phase must take into account the priorities of the bid commission members, as they will ultimately make the decision on the winning bid.

To understand the evaluation criteria used by bid evaluation committee members, a review of the literature has identified several factors that appear to be critical in winning the bid process. These critical factors are outlined in the next section.

WHAT ARE THE CRITICAL FACTORS IN A SUCCESSFUL BID?

The literature outlines several factors for successful event bidding; however, different studies describe an assortment of elements that lead you in many directions. I will review the key factors for success offered by researchers such as Emery (2002), Persson (2000), Hautbois, Parent and Séguin (2012) and Westerbeek, Turner and Ingerson (2002). Then this text puts forward the proposition that the natural environment is another key factor in bidding and that there is one further element that is vital to successful bidding.

To begin, Emery (2002, p. 323) suggested five essential factors for event bid success. These factors include:

1   relevant professional credibility;
2   fully understanding the brief and formal/informal decision-making process;
3   not assuming decision makers are experts, or that they use rational criteria for selection;
4   customizing professional (in)tangible products and services, and exceeding expectations;
5   knowing your strengths and weaknesses relative to the competition.

Emery (2002) postulated that "credibility and capacity to deliver are fundamental to any application, but not normally the discriminating factor between success and failure" (p. 323). Emery emphasized that bid success was "dependent upon in-depth knowledge of networks, processes and people – in other words external political support at the very highest levels of government and the commercial sector" (p. 329). Therefore, the organizing team itself is actually an element that could make a difference in the pursuit of a winning bid. Emery suggested that an organizing team should be made up of members who have considerable experience of successful events.

Emery (2002) also stated that "the information process and protocol must never be underestimated" (p. 329). Some of the bid organizing teams must have experience in the political aspects of bidding, as this area is an important element in the bid process. According to Emery, this means that a bid needs to be politically positioned for success. In addition, Emery suggested that an assumption concerning the use of rational and consistent criteria to select the winning bid may not be correct. An interpretation of this view is that the key factors for winning a bid may actually change depending on the members in a bid commission who are evaluating a submission. Each member's personal perspective on the priorities for the bid must be somehow ascertained and then met. Thus, trying to anticipate the receptivity of a bid commission with several different members is a complex task that is underscored with uncertainty, but it is a necessary part of a successful bid process.

Another researcher, Persson (2000), suggested that a success factor for an Olympic Games bid involved "the fit between the bidder's and the IOC members' perceptions of the bid offers" (p. 27). This implies that the bid committee members must anticipate what the IOC will perceive as important in a bid. The IOC bid commission has several members, and the priorities of a bid are therefore subject to personal bias or agenda. Thus,

204

Persson (2000) and Emery (2002) assert that a key component to achieving success in a bid is gaining an understanding of the priorities of the bid commission members and meeting those priorities through political positioning of the bid.

Persson (2000) further offered the finding that infrastructure is important to the success of a bid. Infrastructure, according to Persson, involves the capacity for the provision of appropriate accommodation, transportation, venues, finances, telecommunications and technology, as well as a top-notch media centre.

Ingerson and Westerbeek (2000) found that experience in event hosting is a key element for success, along with the scope of knowledge of the members on the bid team. This finding was based on the contention that the more experience a member has, the greater the opportunity they have previously had to develop relationships that may drive the success of the current bid and ultimately the event itself. As Westerbeek et al. have stated, "The ability to organize an event is evidenced by having a solid track record in organizing similar events" (2002, p. 318). Thus, another theme arising from the literature is that experience of hosting previous events is a key factor for future success in bidding.

There is a general consensus on the part of Emery (2002), Ingerson and Westerbeek (2000) and Persson (2000) that the political aspects of a bid are vitally important to bid success. However, other researchers have continued to point to additional success factors.

Westerbeek et al. (2002) promote stability as a key factor for bid success. Stability is defined as involving politics, but from a different perspective than being politically positioned for advantage with the bid commission. The political reference in this instance means the stability of the country and municipal politics of the city, along with the stability of the financial support for an event.

Westerbeek et al. (2002) outlined eight factors that were important in the process of bidding. Although these researchers emphasized sport event bidding, these factors are also very applicable to recreation and tourism events. The eight factors outlined by Westerbeek et al. were as follows:

1   *Ability to organize events.* This element involves multiple items such as the intraorganizational network established to manage an event, the technical expertise within the network, the equipment, and the overall financial support for the bid.

2   *Political support.* This element involves support from the government for the event bid. This support is used to assist in gaining access to financial and human resources, as well as access to facilities.

3   *Infrastructure.* This element involves providing convincing proof of the availability of excellent facilities and an ability to meet event component requirements to deliver the transportation, accommodation and so on to produce an event.

4   *Existing facilities.* This element involves the current status of the major event facilities at the time of the bid submission.

5   *Communication and exposure.* This element involves the host city's reputation as a destination and the available support system to handle the technological communication system requirements for hosting and promoting the event.

6   *Accountability.* This element involves proof of the event's reputation, presence and support in the event market, previous success in hosting events, and excellent venues.

7   *Bid team composition.* This element views the talent mixture of the members involved in the development of the bid as important for favourably influencing the bid evaluators. The bid team members should be able to provide a high profile, build relationships, have the skill to manage the complexity of a bid and provide credibility concerning expertise to host.

8   *Relationship marketing.* This element involves the ability to gain access to the members of a bid evaluation team and to influence these members to promote a bid through the development of "friendship."

These eight factors for success in bidding are listed in order of priority. Thus, Westerbeek et al. suggest that the most important factor in bidding is proof of one's ability to organize the network of personnel and the finances for an event.

Management effectiveness, as indicated by Kerzner (1995), was dependent upon an ability to balance a number of items such as time constraints, cost and performance with the pressures of the environment, including political pressures. While Kerzner was discussing project management, the link between the fields of project management and event management is apparent and represents one of the focal points in this text.

Hautbois et al. (2012) find that the bid environment is very complex. They suggest that it is the involvement of both public officials and athletes that makes the difference for a winning bid. These researchers conclude that from "a political, symbolic and strategic point of view, public officials

206

were central in the network of stakeholders" (p. 11). Yet they deem it important to ensure that all groups or stakeholders involved are engaged in the bid process, "as opposed to one single actor (i.e. mayor)" (p. 11). The participants are noted as being instrumental in ensuring that an event is designed for their needs.

A relatively new element gaining prominence in the literature, and promoted in this text as an important factor in event bid success, is environmental sustainability. Over the past 10 years, environmentalism has moved onto the agenda. The authoritative United Nations Environment Programme (UNEP) Intergovernmental Panel on Climate Change has generated a document called *Global Environment Outlook 4* (IPCC, 2007). This document was developed with input from leading researchers from around the globe. Their research on the world's natural resources, including forests, fisheries, water, soil and air, indicates that those resources are at risk: a social and environmental challenge has arisen. Consequently, there is a need to a shift to sustainable practices (Gadenne, Kennedy & McKeiver, 2009; Mitchell & Saren, 2008). This shift to sustainability has been used as one key factor in bid success. For example, the Fédération Internationale de Football Association (FIFA) released a legacy report on the environmental practices from the World Cup held in Germany (FIFA, 2006). This report illustrates the efforts made by event organizers to promote sustainable environmental practices. The International Motorcycling Federation (2006) produced a code for protecting the environment that is to be followed when producing events and is now instituted for all races. In addition, in 1999 the International Olympic Committee (IOC) established *Agenda 21*, a document designed to bring its members into a program that supports the environment (IOC, n.d.). *Agenda 21* was promoted on the IOC website as "putting sport at the service of humanity." IOC (2006) is a code of conduct (2006), which states that athletes are environmental role models. The IOC code of conduct presents six key principles: avoid wasting water, avoid wasting energy, travel as efficiently as possible, consume responsibly, dispose of waste properly and support environmental conservation and education. The IOC expects event organizers and athletes to protect and promote sustainability of the environment. Further, as major events can be a driver for tourism, the IOC code of conduct for environmental sustainability can be extended to tourists, and this element can also be outlined in bids.

There is, however, an issue concerning bids that have stated provisions for safeguarding the natural environment in the initial bid phase of an event.

The issue is that the bid plans have not always been translated into reality during the Implementation, Monitoring and Management phase of an event. The natural environment has been positioned as a priority in the up-front bid phase but has then become a non-priority in the hosting phase. Does this constitute lying in the bid process? Generally, no punishments have been enacted for events that have found themselves in this position, although the negative media publicity is a type of punishment. Where do you stand on this issue? How would you resolve this issue during bidding and event implementation?

Overall, the research literature has suggested that there are a number of critical factors for success in bid evaluation. The suggestions are multidirectional, which increases the complexity of the bid and the uncertainty of bidding success. The complexity stems from the need for multiple groups that must come together to create a cohesive event bid.

Multiple areas of emphasis contained within a bid create a complexity that can strain the cohesiveness of any given committee and thereby compromise the potential for success. In addition, there is political complexity. This means that while the guiding documents outline the bid requirements, intangibles such as underlying political requirements are not explicitly stated in a bid questionnaire. These intangibles need to be anticipated, as they may be important in the final decision-making. Thus, uncertainty is inherent in the bidding process. In the end, only one group is awarded the prize in a bid competition. Unfortunately, the rest have to bear the cost of competing in the process without receiving anything in the end.

To assist in working through the complexity and uncertainty of the bid process, the question is posed: Is there one critical factor that can be used to enhance the opportunity for a successful bid? This book promotes the view that there is *one* critical factor in event bidding.

WHAT IS THE ONE CRITICAL FACTOR FOR BID SUCCESS?

This text puts forward the proposition that *communication* has been underplayed in the literature and should be positioned as *the one critical factor* in event bidding. Greenberg (2002) defined communication as "the process through which people send information to others and receive information from them" (p. 217). An application of this definition means that a bidding process "constitutes a communication process between the actors involved" (Persson, 2000, p. 139). Thus, event bidding is conducted within a social context, and this vital communication element is the key factor in the process of winning an event bid.

Communication in event bidding is discussed in the literature, although the support is not emphatic that communication is the key factor in successful bidding. The literature indicates that "event bidding is about communication to a degree, initially you have got to have communication, and you've got to be a really, really sharp communicator" (Horte & Persson, 2000, p. 67). Westerbeek et al. (2002) included communication as one of the eight key factors in bidding, but as one of a group of elements that are "more likely to be supporting rather than vital factors" (p. 317). Thus, they positioned communication as important in event bidding; however, they discussed communication from the perspective of providing contemporary technology for use in facilitating communication during the event.

This text, however, positions communication as the one key factor in successful bidding, because the event context is teeming with opportunities to advance the success of a bid with the use of written, verbal and visual communication. An ability to communicate underlies every task in the bid process and can therefore be a deciding factor in the success of a bid dossier, a bid tour and all other components in the bid process.

Communication is critical in a bid dossier. A dossier must clearly and succinctly express the intention to host and provide answers to a bid questionnaire. This document communicates the proposed plan for hosting an event. The level of planning detail communicated (level 1, 2 or 3) in the document can hinder or enhance the success of the articulated plans and can influence the interpretations concerning bid activities made by the bid commission members in their assessment. Depending on the event, a bid dossier may also require written communication in more than one language. An ability to clearly express the bid details and the subtle nuances of the bid in multiple languages is an opportunity to position the bid for success.

Communication is a critical factor in conducting a bid tour. A written operational plan for a bid tour explicates the activities to be conducted. In addition, verbal communication is used to aid the network members implementing the bid tour plans to clearly understand the tasks. Poor communication can impact the success of a bid tour, illustrating that communication is a critical factor.

Formal and informal verbal communication is a critical factor in a successful bid. Examples of formal verbal communication opportunities include structured meetings with the bid commission members to present the highlights of the bid, meetings with key stakeholders such as the key sponsors or venue managers, and meetings used to build relationships with the grassroots supporters such as volunteers, small businesses and organizations. Examples of informal verbal communication include casual conversations with the bid commission members evaluating the bid or with grassroots supporters of a bid. Each formal and informal communication opportunity can facilitate the transfer of knowledge concerning the bid or bid tour to all members in the bid network and to the bid commission members. Poor formal and informal communication can, from this viewpoint, profoundly impact the success of a bid.

Visual communication is also a critical factor in bid success. The inclusion of visual elements in presentations, such as the use of diagrams in the bid dossier, video presentations or fireworks in the bid tour, can enhance either the understandings of the bid detail or the enthusiasm for a bid. Visually communicating the bidder's message can have a significant impact on the success of a bid.

Communication technology is a critical factor in bid success. The use of the latest technology that allows for excellent verbal, written and visual communication can clearly demonstrate the host's ability to maximize the use of technology in the conduct of the event.

Communication is also an underlying critical factor in the majority of bid activities that go beyond the topics covered in this text. For example, the financial component of a bid relies on an ability to communicate facts and figures that will attest to the host's financial capacity to host the event successfully, with no negative long-term impact on the community following the event. Marketing and sponsorship in event bidding rely heavily on the ability to enticingly convey the opportunity to be a partner in the event as well as what marketing and sponsorship opportunities might be secured. Written, oral and visual communications, along with the communication technology, are all critical factors in the success of marketing and sponsorship proposals.

The bid process involves communicating to groups such as the network members, the potential sponsors and the bid commission members. Communication is the critical factor in event bidding and must be facilitated in a manner that enhances the overall bid effort. Your facilitation skills will be tested throughout the bid process. A focus on enhancing communication at all levels when facilitating an event bid is a critical factor for success.

CONCLUSION

Overall, this chapter has defined a feasibility study, candidature document, bid questionnaire, bid dossier and bid tour. The viewing of a number of candidature documents, bid submissions and bid questionnaires was encouraged to develop your common knowledge about the requirements of bidding. You can follow a variety of bids on the World Wide Web at www.gamesbids.com. The research literature discussed indicated that there is a complex array of critical factors for successful bids outlined in the literature. As well, it was indicated that environmental sustainability is a new key factor in bidding. Importantly, this text proposes that communication is the most critical factor for success in event bidding. Without a clear consensus, and the fact that each bid is unique, it is important for you to weigh the key factors to win a bid, to analyze the requirements and then to apply the factors based on your own conclusions.

CHAPTER QUESTIONS

1   Describe a feasibility study, a candidature document, a bid questionnaire and a bid dossier.
2   List at least five key elements of successful bidding that have been outlined in the literature.
3   Do you feel that concern for the natural environment should be part of the bid process? If so, how should the natural environment be safeguarded at events?
4   Do you agree with the author's assertion that communication is the one key factor in successful event bidding? If you disagree, say why. If you agree, explain how you see the ways in which communication can be utilized in the process of facilitating an event bid.

CHAPTER 11

POLITICS IN EVENT BIDDING AND HOSTING

TRISH CHANT-SEHL

This chapter focuses on the underlying political aspects of event bidding and hosting. Managing and mitigating the political aspects of events is a key skill for an event manager. It would be ideal if I could tell you how to manage each type of political situation. Because of the complexity of place, people and scenarios, however, this is not possible. To become a skilled political manager of events, you must develop knowledge and experience concerning where to expect political manoeuvres and how they could come into play, and then devise personalized management strategies based on personal knowledge and experience. To aid you in acquiring the foundational knowledge necessary to gain this skill, this chapter defines "politics"; applies the definition to bidding and event-hosting experiences; explains the role that politics plays through the event continuum in three distinct phases, including bidding, transition and review, and event hosting; examines scenarios; and offers some (hopefully) insightful ways in which the political effect can be mitigated. A case study in event bidding is included to guide the reader in developing personal insights concerning politics, and a series of questions are posted to encourage the reader to contemplate how they might choose to navigate the complex world of politics in event bidding and hosting.

WHAT IS MEANT BY "THE POLITICS OF EVENTS"?

It is not necessary to look far to discover numerous definitions for "politics." Many definitions include a connection to government and/or government policy. The Merriam-Webster dictionary (www.merriam-webster.com) defines politics as "3a: political affairs or business; *especially*: competition between competing interest groups or individuals for power and leadership"; and "5a: the total complex of relations between people living in society." In addition, Trevor Taylor defines politics as that which "involves matters of power, of control and of influence over people's behaviour" (Allison, 1986, p. 30). These definitions guide the discussion within this chapter. Therefore, "politics" is understood as encompassing the competing relationships and interests between individuals and groups, as well as the political environment as it relates to the event organization and/or government's interest.

POLITICS IN THE DECISION TO BID OR NOT TO BID

The world of event bidding is fraught with political agendas from the very beginning of the process. This is not surprising, given that bids are human initiatives. It is almost impossible to discern a time throughout the bid process when politics is not involved. From the moment that the idea to bid for a specific event is conceived, politics plays a role.

As the world of international event bidding becomes more sophisticated and costly, it is incumbent upon interested bidders to spend time and energy on assessing the "winnability" (the likelihood of their bid being successful) of a bid prior to formally launching a bid for a specific event. There are a number of items to consider when assessing a bid's winnability, many of which are political in nature. For example:

- Is there a competitor that is already being seen as the likely next host?
- Has your area or region recently hosted the same event, or an event of similar size and scale?
- Do you have the full support of the necessary levels of government or organizational bodies?
- Is there a regional rotation at play for the event?
- Have other interested cities previously bid for the same event and feel that it is their turn to host?
- Is there an influential champion for your bid and, just as importantly, for a competitor's bid?
- Who can influence the decision-making process?

These questions are important to ask and answer before making a final decision on whether or not to proceed with launching a formal bid. It is worth noting, however, that despite doing the due diligence on winnability, the outcome of a bid process is never certain, and political influences play a part in this uncertainty.

If the bidder's assessment of the winnability of their initiative is favourable, then it is time to proceed with completing the necessary bid requirements, as well as preparing for the inevitable politics that will now arise. It is imperative that the bidders accept the role that politics plays throughout the entire process and enter into the bid environment knowing that they must understand, navigate and mitigate the political aspects of bidding and hosting events. Consider strategies you could engage in to improve your knowledge and ability to manage politics in event management.

POLITICS IN THE EVENT BID PHASE: THE COMMITTEE

Before we delve into the politics involved within the bidding process, it is important to identify the governance structure for an event, whether it is an international, national or small-scale local event. The larger-scale events have formalized bid formats; however, smaller-scale events can have many governance structure options that range from there being no formal bid protocols to fairly well-established processes that mirror some international bid processes. For example, for some national events there is a regional rotation whereby it is known each year which region will host, but not which specific community or city. At the local and regional level, there may not be a formal bid process but rather expressions of interest by different leagues or communities. In these situations, the decision may be made by a staff representative, a committee or perhaps a board of directors.

For the purpose of this chapter, we are assuming that a national governing authority has endorsed a competitive bid process for an international event. Perhaps the easiest place to start when discussing the role of politics in this scenario is with the bid committee itself.

If you recall, the earlier definition of politics was "competition between competing interest groups or individuals," which situates politics within a bid committee. The determination of both who and what is represented on a bid committee is not an easy decision – and is open to political manoeuvring from those interested in serving on this committee. Large

214

events are seen as exciting to be a part of, as well as being thought of as potential once-in-a-lifetime opportunities. For these reasons, and many others, there are many people and organizations who want to be represented on a bid committee, to serve and/or to ensure that their opinions and interests are given due consideration. Oftentimes, the specific event program is not predetermined, and thus organizations see the bid phase as a significant opportunity to influence the inclusion of their focus within the program. Being represented on a bid committee is then considered an excellent means by which to achieve this objective. What criteria would you use to make selections?

In Senn's book *Power, Politics, and the Olympic Games* (1999), an excellent example of the politics involved in committee membership is presented. This example is focused on the International Olympic Committee (IOC) and not a particular bid committee, but is applicable. Senn indicated that

> with the inclusion of the [former] Soviet Union and the newly emerging countries of the Third World, the Committee came to tolerate a much more active role on the part of governments. It has also recognized that its members work basically in states, rather than regions. Although it still refuses to give a seat to every state, it makes an effort to represent the various parts of the world. It rejects thoughts that any country has the "right" to be represented or even the right to name its own representative; but it has often accepted official nominees. The Old Guard in the IOC long insisted that they were freely electing their colleagues, but in 1951, for example, when the Soviet Union demanded a seat and nominated its own candidate, the IOC simply yielded. In dealing with the United States, in contrast, it has shown considerably more independence in choosing its membership.
>
> (p. 7)

This example indicates that bid committee membership has been rife with political scenarios over the decades. Overall, when establishing a bid committee, it is important to remember that the goal of bidding is to win the right to host the event. This may seem like a simple point, but it is one that is often overlooked when community and event leaders and/or government representatives try to influence the committee membership. Pulling together a bid is a major undertaking and one that is usually done within a tight time frame. In short, there is a significant amount of work to be done. It is important that each bid committee member should be able to deliver value to the bid process.

This value includes the criteria of being able to provide guidance and oversight, as well as completing the work requirements. To mitigate some of the politics of membership on a bid committee, another criterion is to meet the necessary options for strategically placing individuals and groups to be engaged with the bid process without being named to the formal bid committee. The volume of work to be completed for a bid necessitates the development of subcommittees associated with a bid. Of key importance, however, is to weigh the placement of members who can complete the tasks and ensure the cooperation of subcommittees above the political appointments.

POLITICS IN THE EVENT BID PHASE: THE PROPOSAL

Despite the prescriptive nature of a national or international bid dossier, there are still many important decisions that a bid committee needs to make, and these are open to political manoeuvring. One particular item is the venue or facility. International events are often seen as a way in which a community can benefit from new facilities, including sport, recreational and tourism venues. The construction of new venues requires many questions to be answered. For instance:

- Where should the new facility be built?
- Who should own and operate the facility?
- Who will pay for ongoing facility maintenance?
- Who will have access to the facility?
- What type of amenities should be included in the new facility?
- Can locating facilities in a specific area of the city help further a political or community interest?

It is easy to see how politics can come into play when attempting to answer the questions posted. A recent example to illustrate this point is the 2012 Olympic Games, held in London. It was noted during the bid process that

> the BOA [British Olympic Association] refused to give up and had already won the support of the Mayor of London, Ken Livingstone,

216

provided the bid fulfilled his vision for transforming the desperately deprived East End and increased investment in the capital.

(Lee, 2006, p. 7)

The bid committee was, thus, open to political manoeuvring concerning social issues and not just concerned with the best construction of facilities for the staging of the event.

If facilities do not need to be constructed, the use of existing venues still poses some opportunities for political manoeuvring. For example, when existing facilities are utilized, decisions need to be made concerning a number of elements, such as:

- Which facilities will receive upgrades and/or renovations as part of their participation in the event?
- What level of service is the facility owner expected to provide for the event?
- Will a facility be compensated accordingly for the services?

These questions are important to consider during the bid phase to ensure that political issues are mitigated and that facility owners and operators have reasonable expectations of their participation within a bid, and ultimately as an event host.

Facility decisions are not the only ones for which politics comes into play during the proposal phase. Decisions around delegate accommodations require careful consideration and political savvy. For instance:

- Which hotel should be named as the "host hotel"?
- Who has priority access to the limited rooms available at the premier hotel?

In instances where an event has a cultural or festival component, there are many additional questions to answer, such as:

- Which cultural communities will be involved in the event?
- Who will speak at the opening ceremonies and/or formal dinners?

In the case of a large international sport or tourism event that attracts significant sponsorship dollars and television audiences, the politics involved is even more demanding. In this case, questions include:

- Who can be an event sponsor?
- Which broadcasting entity should be a partner?

Political manoeuvring in determining the answers to these questions requires careful attention.

POLITICS IN THE EVENT BID PHASE: THE DECISION MAKERS

In event bidding, perhaps the most likely example of politics stems from the decision-making process whereby people are responsible for making final decisions concerning the event. The Salt Lake City scandal surrounding the selection process for the 2002 Winter Olympic Games shone light on the political games of corruption and bribery inherent in the IOC bid process at the time. Significant reform has taken place within the IOC, and the bidding process is now more structured and transparent; however, the final decision still rests with individual IOC members. That is to say, the human element cannot be overlooked when it comes to decision making within a bid process. The IOC is not the only international governing body to utilize membership voting as the means by which it chooses the successful bid. The Commonwealth Games Federation (CGF) and the Pan American Sport Association (PASO) are two other examples of organizations that have their membership vote to determine a winning bid.

The IOC, as well as the CGF and PASO, have documented bid guidelines and protocols that must be adhered to by all bid candidates. There are, however, many opportunities for politics to come into play with both the voting delegates and bid committee members. In some instances, the politicking will fall outside the scope of the rules, and could be subject to disciplinary action by the governing body. In other scenarios, the politics at play are more subtle. A region or group of nations may plan to bid for the subsequent event and thus have a vested interest in where the current bid will be situated. Their votes may then have little to do with the quality of the bids, and more to do with geography and planning for their own future.

Another example of the politics within bidding is with the bid decision process itself – which typically is secretive in nature. Whether a bid is local or international in scope, if individuals are required to vote for one bid over another, then politics will come into play. Enthusiastic and hardworking bid teams will do their best to develop and present an excellent

218

bid package to the voting delegates. Each bid committee will do its best to convince the voters to choose its bid over its competitors'. If there is a secret ballot, there is no negative consequence for a voting delegate who pledges their support to all candidates, as it is never known who votes for which bid. This makes the bidding environment vulnerable to politically motivated activities such as voting delegates asking for special favours or bid committee representatives promising more than they can deliver.

In John Furlong's book *Patriot Hearts: Inside the Olympics That Changed a Country* (2011), the former CEO of the 2010 Vancouver Olympic and Paralympic Winter Games shares personal stories of his time with the Vancouver bid team and the host organizing committee. He supported the concept of potential politics in the voting strategy when he indicated his thoughts concerning his city's win for the rights to host. The fact that he mentions this scenario means that it was a political point of potential importance. His statement is as follows:

> I was surprised at how close the final vote was. Three votes. We were behind after round one but grabbed all of Austria's 16 votes to sneak by the Koreans 56–53. Scary close. Only a couple of other decisions in IOC history had been closer than ours – both those determined by one vote. There would be a lot of talk about the role geopolitics played in our victory. How European countries wanted the 2012 Summer Games, so were not going to vote for a European city to win the 2010 Games. I never put much stock in that theory.
>
> (p. 75)

It does not need to be a large event for this type of politics to come into play. Small and medium-sized events also have to manoeuvre through the politics from some of the decision makers.

POLITICS IN THE EVENT BID TRANSITION AND REVIEW PHASE

Eventually, decision day will arrive and one city's bid will be selected, making it the next host city for the event. After months, and sometimes years, of hard work, the bid process is complete. Now what? Depending on the outcome of the specific bid, the next steps are very different. Next steps for unsuccessful bids include financial reconciliation, closing down the bid office, file storage and documentation, filing of any necessary legal paperwork, the bid committee post-mortem and the writing of a final report. In view of the time, money and resources put into bidding for events, it is not surprising to see politics at play even after a bid has been lost. There can be a tendency for blame and second-guessing of decisions that were made during the bid process. How would you manage these types of political situations? It is important that the bid team takes time to evaluate the bid process and document areas in need of improvement and general thoughts on why the bid was not successful. This type of analysis and documentation will be an asset for future bid committees. This falls within the transfer of knowledge concept and should be common practice for all bid processes – win or lose.

For those bid committees fortunate enough to win the bid competition and have their city named as the next host city, the next steps and the politicking can be daunting. Transitioning from a bid committee to a host organizing committee can be very stressful, given that few people have had an opportunity to be involved in such a complex undertaking. For larger, international events, the bid committee is usually well structured, with full-time staff, office space, formalized policies and procedures as well as financial and legal accountabilities. Small and medium-sized events, though, do not generally get away without having to deal with bid transition politics.

The bid committee is now no longer needed and a host organizing committee is required to take its place. While the bid committee is winding down and the transition team is planning for the future host committee, there is an expectation that work continues with planning for the event. This is a key challenge as there is no shortage of politics at play concerning who is leading the process. Interested candidates may campaign strongly, and publicly, for their preferred position within the new host organizing committee structure. Individuals who may have been colleagues on the bid committee may now be adversaries in competing for a specific position on the organizing committee. Leaders within key stakeholder groups, including governments, who have significant interests in the success of an event may try to wield their influence over the decision-making process.

The composition of the new organizing committee is not the only forum where politics plays a role in the transition and planning phase of an event. Perhaps one of the most politically charged tasks within any event planning process is the final determination of the venue plan. Although bid dossiers are required to include full details on all venues, once a bid is won the host committee has an opportunity to revisit the original plans.

Despite everyone's best efforts at planning during the bid phase, there will inevitably be changes once a bid has been won. These changes happen for reasons such as a change in government officials or priorities, revisited cost estimates, a change in the program and issues with land acquisition, or pressure from the public or other special interest groups.

Changes in government will happen, and neither bid committees nor host committees can control these changes. A particular change could have a positive effect on the event in the form, say, of available office space or personnel secondments. Or it could have a negative effect, such as a demand to change a venue location. For example, a new ward councillor may not support a bid plan for the construction of a new building in their ward and may publicly campaign for a move to a different site within a city. This type of discussion opens the door for political jockeying as other ward councillors, landowners, neighbourhood associations and busi-nesses begin to lobby the organizing committee for their preferred site. Further, there are compounding effects on the event plans, as delays in site selection can result in increased construction costs due to shortened time-lines and later-than-anticipated opening of the venue, resulting in less time for testing of the venue and its systems for the event.

What additional political scenarios can you envision for the transition phase of an event in which you may be involved?

Host organizing committees will be faced with significant change through-out the planning process, some of which will be political in nature. The key for any committee is how its members choose to deal with the politics. This will be discussed again later in this chapter.

POLITICS IN THE EVENT HOSTING PHASE

This chapter has discussed the politics evident throughout the bid phase and the transition phase of planning an event. Given the amount of time spent on these activities, it is not surprising that politics plays a more significant role in the lead-up to the hosting of an event than during the actual event hosting period. Events can last for one day or longer, such as tourism events that last up to 30 days; regardless, the hosting time frame is dramatically less than the time taken to bid and to plan. As a result, there are fewer opportunities for politics to come into play. The event production time period, however, is not exempt from political manoeuvring.

One area where politics may come into play is with the very important persons (VIPs) attending the event. These VIPs could be government officials, sponsors or media or other organizational representatives. Some events will have established protocols for VIP management, while others will not. Regardless, VIPs may have unrealistic expectations of the event organizers and can use their influence and strong connections to the event to try to get what they want. The event management team members need to pay careful attention as to how they handle this group of individuals. VIPs may engage in politics by trying to use their influence to obtain free tickets to the event, or merchandise, or to participate in ceremonies. Ensuring a sense of fairness for all VIPs is an important task for the event management team.

In addition to recognized VIPs, there may be individuals who believe they should be considered VIPs, and should be entitled to special treatment. These types of requests may seem like minor headaches. However, how an organizer deals with them can have an impact on the success of an event, as their sharing of negative perceptions with the public and others can have a significant impact. It is, thus, important for event organizers to anticipate these types of scenarios during the planning process, and to have planned messaging in place prior to being confronted with the reality.

Another example of how politics can come into play at events involves the performers. Organizations and advocates may use the performers as a vehicle to lobby for additional funding. For instance, if a performer gains a high level of success, government funders may utilize the publicity as a demonstration of their government's commitment to and support of the program, or a group may use it to promote their next bid and hosting initiative.

OVERCOMING POLITICS IN EVENT BIDDING

This chapter has examined how politics plays a role in the bidding for and hosting of events. A range of examples have been provided within the three distinct phases: bidding, transition and planning, and event hosting. Understanding the role that politics can play in bidding and hosting is important, and learning how to be successful in spite of the politics

222

is critical. It is naïve to believe that event bidding and hosting can occur without politics coming into play, given the working definition we have been using, with politics as "the total complex of relations between people living in society," according to the Merriam-Webster definition.

It is proposed, then, that eliminating politics from the bidding and hosting process is impossible. Thus, having the skill to deal with the politics effectively is important.

A key factor in managing event politics: consistent communication messaging

Consistent communication is the first tenet for successfully dealing with the politics involved in the bidding and hosting experience. One of the reasons why people and organizations engage in politics is because this type of activity can yield their desired result even if it is not in the original bid or event plans. Oftentimes, this success is achieved because of a lack of consistency within the messaging, or in understanding what the committee or organization is trying to achieve. This provides opportunities for political manoeuvring by outside groups or individuals who exploit the inconsistency in communication.

Bid committee and event hosts need to spend time developing their vision for the event, and the strategy by which they plan to fulfill the vision. They must spend time as a team ensuring that all members of their respective organizations understand what they are trying to achieve and how they plan to get there. Doing so requires consistent communication within the entire bid team, as well as the external stakeholders. Communication not only needs to be consistent over time, but also must be honest, open and transparent, and two-way, to allow for feedback and questioning.

A key factor in managing event politics: establishing core values

The second tenet for successfully dealing with the politics of bidding and hosting is the establishment of core values. One of the first steps that a small or large event bid or host committee should take is to identify what their core values are, and commit to having their values guide their decision making and their actions. Examples of these values include promoting and encouraging diverse participation; a commitment to develop competencies, leadership and personal development; contributing positively to the tourism, sport and recreation industries; developing and advancing mutually beneficial partnerships; and behaving ethically and with integrity. It is often difficult, however, to abide by the values when it is close to bid decision day and a political manoeuvre or the promise of a vote in return for a favour is presented.

The leadership of an event bid must clearly articulate the importance of their organization's values and ensure that they will lead by example in demonstrating the values in each and every decision. The values must be more than a poster on the wall in the lunch room, and all team members must ensure that their behaviours are reflective of the values in their everyday work. A good question to ask when in a difficult situation is: would you be comfortable if this decision or action was on the front page of the newspaper? This is an effective way to remind yourself of the importance of being true to the values that are important to you and your team. It is much easier to deal with the politics involved in the bidding and hosting process when you have a strong set of values to help navigate your way through the murky waters of political manoeuvring.

The only way to develop management skills for politics in event bidding and hosting is to develop understandings of the types of political manoeuvres that can come into play and to practise considering potential responses. Figure 11.1 offers a case study for you to read in small groups, to consider different potential responses and to determine the impact of each response on a bid and, ultimately, on the hosting of the event.

CONCLUSIONS

This chapter examined the role of politics in both event bidding and hosting. The notion of politics has been defined, and broken into three phases for discussion. First, the bidding phase was explored. It included the initial assessment concerning whether or not to bid for a specific event, the bid committee competition, development of the bid proposal and the decision makers involved in determining the successful bid. Second, the transition and planning phase between bidding and hosting was discussed, followed by the event hosting period. Finally, two key tenets for dealing with the politics of bidding and hosting were noted. The first factor, consistent communication, supports the work of Mallen and Adams (2008), which also promoted communication as a key element in

224

Read the scenario below and consider the questions posed at the end.

ABC Bid Committee had been working on their bid proposal for the 74th International Multisport Games for nineteen months and were ready to do the final review before sending it to print. The bid dossier was over 250 pages long and covered all of the required components for bidding. The Bid Committee had worked tirelessly to put together a sport and venue plan that would appeal to the voting delegates, yet still provide a meaningful legacy for the community. The jewel of their bid was a world-class basketball and volleyball facility with an adjacent indoor football pitch that was to be built in an economically depressed area of the city. The Bid Committee had the support of both the local and the regional elected officials to construct the arena complex on the desired site. As a courtesy, the Bid CEO had agreed to share the bid dossier with the local, regional and national sport organizations for basketball, volleyball and football before sending the final version to print. The day after sending the final version of the bid dossier to these officials for review, the Bid CEO received a call from one of the national offices demanding that the seating for the facility be expanded by 5,000 seats in order to accommodate plans for a future professional league. This national office noted that their president was an influential member of the executive committee of the Multisport Games organization during the call. The addition of 5,000 seats to the facility had significant financial implications, as well as a major impact on the amount of land needed, and the relationship with the proposed adjoining indoor football pitch.

Questions:

1 Describe the politics at play in the above scenario.
2 If you were the Bid Committee CEO, what would you do in response to the official's telephone call to increase the seating capacity by 5,000 seats?
3 Identify the actions that could have been taken to prevent the official from making such a demand of the bid committee.
4 On the basis of the information outlined in this chapter, do you feel that politics in event bidding and hosting can have a positive impact on the process?

Figure 11.1 Case study assignment in event bid politics

successful bidding. The second factor was the establishment of core values. Overall, the discussion in this chapter underscores that it is crucial that event managers develop their understandings and abilities to become skilful at dealing with event politics.

CHAPTER QUESTIONS

1 Select a major event that has been held in your area and record the event name and host site. Next, record five potential political scenarios

that could arise during the bidding phase to gain the rights to host this event. What strategies could be used to mitigate or reduce the severity of each political situation?

2 Consider the same event selected in question 1. Suppose that you have now been awarded the right to host this event. What complexity could you expect as you transition to set up the hosting of the event? List five potential political scenarios that you could face and detail how you would deal with each.

3 Again, for the same event selected in question 1, you are now in the hosting phase. What five political manoeuvres could arise and how would you mitigate and manage these issues?

CHAPTER 12

CONCLUSIONS

LORNE J. ADAMS

Event management – it sounds finite. It sounds like a discrete point in time. Indeed, it has a beginning and an end point, but event management is certainly not static. It is best to view events as dynamic, complex and ever-changing entities. No two events are the same; what worked in one situation may not necessarily work in a different but similar situation. That is why this text does not provide you with a series of prescribed checklists that you can simply mark off as you go along. While checklists are helpful, they are static and do not – cannot – take into account every contingency that you will have to deal with. We have spent some time introducing you to some theories that support the notions of change, contingency and complexity. We suggest that you do some further reading in that area. A sound theoretical framework will provide you with an anticipatory set that will help you deal with deviation and the inevitable unforeseen issues. In fact, a message that we have delivered is the need for anticipation in the short term and anticipation in the long term. As a critical element in the dynamic system of event management, you should now understand that anything you do has the potential to affect many other things. Some of those outcomes will be positive, others will create unforeseen outcomes.

We have also stressed the importance of setting goals and writing them with clarity. Goals need to be communicated clearly to everyone involved. The less clarity, the greater the chance for misinterpretation, and we want everyone to be on the same page and heading in the same direction. You will note throughout the text how often the need for clear goals is expressed both directly and indirectly.

We also have spent a good deal of time talking about planning, and committing that planning to paper. You should be aware that planning exists on a continuum, with over-planning and under-planning as polar opposites. The more uncertain we are, the greater the tendency to over-plan. The concrete act of planning can become a trap; it can become an end in itself. Immersing yourself in the process feels good, it feels as though you are actively involved in problem solving and it produces a highly detailed, visible product: the plan of the event. The more certain we are about an event, perhaps by having done it a number of times, the greater the tendency to under-plan. You know what to do because you've been there before, or "this is the way it has always been done." Unfortunately, this approach leads to many assumptions about, for instance, who is responsible for what, or what needs to be done. Because the plan is unstated, the chance for oversight or misinterpretation increases dramatically.

Somewhere between these polar extremes is the amount of planning that is right, not only for the event but also for the people involved. Where is that magic place that is not too much and not too little? Unfortunately, there is no way of prescribing where that might be. It is, as we have referred to, in those indeterminate zones (Schön, 1983) that go beyond simply what you have been taught. Experience will help you find that place. As an emerging professional, take the opportunity to volunteer at different events and to do as many different jobs as you can. As you begin to see events from different perspectives, you will see how written plans affect your particular function. You will then be developing "event sense," in the same way as experiences in the lived world help you develop common sense. You will learn that there are very few absolutes either in life or in event management. There are lots of instances of "sometimes," "in many cases," "in general," "based on my experience." You will see the need for establishing priorities but will also come to understand that priorities too can change. You have probably already experienced that as part of your academic journey. Ask yourself whether your priorities are the same now as when you first entered university. In fact, you could look at getting a degree as personal event management. Goals, plans, priorities are all important but subject to change and deviation. Many things can cause change, and they all can provide different effects. You have had to manage all those things in the pursuit of your degree and probably have been fairly successful thus far.

We have also pointed out the need to analyze events. It is essential to analyze errors: where they might have come from, what processes were in place that set the stage for their occurrence, and so forth. At some point in time, you will accept your own fallibility – that sometimes errors are a direct result of our own action or inaction; that we tend to court disaster in our own unique ways through prior experience, bias or ability. Error, however, is only a small part of the overarching need for evaluation. Once again, though, evaluation needs to be placed in context. For what purpose, to what end, is evaluation being conducted? What is or should be evaluated? These questions have been posed in previous pages, and we have tried to give you a reasonable starting point to answer them.

We live in a dynamic, changing world and we now recognize that what we do in the name of event management can have long-lasting, indeed permanent, effects on our most valuable resource: the environment we live in. It is essential that we consider carefully what these impacts might be and how they might be mitigated. While it might seem that this is just one more thing to consider, concern for the environment is now a central focus for event organizers, hosts and the communities that are potentially impacted. The chapter on environmental sustainability should provide you with a sense of the reach events can have and also how you might manage some of the responsibilities that ensue.

Event management is a human initiative with many interested stakeholders, both within and outside of the event management team. Not everyone has the same agenda, and indeed there may even be some opposition to what you are trying to accomplish. Trying to navigate your way through and around some of these political issues will challenge you as an event manager. While some of the "politics" can be anticipated readily, some other political concerns can be far less obvious and require an anticipatory set, or that you "read" the situation properly. It is a skill set that will be developed over time as you increase your base of knowledge and experience.

Finally, you will note that many of the examples that we have used pertain to big events, such as the Olympic Games or other major attractions. These examples clearly provide information about the multilevel detail and advanced preparation required to host these spectacles successfully. It would be a mistake, however, to conclude that events on a much smaller scale require little thought and would not benefit from the processes described in this text. From a charity dance to a banquet or to a small golf tournament, the process is the same; only the scale differs. We are confident what you have been provided with will equip you to be a successful event manager.

Many different authors have tried to bring to bear their experience and to condense a vast amount of knowledge into manageable and useful sketches that will help you develop the tools to be a successful event manager. None of the chapters is intended to be conclusive. We have recommended throughout the text that you continue to read in the several areas – to develop common knowledge that will help you develop advanced knowledge. Some of the chapters will seem as though they are speaking directly to you: they will resonate with your experience, skills and present abilities. Some of the chapters you will struggle with. They will take you outside the comfort zone of your present skills and abilities. This is the place you want to be; it is where the most development will take place. Spend time with these chapters until you are comfortable, and then seek out the next place of discomfort. We have mentioned in several places that events will grow and evolve – and so will you. If the previous pages have been or can be an agent in that evolution, we have done our job.

REFERENCES

1 TRADITIONAL AND NICHE EVENTS IN SPORT, RECREATION AND TOURISM

Bell, D. (1973). *The coming of post-industrial society*. New York: Basic Books.

Choo, C. W., & Bontis, N. (Eds.). (2002). *The strategic management of intellectual capital and organizational knowledge*. New York: Oxford University Press.

Cobb, P., Confrey, J., diSessa, A., Lehrer, R., & Schauble, L. (2003). Design experiments in educational research. *Educational Researcher, 32* (1), 9–13.

Gallagher, W. (2012). *New: Understanding our need for novelty and change*. New York: Penguin Press.

Hirschhorn, L. (1984). *Beyond mechanization: Work and technology in a postindustrial age*. Cambridge, MA: MIT Press.

Homer-Dixon, T. (2001). *The ingenuity gap: Can we solve the problems of the future?* Toronto: Vintage Canada.

Jensen, R. (1999). *The dream society: How the coming shift from information to imagination will transform your business*. New York: McGraw-Hill.

Limerick, D., Cunnington, B., & Crowther, F. (1998). *Managing the new organisation: Collaboration and sustainability in the post-corporate world* (2nd ed.). Sydney: Business and Professional Publishing.

Sproull, L., & Kiesler, S. (1991). *Connections: New ways of working in the networked organization*. Cambridge, MA: MIT Press.

Zuboff, S. (1988). *In the age of the smart machine: The future of work and power*. New York: Basic Books.

2 THE CONCEPT OF KNOWLEDGE IN EVENT MANAGEMENT

Bell, D. (1973). *The coming of post-industrial society: A venture in social forecasting*. New York: Basic Books.

Blackler, F. (1995). Knowledge, knowledge work and organizations: An overview and interpretation. *Organization Studies, 16* (6), 1021–1046.

Boisot, M. (2002). The creation and sharing of knowledge. In C. W. Choo & N. Bontis (Eds.), *The strategic management of intellectual capital and organizational knowledge* (pp. 65–77). New York: Oxford University Press.

Carney, M. (2001). The development of a model to manage change: Reflection on a critical incident in a focus group setting: An innovative approach. *Journal of Nursing Management, 8* (5), 3–9.

Castells, M. (2000). Toward a sociology of the network society. *Contemporary Sociology, 29* (5), 693–699.

Collins, H. (1993). The structure of knowledge. *Social Research, 60*, 95–116.

Conner, K., & Prahalad, C. K. (2002). A resource-based theory of the firm: Knowledge versus opportunism. In C. W. Choo & N. Bontis (Eds.), *The strategic management of intellectual capital and organizational knowledge* (pp. 103–131). New York: Oxford University Press.

Drucker, P. (1994). The age of social transformation. *Atlantic Monthly, 275* (5), 53–80.

Edvinsson, L., & Malone, M. S. (1997*). Intellectual capital: Realizing your company's true value by finding its hidden brainpower.* New York: HarperBusiness.

English, M. J., & Baker, W. H., Jr. (2006). *Winning the knowledge transfer race.* New York: McGraw-Hill.

Grant, R. M. (1996). Prospering in dynamically competitive environments: Organizational capability as knowledge integration. *Organization Science, 7*, 375–387.

Gupta, A., & MacDaniel, J. (2002). Creating competitive advantage by effectively managing knowledge: A framework for knowledge management. *Journal of Knowledge Management Practice, 3* (2), 40–49.

Hall, H. (2001). Input-friendliness: Motivating knowledge sharing across intranets. *Journal of Information Science, 27* (3), 139–146.

Harris, L., Coles, A.-M., & Dickson, K. (2000). Building innovation networks: Issues of strategy and expertise. *Technology Analysis and Strategic Management, 12* (2), 229–241.

Kogut, B., & Zander, U. (1992). Knowledge of the firm, combinative capabilities, and the replication of technology. *Organization Science, 3* (3), 383–397.

Krogh, G. von, and Grand, S. (2002). From economic theory toward a knowledge-based theory of the firm. In C. W. Choo & N. Bontis (Eds.), *The strategic management of intellectual capital and organizational knowledge: Conceptual building blocks* (pp. 163–184). New York: Oxford University Press.

Leonard, D., & Sensiper, S. (2002). The role of tacit knowledge in group innovation. In C. W. Choo & N. Bontis (Eds.), *The strategic management of intellectual capital and organizational knowledge* (pp. 485–499). New York: Oxford University Press.

Nelson, R. R., & Winter, S. G. (1982). *An evolutionary theory of economic change.* Cambridge, MA: Belknap.

Nonaka, I., & Takeuchi, H. (1995). *The knowledge-creating company: How Japanese companies create the dynamics of innovation.* New York: Oxford University Press.

Nonaka, I., Toyama, R., & Konno, N. (2000). SECI, *ba* and leadership: A unified model of dynamic knowledge creation. *Long Range Planning, 33*, 5–35.

232

Schorr, L. B. (1997). *Common purpose: Strengthening families and neighborhoods to rebuild America.* New York: Doubleday, Anchor Books.

Spender, J.-C. (1996). Making knowledge the basis of a dynamic theory of the firm. *Strategic Management Journal, 17* (S2), 445–462.

Spender, J.-C. (2002). Knowledge management, uncertainty, and the emergent theory of the firm. In C. W. Choo & N. Bontis (Eds.), *The strategic management of intellectual capital and organizational knowledge: Conceptual building blocks* (pp. 149–162). New York: Oxford University Press.

Winter, S. G. (1987). Knowledge and competence as strategic assets. In D. J. Teece (Ed.), *The competitive challenge: Strategies of industrial innovations and renewal* (pp. 159–184). Cambridge, MA: Ballin.

Zack, M. H. (1999). Developing a knowledge strategy. *California Management Review, 41* (3), 125–145.

3 THE EVENT PLANNING MODEL: THE EVENT DEVELOPMENT PHASE, PART I

Bens, I. (2000). *Facilitating with ease! A step-by-step guidebook.* San Francisco: Jossey-Bass.

Drucker, P. (1946). *Concept of the corporation.* New York: John Day.

Greenberg, J. (2002). *Managing behaviour in organizations.* Upper Saddle River, NJ: Prentice Hall.

Kilmann, R. H., Pondy, L. R., & Slevin, D. P. (Eds.) (1976). *The management of organization design*, Vol. 1: *Strategies and implementation.* New York: North-Holland.

Laird, D. (1985). *Approaches to training and development.* Reading, MA: Addison-Wesley.

Lambert, V., & Glacken, M. (2005). Clinical education facilitators: A literature review. *Journal of Clinical Nursing, 14*, 664–673.

Peel, D. (2000). The teacher and town planner as facilitator. *Innovations in Education and Training International, 37* (4), 372–380.

Rogers, C., & Freiberg, H. J. (1994). *Freedom to learn* (3rd ed.). New York: Charles E. Merrill.

Sawyer, K. R. (2006). Group creativity: Musical performance and collaboration. *Psychology of Music, 34* (2), 148–165.

Scribd.com. (2012). The Olympics in London 2012. Retrieved from http://www.scribd.com/doc/16208292/The-Olympics-in-London-2012

Slack, T., & Parent, M. M. (2006). *Understanding sport organizations: The application of organization theory* (2nd ed.). Champaign, IL: Human Kinetics.

Thomas, G. (2004). A typology of approaches to facilitator education. *Journal of Experiential Education, 27* (2), 123–140.

Vancouver 2010 (2007). *Organizing committee.* Retrieved May 25, 2007 from: http://www.vancouver2010.com/en/OrganizingCommittee

Vidal, R. (2004). The vision conference: Facilitating creative processes. *Systemic Practice and Action Research, 17* (5), 385–405.

4 THE EVENT PLANNING MODEL: THE EVENT DEVELOPMENT PHASE, PART II

Bain, L. L. (1990). Critical analysis of the hidden curriculum in physical education. In D. Kirk & R. Tinning (Eds.), *Physical education, curriculum and culture: Critical issues in the contemporary crisis* (pp. 23–42). London: Falmer Press.

Canadian Survey of Giving, Volunteering and Participating. (2010). Retrieved from http://www.statcan.gc.ca/daily-quotidien/120321/dq120321a-eng.htm.

Graff, L. (1997). Excerpted from *By definition: Policies for volunteer management.* Graff & Associates.

Hager, M. A., & Brudney, J. L. (2004a). *Volunteer management practices and retention of volunteers.* The Urban Institute. Retrieved from http://www.nationalservice.gov/pdf/Management_Brief.pdf

Hager, M. A., & Brudney, J. L. (2004b). *Balancing act: The challenges and benefits of volunteers.* The Urban Institute. Retrieved from http://www.urban.org/uploadedpdf/411125_balancing_act.pdf

Kotler, P., & Lee, N. (2005). *Corporate social responsibility: Doing the most good for your company and your cause.* Hoboken, NJ: John Wiley.

Lanigan, R. L. (1988). *Phenomenology of communication: Merleau-Ponty's thematics in communicology and semiology.* Pittsburgh, PA: Duquesne Press.

Lanigan, R. L. (1992). *The human science of communicology: A phenomenology of discourse in Foucault and Merleau-Ponty.* Pittsburgh, PA: Duquesne University Press.

Merleau-Ponty, M. (1962). *Phenomenology of perception,* C. Smith, Trans. London: Routledge & Kegan Paul.

Merrill & Associates. (2006, November). *Five emerging patterns of volunteerism.* CharityVillage.com. Retrieved from https://charityvillage.com/Content.aspx?topic=five_emerging_patterns_of_volunteerism&last=166

Penner, M. (2002). *Coping with change.* CharityVillage.com. Retrieved from http://www.charityvillage.com/cv/research/rvol39.html

Quirk, M. (2009). *14 steps to develop a top-notch volunteer program.* Charity Village.com. Retrieved from http://www.charityvillage.com/cv/research/rvol62.html.

Volunteer Canada. (2006a). About volunteerism. Retrieved from http://volunteer.ca/about-volunteerism

Volunteer Canada. (2006b). The Canadian code for volunteer involvement. Retrieved from http://www.volunteer.ca/files/CodeEng.pdf

Volunteer Canada. (2006c). *The Canadian code for volunteer involvement: An audit tool.* Retrieved from http://volunteer.ca/files/ManagementAuditEng.pdf

Webster's new collegiate dictionary. (1985). Markham, ON: Thomas Allen.

Wendell, S. (1996). *The rejected body: Feminist philosophical reflections on disability.* New York: Routledge.

5 THE EVENT PLANNING MODEL: THE EVENT OPERATIONAL PLANNING PHASE

Bowen, H. (2006, February). *The Salt Lake organizing committee: 2002 Olympics*. Boston: Harvard Business School Publishing.

Doherty, N., & Delener, N. (2001). Chaos theory: Marketing and management implications. *Journal of Marketing Theory and Practice, 9* (4), 66–75.

Eisenhardt, M. K. (1989). Agency theory: An assessment and review. *The Academy of Management Review, 14* (1), 57–74.

Grant, R. (2001). The knowledge-based view of the firm. In C. W. Choo & N. Bontis (Eds.), *The strategic management of intellectual capital and organizational knowledge* (pp. 133–148). New York: Oxford University Press.

Keirsey, D. (2003). *Existence itself: Towards the phenomenology of massive dissipative/replicative structures*. Retrieved May 27, 2003 from http://edgeof order.org/pofdisstruct.html

Matusik, S. F. (2002). Managing public and private firm knowledge within the context of flexible firm boundaries. In C. W. Choo & N. Bontis (Eds.), *The strategic management of intellectual capital and organizational knowledge*. New York: Oxford University Press.

Owen, R. G. (2001). *Organizational behavior in education*. Boston: Allyn & Bacon.

Stacey, R. D. (1996). *Complexity and creativity in organizations*. San Francisco: Berrett-Koehler.

Wijngaard, J., & de Vries, J. (2006). Performers and performance: How to investigate the contribution of the operational network to operational performance. *International Journal of Operations and Production Management, 26*, 394–411.

6 THE EVENT PLANNING MODEL: THE EVENT IMPLEMENTATION, MONITORING AND MANAGEMENT PHASE

Buchanan, L., & O'Connell, A. (2006, January). A brief history of decision making. *Harvard Business Review*, 32–41.

Dörner, D. (1996). *The logic of failure: Recognizing and avoiding error in complex situations*, R. Kimber & R. Kimber, Trans. Cambridge, MA: Perseus Books.

Garvin, D. A., & Roberto, M. A. (2001, October 15). What you don't know about making decisions. *Harvard Business Review*, pp. 1–8.

How to stay on course: Sensing and responding to deviations from plan. (2006). *Harvard Business School Press*, 1–19.

Keeping on track: Maintaining control. (2004, February 18). *Harvard Business Review*.

Konijnendijk, P. A. (1994). Coordinating marketing and manufacturing in ETO companies. *International Journal of Production Economics, 37*, 19–26.

Mallen, C. (2006). Rethinking pedagogy for the times: A change infusion pedagogy. Unpublished Ed.D. dissertation, University of Southern Queensland, Toowoomba, Australia.

Mintzberg, H., Raisinghani, D., & Theoret, A. (1976). The structure of "unstructured" decision processes. *Administrative Science Quarterly, 21* (2), 246–275.

Schön, D. (1983). *The reflective practitioner: How professionals think in action.* London: Temple Smith.

Wijngaard, J., & de Vries, J. (2006). Performers and performance: How to investigate the contribution of the operational network to operational performance. *International Journal of Operations and Production Management, 26,* 394–411.

7 THE EVENT PLANNING MODEL: THE EVENT EVALUATION AND RENEWAL PHASE

Chelimsky, E. (1997). The coming transformations in evaluation. In E. Chelimsky & W. R. Shadish (Eds.), *Evaluation for the 21st century: A handbook* (pp. 1–26). Thousand Oaks, CA: Sage.

Dudley, J. R. (2009). Crafting goals and objectives. In J. R. Dudley, *Social Work Evaluation: Enhancing What We Do* (pp. 138–156). Chicago: Lyceum Books. Retrieved from http://lyceumbooks.com/pdf/Social_Work_Eval_Chapter_07.pdf

Erwin, T. D. (1993). Outcomes assessment. In M. J. Barr & Associates, *The handbook of student affairs administration.* San Francisco: Jossey-Bass.

Fetterman, D. M., Kaftarian, S. J., & Wandersman, A. (Eds.). (1996). *Empowerment evaluation: Knowledge and tools for self-assessment and accountability.* Thousand Oaks, CA: Sage.

Getz, D. (1997). *Event management and event tourism.* Elmsford, NY: Cognizant Communication Corporation.

Gotlieb, L. (2011). *Evaluation: Your tool for success.* Retrieved from http://www.charityvillage.com/cv/resureach/rvol84.html

Henderson, K. A., & Bialeschki, M. D. (2002). *Evaluating leisure services: Making enlightened decisions.* State College, PA: Venture Publishing.

Isaac, S., & Michael, W. (1981). *Handbook in research and evaluation.* San Diego, CA: Edits.

Jones, G., George, J., & Langton, N. (2005). *Essentials of contemporary management* (1st Canadian ed.). Toronto: McGraw-Hill.

McDavid, J. C., & Hawthorn, L. (2006). *Program evaluation and performance measurement: An introduction to practice.* Thousand Oaks, CA: Sage.

Rossi, P. H., Lipsey, M. W., & Freeman, H. E. (2004). *Evaluation: A systematic approach* (7th ed.). Thousand Oaks, CA: Sage.

Rossman, J. R., & Schlatter, B. E. (2003). *Recreation programming: Designing leisure experiences* (4th ed.). Champaign, IL: Sagamore.

Schuh, J., & Upcraft, M. L. (1998, November–December). Facts and myths about assessment in student affairs. *About Campus,* 2–8.

Scriven, M. (1972). Pros and cons about goal-free evaluation. *Evaluation Comment, 3,* 1–7.

Stake, R. E. (1975). *Evaluating the arts in education: A responsive approach.* Columbus, OH: Merrill.

Stufflebeam, D. L. (1971). The relevance of the CIPP evaluation model for educational accountability. *Journal of Research and Development in Education, 5,* 19–25.

Worthen, B. R., Sanders, J. R., & Fitzpatrick, J. L. (1997). *Program evaluation: Alternative approaches and practical guidelines* (2nd ed.). White Plains, NY: Longman.

8 SAFEGUARDING THE NATURAL ENVIRONMENT IN EVENT MANAGEMENT

Alexander, J. (2007). Environmental sustainability versus profit maximization: Overcoming systemic constraints on implementing normatively preferable alternatives. *Journal of Business Ethics, 76* (2), 155–162.

Barrett, J., & Scott, A. (2001). The ecological footprint: A metric for corporate sustainability. *Corporate Environmental Strategy, 8* (4), 316–325.

Cantelon, H., & Letters, M. (2000). The making of the IOC environmental policy as the third dimension of the Olympic Movement. *International Review for the Sociology of Sport, 35* (3), 294–308.

Collins, A., Jones, C., & Munday, M. (2009). Assessing the environmental impacts of mega sporting events: Two options? *Tourism Management, 30* (6), 828–837.

Collins, A., Flynn, A., Munday, M., & Roberts, A. (2007). Assessing the environmental consequences of major sporting events: The 2003/04 FA Cup Final. *Urban Studies, 44* (3), 457–476.

Fédération Internationale de Football Association (FIFA). (2006). *Green goal – Environmental goals for the 2006 FIFA World Cup.* Öko-Institut e.V., Institute for Applied Ecology, Berlin. Retrieved from http://www.oeko.de/oekodoc/169/2003-044-en.pdf

Finnveden, G., Hauschild, M. Z., Ekvall, T., Guinée, J., Heijungs, R., Hellweg, S., & Suh, S. (2009). Recent developments in life cycle assessment. *Journal of Environmental Management, 91* (1), 1–21.

Government of Canada. (2010). *Fifth National Communication on Climate Change.*

Hollender, J., & Breen, B. (2010). *The responsibility revolution: How the next generation of businesses will win.* San Francisco: Jossey-Bass.

Hums, M. A. (2010). The conscience and commerce of sport management: One teacher's perspective. *Journal of Sport Management, 24*, 1–9.

Ingebrigtsen, S., & Jakobsen, O. D. (2006, November/December). Environment and profitability in the reprocessing of paper in Norway: Contradictory research reports in the context of circulation economics. *Business Strategy and the Environment, 15* (6), 389–401.

IPCC. (2007). *IPCC Fourth Assessment Synthesis Report: Climate Change 2007.* Cambridge: Cambridge University Press.

ISO. (2006). *ISO 14044:2006 Environmental management – Life cycle assessment – Requirements and guidelines* (First.). Geneva, Switzerland: ISO. Retrieved from http://www.iso.org/iso/catalogue_detail?csnumber=38498

Jolliet, O., Margni, M., Charles, R., Humbert, S., Payet, J., Rebitzer, G., & Rosenbaum, R. (2003). IMPACT 2002+: A new life cycle impact assessment methodology. *International Journal of Life Cycle Assessment, 8* (6), 324–330.

Jones, C. (2008). Assessing the impact of a major sporting event: The role of environmental accounting. *Tourism Economics, 14* (2), 343–360.

Jones, M. (2011, Spring). Sustainable event management, ISO 20121. *The Business of International Events.* Retrieved from http://sustainable-event-alliance.org/wp-content/uploads/2011/04/Sustainable-Event-Management-Vol-22-IS-11.pdf

Lothe, S., Myrtveit, I., & Trapani, T. (1999, November/December). Compensation systems for improving environmental performance. *Business Strategy and the Environment, 8* (6), 313–321.

Mallen, C., & Chard, C. (2011). A framework for debating the future of environmental sustainability in the Sport Academy. *Sport Management Review, 14,* 424–433.

Mallen, C., Stevens, J., Adams, L., & McRoberts, S. (2010). The assessment of the environmental performance of an international multi-sport event. *European Sport Management Quarterly, 10* (1), 97–122.

McDonough, W., & Braungart, M. (2002, August). Design for the triple top line: New tools for sustainable commerce. *Corporate Environmental Strategy, 9* (3), 251–258.

Mulgan, R. (2000). "Accountability": An ever-expanding concept? *Public Administration, 78* (3), 555–573.

Ness, B., Urbel-Piirsalu, E., Anderberg, S., & Olsson, L. (2007). Categorising tools for sustainability assessment. *Ecological Economics, 60* (3), 498–508.

Perelman, M. (2003). Myths of the market: Economics and the environment. *Organization and Environment, 16* (2), 168–226.

Randjelovic, J., O'Rourke, A., R. & Orsato, R. J. (2003, July/August). The emergence of green venture capital. *Business Strategy and the Environment, 12* (4), 240–253.

Robinson, J. (2004). Squaring the circle? Some thoughts on the idea of sustainable development. *Ecological Economics, 48* (4), 369–384.

Scharwath, K. (2012, February 3). The super green bowl. Environmental News Network. Retrieved from http://www.enn.com/lifestyle/article/43947

Sobhana, K. (2010, September 7). Games committee ropes in players to counter carbon footprint in 2010. Retrieved from http://www.indianexpress.com/news/games-committee-ropes-in-players-to-counter-carbon-footprint-in-2010/513827/0

Tian, Q. T., & Brimblecombe, P. (2008). Managing air in Olympic cities. *American Journal of Environmental Sciences, 4* (5), 439–444.

United Nations (UN) Brundtland Report (1987). 96th Plenary meeting, United Nations General Assembly, *Report of the World Commission on Environment and Development: Our common future.* Retrieved from http://www.un-documents.net/our-common-future.pdf

United Nations (UN). (2010). United Nations Environment Programme: Sport and environment. Retrieved March 21, 2012 from: http://www.unep.org/sport_env/

United Nations Environment Programme (UNEP). (n.d.) Climate Neutral Network. Retrieved March 15, 2012, from http://www.unep.org/climateneutral

United Nations Environment Programme (UNEP). (2007). *Global Environment Outlook GEO-4: Summary for Decision Makers.* Valletta, Malta: Progress Press.

United Nations Environment Programme (UNEP). (2011). Climate Neutral Network. Retrieved from http://www.unep.org/climateneutral/

Wackernagel, M., & Rees, W. E. (1996). *Our ecological footprint: Reducing human impact on the Earth.* Gabriola Island, BC: New Society Publishers.

Weidema, B. P., Thrane, M., Christensen, P., Schmidt, J., & Løkke, S. (2008). Carbon
Footprint: A catalyst for life cycle assessment? *Journal of Industrial Ecology, 12*
(1), 3–6.
Wright, L. A., Kemp, S., & Williams, I. (2011). "Carbon footprinting": towards a
universally accepted definition. *Carbon Management, 2* (1), 61–72.
WWF. (2010). *Living Planet Report 2010: Biodiversity, biocapacity and development.* Gland, Switzerland: WWF International.

9 FACILITATING QUALITY IN EVENT MANAGEMENT

Crosby, P. B. (1979). *Quality is free: The art of making quality certain.* New York:
McGraw-Hill.
Garvin, D. A. (1988). *Managing quality: The strategic and competitive edge.* New
York: The Free Press.
Ford, H., & Crowther, S. (1922). *My life and work.* New York: Doubleday Page.
Reeves, C. A., & Bednar, D. A. (1994). Defining quality: Alternatives and impli-
cations. *Academy of Management Review, 19* (3), 419–445.
Saad, G. H., & Siha, S. (2000). Managing quality: Critical links and a contingency
model. *International Journal of Operations & Production Management, 20* (10),
1146–1163.
Watkins, D. K. (2006). Reflections on the future of quality. *Quality Progress, 39* (1),
23–28.
Yoshida, M., & James, J. D. (2011). Service quality at sporting events: Is aesthetic
quality a missing dimension? *Sport Management Review, 14*, 13–24.
Zeithaml, V. A., Parasuraman, A., & Berry, L. L. (1990). *Delivering quality service:
Balancing customer perceptions and expectations.* New York: The Free Press.

10 EVENT BIDDING

Emery, P. R. (2002). Bidding to host a major sports event: The local organizing
committee perspective. *International Journal of Public Sector Management, 15*,
316–335.
Fédération Internationale de Football Association (FIFA). (2006). *Green goal: The
environmental concept for the 2006 FIFA World Cup.* Frankfurt am Main: Report
published by the Organizing Committee, 2006 FIFA World Cup.
Gadenne, D. L., Kennedy, J., & McKeiver, C. (2009). An empirical study of environmental awareness and practices in SMEs. *Journal of Business Ethics, 84* (1),
45–63.
Greenberg, J. (2002). *Managing behaviour in organizations.* Upper Saddle River,
NJ: Prentice Hall.
Hautbois, C., Parent, M. M., & Séguin, B. (2012). How to win a bid for major sporting
events? A stakeholder analysis of the 2018 Olympic Winter Games French bid.
Sport Management Review, 15 (3), 263–275.
Horte, S. Å., & Persson, C. (2000). How Salt Lake City and its rival bidders
campaigned for the 2002 Olympic Winter Games. *Event Management, 6*, 65–83.

Ingerson, L., & Westerbeek, H. M. (2000). Determining key success criteria for attracting hallmark sporting events. *Pacific Tourism Review, 3*, 239–253.

Intergovernmental Panel on Climate Change (IPCC) (2007). *Global environment outlook 4: Summary for decision makers.* Retrieved from http://www.unep.org/geo/geo4/media/GEO4%20SDM_launch.pdf

International Motorcycling Federation (Fédération Internationale de Motocyclisme, IFM). (2006). *Environmental code.* Mies, Switzerland.

International Olympic Committee. (2006). *IOC guide on sport, environment and sustainable development.* Lausanne, Switzerland.

International Olympic Committee (IOC) Sport and Environment Commission. (n.d.). *Olympic Movement's Agenda 21: Sport for sustainable development.* Retrieved from http://www.olympic.org/Documents/Reports/EN/en_report_300.pdf

Kerzner, H. (1995). *Project management: A systems approach to planning, scheduling, and controlling* (5th ed.). Princeton, NJ: Van Nostrand Reinhold.

Mitchell, I. K., & Saren, M. (2008). The living product: Using the creative nature of metaphors for sustainable marketing. *Business Strategy and the Environment, 17* (6), 398–410.

Persson, C. (2000). The International Olympic Committee and site decisions: The case of the 2002 Winter Olympics. *Event Management*, 6, 135–153.

Westerbeek, H. M., Turner, P., & Ingerson, L. (2002). Key success factors in bidding for hallmark sporting events. *International Marketing Review, 19*, 303–322.

11 POLITICS IN EVENT BIDDING AND HOSTING

Allison, L. (Ed.). (1986). *The Politics of Sport.* Manchester: Manchester University Press.

Furlong, J. (2011). *Patriot hearts: Inside the Olympics that changed a country.* Vancouver: Douglas & McIntyre.

Lee, M. (2006). *The race for the 2012 Olympics: The inside story of how London won the bid.* London: Virgin Books.

Mallen, C., & Adams, L. J. (2008). *Sport, recreation and tourism event management* (1st ed.). Oxford: Butterworth-Heinemann.

Senn, A. E. (1999) *Power, politics, and the Olympic Games: A history of the power brokers, events, and controversies that shaped the Games.* Champaign, IL: Human Kinetics.

12 CONCLUSIONS

Schön, D. (1983). *The reflective practitioner: How professionals think in action.* New York: Basic Books.

INDEX

242